Saunders

The Visitor'
to
FRANCE: MASS

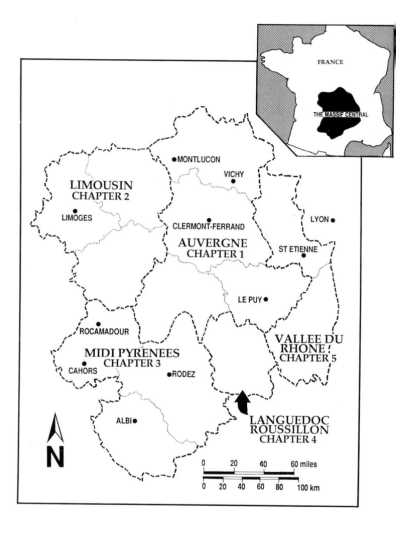

THE
VISITOR'S GUIDE TO
FRANCE:
MASSIF CENTRAL

Barbara Mandell

MPC
HUNTER
PUBLISHING INC

Published by:
Moorland Publishing Co Ltd,
Moor Farm Road,
Airfield Estate,
Ashbourne,
Derbyshire DE6 1HD
England

British Library Cataloguing in Publication Data:
The Visitor's guide to France.
Massif Central.
  1. France. Massif Central -
  Visitor's guides
  I. Mandell, Barbara
  914.4'59

ISBN 0 86190 347 1 (paperback)
ISBN 0 86190 346 3 (hardback)

Colour and black & white origination by:
Scantrans, Singapore

Printed in the UK by:
Richard Clay Ltd, Bungay, Suffolk

Cover photograph: *St Robert, Limousin* (Peter Baker, International Photobank).

Illustrations have been supplied as follows: Martin Gray: pp 22, 23, 30 (both), 31, 34, 35, 42 (bottom), 43, 55, 58, 59, 66, 67, 70, 75, 78, 79, 98, 110, 126-7, 138, 139, 142, 143, 162, 163, 166, 174, 175, 178, 179, 191, 195, 198, 202, 206, 210, 214; Regional Tourist Office, Clermont-Ferrand: pp 11, 19, 42 (top), 54, 71, 74; Regional Tourist Office, Limoges: pp 87, 90, 91, 99, 122, 146; Tourisme Attelé Diffusion: pp 111, 167; Château de Boussac: pp 118, 119; Barrie Monk: pp 147, 171; Ron Scholes: pp 154, 155, 170, 179, 186, 187 (both), 203.

Acknowledgements

The author would like to express her thanks to the many people who gave her invaluable help and advice, especially: Pascale Girod at the Comité Régional de Tourisme en Auvergne; Catherine Fossati, Comité Régional de Tourisme, Limoges; Thérèse Gutierrez, Comité Départmental de Tourisme, Mende.

Published in the USA by:
Hunter Publishing Inc,
300 Raritan Centre Parkway,
CN 94, Edison, NJ 08818
ISBN 1 55650 232 X (USA)

CONTENTS

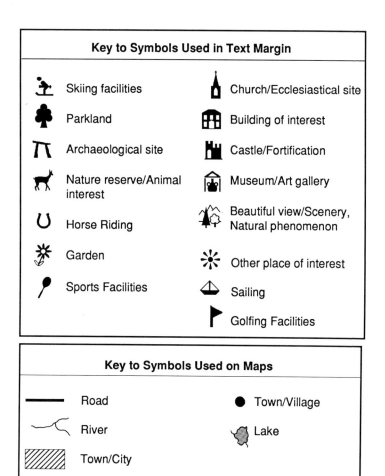

Key to Symbols Used in Text Margin

Skiing facilities

Parkland

Archaeological site

Nature reserve/Animal interest

Horse Riding

Garden

Sports Facilities

Church/Ecclesiastical site

Building of interest

Castle/Fortification

Museum/Art gallery

Beautiful view/Scenery, Natural phenomenon

Other place of interest

Sailing

Golfing Facilities

Key to Symbols Used on Maps

Road

River

Town/City

Town/Village

Lake

Note on the maps
The maps drawn for each chapter, while comprehensive, are not designed to be used as route maps, but rather to locate the main towns, villages and places of interest.

INTRODUCTION

W hen two or three travellers are gathered together and the conversation turns to the Massif Central one thing is more or less certain — each will have a different idea of precisely where this vast collection of mountains, plateaux, valleys, lakes and rivers actually begins and ends. A geologist will define the region with map-like precision as a landlocked area in the southern half of France, covering about one-sixth of the entire country. However, the outline resembles a giant slice of cheese at whose edges mice have been nibbling away for thousands of years and, as far as the average person is concerned, the answer is not nearly so obvious.

The Vallée du Rhône provides a fairly well defined border to the east, the Cévennes serve the same purpose further south but the western approaches are infinitely more complicated. The mountains tend to peter out into foothills, scored by river courses, leaving a jagged edge which ignores man-made boundaries altogether. Nevertheless, it is generally agreed that Auvergne is at the heart of the Massif Central with Limousin, to the west, running a close second. A sliver of Aquitaine seals off the south-west while the Midi-Pyrénées, in spite of its name, contributes part of the northern *départements* of Lot and Aveyron. Languedoc-Roussillon weighs in with Lozère and a fragment of Gard skirting the border with Ardèche in the Vallée du Rhône. Little pieces of Ardèche and Loire are also included while the Morvan Hills nose their way into Nièvre, leaving Val de Loire to complete the circle.

Everyone is expected to draw a line somewhere and, because the various tourist offices concerned will help in defining the Massif sections of their own territories but seldom those of their neighbours, this guide has been left on occasions to make up its own mind. The result is that it includes the different regions and *départements* already mentioned, with an occasional glance down an inviting valley that has pushed back the hills on either side until they all but disappear from view. At the same time it only lingers briefly in areas which have little of interest for the visitor.

Inevitably opinions differ when it comes to pinpointing the exact spot at which a river, travelling from its source in the mountains, ceases to be part of the Massif Central and starts to invade fresh territory. For ease of reference, a medium-sized town on the banks, not too far from its provincial boundary, qualifies as a good landmark for the first-time visitor. These centres include Roanne on the Loire, Vichy beside the Allier, Limoges threaded through by the Vienne and Souillac on the northern bank of the Dordogne. They are all easily accessible, have their own individual attractions and are well placed for exploring the surrounding countryside, whether out on a wandering spur of the Massif or well within the prescribed area.

Geography

The Massif Central, as its name implies, is a mountainous region bridging the gap between the Alps and the Pyrénées but belonging to neither of them. The most widely known section is probably the volcanic area round Clermont-Ferrand and Le-Puy-en-Velay in Auvergne. Much of it is extremely ancient although there are some grass-covered volcanoes which only became extinct about 10,000 years ago. In the dim and distant past, Mont-Dore and Cantal were approximately the size of Vesuvius and Etna respectively and from one viewpoint it is still possible to make out a crater roughly 64km (40 miles) across with the remains of smaller eruptions in the middle. There are cones to be seen in every direction, rising in places to a height of about 1,860m (6,000ft), flows of pumice reputedly unequalled anywhere in the world apart from New Zealand and Alaska as well as rocky pinnacles that reach pointedly for the sky.

Generally speaking, the area has a base of crystalline rocks, such as granite, with a covering of sand and clay to the north and limestone further south. The Ice Age contributed a few glaciers after which the main rivers and their tributaries carried on the good work by creating gorges which can be anything up to 620m (2,000ft) deep in places.

The scenery along the river courses varies considerably, from stretches where the water meanders sedately between grassy banks flanked by farmlands, through wooded hills which force it to quicken the pace somewhat, to ravines where it surges over the rocks in rainbowed clouds of froth and spray. Streams abound everywhere except in the deep south, accompanied by ice cold waterfalls that cascade down among the rocks while warm water springs attract crowds to the various spas, as one or two of them have been doing since Roman times.

The rivers set off in all directions. The Allier rises in Auvergne and heads north while the Loire emerges through a small pipe just over the border in Ardèche and makes its way to Le Puy and Roanne before eventually striking out towards the Atlantic Ocean, passing Orléans, Tours and Nantes on its way to St Nazaire. The Cher, the Creuse and the Vienne all begin life in Limousin and flow roughly north-eastwards, leaving the Dordogne, the Lot and the Tarn to head for Aquitaine in the south-west. Smaller rivers make shorter and less spectacular journeys to swell the Rhône and the Saône.

The plateaux, some of them more in the nature of extensive plains, vary quite surprisingly, usually according to their different altitudes. The highest ground consists mainly of heath and moorland where sheep and cattle graze during the summer months, to be moved down to more friendly pastures before the onset of winter when the uplands can be decidedly cold and bleak. One step down, and starting at around 1,240m (4,000ft), are forests of natural oak, beech and chestnut to which have been added a variety of conifers.

Farming is mostly restricted to the valleys, where the main crops are wheat, barley, oats, potatoes and sugar beet although orchards and vineyards flourish in some areas and mulberries and olives appear as the Cévennes drop down towards the Mediterranean. Market gardens can be found in the vicinity of some of the larger towns but are usually local affairs rather than large commercial ventures. The ancient Britons would no doubt be fascinated to discover that woad is grown in the countryside round Toulouse.

The combination of fairly high rainfall and a bed of rock means that the water collects in pools and peat bogs, especially in Limousin. These are augmented by barrages across the various rivers, resulting in lakes of different sizes. They are not only part of the hydro-electric system but also come in useful when meeting the ever growing demands for new holiday centres with all their usual facilities including water sports. Further south, in the limestone regions, the water drains away, leaving little in the nature of green pastures but providing good grazing land for sheep. The arid and uninviting uplands of the Causses are strewn with rocks and stones, scoured by strong winds and honeycombed with caves and grottoes full of natural sculptures that dwarf the hundreds of visitors who go to see them every year. Trees reappear in the Cévennes as they sweep up in a curve to the Vallée du Rhône, etched with steep valleys and topped by Mont Mézenc which is part of the volcanic plateau of Velay. As far as minerals are concerned there is a certain amount of coal and pockets of zinc, lead and china clay as well as small quantities of recently discovered uranium.

Population

The Massif Central is not exactly over-populated when compared with other parts of France but it could never be described as the back of beyond. The majority of the inhabitants live in urban communities such at St Etienne which, with Alès and Blanzy, produces much of the local coal, at Clermont-Ferrand or Montluçon, where there are rubber factories, and in the Limoges area of Limousin. Textiles and porcelain are among the principal light industries along with leather, paper, glass, furniture and lace.

The medium-sized towns are fairly well scattered and include Roanne which is kept busy making silk and rayon, Guéret the administrative centre of Creuse, Brive, described as the gateway to the south, Tulle, the chief town of Corrèze, Cahors, Aurillac, Mende and Le Puy. There are also tourist centres such as Vichy, La Bourboule and Royat. All these are interspersed with slightly smaller but equally attractive towns, large villages and hamlets that can be anything from a closely-knit community with a modest *auberge* to a few houses clustered round a tiny and frequently extremely ancient church.

Not all the villages are picturesque although there are several notable exceptions. The most outstanding of these include Collonges-la-Rouge and Conques, whose ancient monastery is one of the most famous in France. The modern houses, and there are a great many of them, tend to be extremely matter-of-fact, set squarely in the middle of small, well tended gardens, closely surrounded by lookalikes. After a time the resulting scene becomes monotonously pretty and, just occasionally, pretty monotonous.

In complete contrast, some of the high plateaux and parts of the Causses are virtually uninhabited and Lozère, in particular, is very

Cross-country skiing at Brioude in Auvergne

short of places to stop for the night. There are exceptions of course, like Florac, La Canourgue and Ste Enimie, the largest village in the Gorges du Tarn, with its decidedly up-market hotel occupying a fifteenth-century château nearby.

History

The history of the Massif Central is as complex as it is fascinating. All too often it has been said that the region was a closed area before the arrival of the railway — a place where it was difficult to move about and where the people eked out an existence to the best of their ability, hampered by poor soil and unhelpful weather conditions. This generalised observation is partly true but it paints a dismal picture which has been contradicted repeatedly down the centuries and, with a few notable exceptions, cannot be said to apply today.

There is plenty of evidence that early man roamed about at will, living in caves and spending a good deal of time building dolmens. The greatest concentration of these can be found in Lot and Aveyron, the latter being particularly rich in prehistoric monuments. There was no shortage of stone for the ancient hunter's spears and axes and when his descendants progressed into the Bronze and Iron Ages they were lucky enough to have adequate supplies of both to hand. This meant that the situation was ideal for the Celts when they invaded Gaul in the sixth century BC. They established themselves in Auvergne, intermarried with the existing residents and before long became known as the Arvernes.

Life was not always a bed of roses in this ancient province of France, but it must have seemed so in retrospect when the Romans forced their way up in 53BC. The Arvernes were not the sort of people to give in easily and their chief, Vercingétorix, was determined to preserve the independence of his part of Gaul for as long as possible. He was reasonably successful to start with, winning an impressive victory against the Roman legions when they attacked his hill fort of *Gerovia*, near Clermont-Ferrand. Eventually, however, he was forced to surrender at *Alesia*.

The Plateau de Puy d'Issolu, near Vayrac in Lot, is thought by some experts to be the site of *Uxcellodunum* where the Gauls made their last stand against the armies of Julius Caesar in 51BC. The Romans consolidated their positions in the area, the Arverni capital was moved to *Augustonemetum*, now Clermont-Ferrand, and, apart from an odd uprising or two, the time passed quite peacefully. Meanwhile, Caesar pressed on westwards, forcing Limousin into the Roman Empire a couple of years afterwards.

In 27BC the Emperor Augustus decided to rationalise the various administrative regions under his control. He did this partly by extending the province of *Aquitania* from its border on the Garonne River in the neighbourhood of Bordeaux northwards to the Loire and then included Berry, the high regions of the Massif Central, the rest of Auvergne and the Cévennes as well. The experiment was not an unqualified success. There were five different capitals to start with, reduced to three in the third century AD, with each one convinced that the others were entirely superfluous.

The introduction of Christianity simply meant that the various archbishops started fighting for supremacy just as hard as all the local warlords and unity was the very last thing any of them had in mind. The Visigoths' invasion in the fifth century added to the general confusion and, although they were defeated in AD507, the local disputes continued unabated. The Saracens were the next on the scene but even after they got their come-uppance in AD732, the feuding and fighting persisted with as much enthusiasm as before.

Finally, Charlemagne took over the whole area and gave it to his son, who was later to become Emperor Louis I.

The next two Frankish kings, Pepin I and Pepin II, were constantly at loggerheads with the Ducs d'Aquitaine — a title which had first been disputed and then assumed by a long string of different people, some of whose claims were dubious to say the least. William I, Comte d'Auvergne and founder of the abbey at Cluny, managed to get hold of it at the end of the ninth century in the face of fierce opposition from the Comtes de Toulouse and Poitiers. Everybody wanted to be crowned Duc d'Aquitaine in Limoges Cathedral and, when the Comte de Poitiers at last achieved his ambition, the family succeeded in keeping a firm hold on the title for something like 200 years.

The last of the line was William X whose daughter Eleanor married Louis VII with the result that the whole region — lock, stock and barrel — became part of the kingdom of France. However, their marriage only lasted for about 15 years. They were divorced and Eleanor married Henry Plantagenet, the Comte d'Anjou, who, 2 years later, succeeded to the throne of England as Henry II. So Aquitaine changed hands again, much to the disgust of all the French nobility involved who decided to ignore the whole thing and parcel out the area amongst themselves. The Comtes de la Marche already had a firm hold in the northern part of Limousin but joined happily in the ensuing battles which resulted in France regaining the area in 1214.

This should have been the end of it but 124 years later England's Edward III laid claim to the kingdom of France and so began the Hundred Years War. There were victories and defeats on both sides, with an occasional breathing space in between. Limousin was overrun after the Battle of Poitiers and secured by the English under the Treaty of Brétigny in 1360, although 14 years later it was back in French hands. Auvergne, meanwhile, was well on the way to becoming the property of the Ducs de Bourbon through a series of advantageous marriages, some of which were skilfully arranged within the family circle.

All this seemed rather pointless when, 5 years after the Battle of Agincourt, Henry V of England was officially recognised as heir to the French throne under the Treaty of Troyes, signed and sealed in 1420. However, before anything practical came out of it, Henry died, Joan of Arc followed her voices into war and, although she was captured and burned to death, she had inspired her countrymen to such an extent that the English were finally thrown out in 1453.

Sad to say, the lands of the Massif Central, and in particular Auvergne, still had a good deal of trouble ahead. The Duc de Bourbon indulged in a spot of treason and promptly had all his property confiscated by Francis I, who immediately made a present of it to his mother, Louise de Savoie. Although the French Crown received most of it back when she died in 1532, the Auvergne title found its way down to Catherine de Médici, who got hold of Clermont as well in 1551. It was not until her daughter, Marguerite de Valois, followed her mother to the grave 64 years later that they were formally annexed by France and have remained in safekeeping ever since.

The next 200 years saw mixed fortunes for the area. Cardinal Richelieu demolished a few fortifications, which was a habit with him, and there were the Wars of Religion and several local disagreements that resulted in bloodshed. However, the inhabitants had, not unreasonably, become extremely tired of being involved in other people's troubles and did their best to ignore them altogether. They even managed to stand aloof from the worst excesses of the Revolution, after which the defeat of Napoleon at Waterloo hardly caused a ripple.

On the credit side, kaolin was discovered in 1771 which gave the craftsmen porcelain to think about; the railway arrived in the mid-nineteenth century and with it all the supplies necessary to revive an interest in agriculture, cattle breeding and other such rural pursuits. Industry got its second wind and before long the area had established itself as the foremost manufacturing centre for china and footwear in France. In fact things were going rather well when World War II broke out in 1939.

The Pétain government, having lost Paris, set up its headquarters in Vichy and in no time at all the general apathy evaporated. Limousin became one of the most active areas of guerrilla warfare in the country and its people paid for their patriotism when whole groups were massacred as the Germans were driven back after the Allied Landings in June 1944. With the return of peace, everyone set about repairing the damage caused by war. Hydro-electric schemes were put into operation, new light industries were introduced and traditional crafts encouraged to expand and improvise. At the same time, the Massif Central woke up to its potential as a holiday region and today it is capitalising on its natural assets, publicising its historical attractions and slowly but surely building up all the amenities required to attract tourists and keep them entertained and happy.

1

AUVERGNE

Auvergne, which occupies a considerable portion of the Massif Central, lies very much to the east of the area, with Limousin taking over in the west. The *départements* of Lozère, Aveyron and, to a certain extent, Lot, seal off its southern boundaries. Ardèche and Loire separate it from the Vallée du Rhône with Saône-et-Loire, Nièvre and Cher side by side to the north.

Much of the province was originally created by volcanic action and because so many craters are still visible there is a tendency to think of it as a wild, rugged place where the visitor is surrounded by bare rocks and total isolation. Nothing, in fact, could be further from the truth. Most of the humps that bubbled up thousands of years ago are covered with grass, trees and scrub. Indeed, there are large, fertile valleys such as the Limagnes, which lies along the Allier between Vichy and Clermont-Ferrand, and green pastures as far as the eye can see. In spite of having the highest peaks in central France and a number of plateaux to match, its winters are cold but not too unkindly, the summers are hot without being unbearably so, while the seasons in between are pleasantly warm if sometimes wet and misty.

Auvergne makes the most of its natural assets. To start with, there are two splendid nature parks, the largest being the Parc Régional des Volcans d'Auvergne . The area extends from well up in Puy-de-Dôme down into Cantal and includes the Puy-de-Sancy, at 1,886m (6,186ft) the highest point of the Massif Central. The Parc Régional du Livradois-Forez is only slightly smaller, taking in the Monts du Forez, the Plaine d'Ambert and the areas of La Chaise-Dieu.

Mineral springs are widespread and give rise to at least ten different spas, the best-known of which is unquestionably Vichy. With

15

rivers and streams, lakes and waterfalls in abundance there are endless opportunities for sports of all kinds, whereas the dedicated history-hunter has something like 500 different castles, châteaux and ruins to choose from in addition to all the churches and chapels, medieval villages and museums.

The history of Auvergne is checkered from its very early days. The ancient province, known as *Arvernia*, was a powerful confederation, led by its chief Vercingétorix, when the Roman legions marched in. Although the Gauls resisted furiously, they were eventually defeated and forced to move their capital from *Gergovie* to Clermont. Most of the area was incorporated into Aquitaine in 27BC, which did not please the inhabitants very much at the time and led to endless problems afterwards. Christianity was introduced during the third century by St Nectaire and St Austremoine, ably assisted by Ste Marie. The Visigoths staged their invasion around AD475 and were followed by the Francs less than 30 years later.

Although the area was still part of Aquitaine, this did not stop the local nobility carrying on frequent disputes among themselves, even after Eleanor of Aquitaine married Henry Plantagenet and made them all vassals of the English king. In the twelfth century, William the Young lost most of his lands to his uncle, William the Old, and only managed to hang on to the area bounded by the Allier and the Coux, known from the end of the thirteenth century as the Dauphiné d'Auvergne. Philip II of France decided to join in the family quarrel and, predictably, came out of it with a large part of the country which he promptly annexed under the name of Terre d'Auvergne. The Bishop of Clermont wisely approved of this and was rewarded with the lordship of the town and the title of Robert I.

As a result of judicious marriages between the more illustrious families in the area, such as the Poitiers and the Bourbons, the boundaries remained more or less static until Charles, the famous Constable of France, reunited by far the greatest part when he became the Duc de Bourbon. It was a matter of treason that led to his downfall and the subsequent confiscation of his property by Francis I who lent it to Louise de Savoie for her lifetime.

Meanwhile, Catherine de Médici, the daughter of Pope Leo X and Madeleine de la Tour d'Auvergne, inherited the countship of Auvergne and appropriated Clermont as well in 1551. However, it all ended happily because she was the wife of the Duc d'Orleans, later Henry II of France, so everything found its way safely back into the hands of the French monarch on the death of her daughter, Marguerite de Valois.

Cardinal Richelieu, who made a habit of destroying fortified castles in order to keep their owners well under control, demolished several in Auvergne early in the seventeenth century. However, apart from that, the province was allowed to get on with agriculture and industry in comparative peace and quiet, even as one Republic succeeded another. In 1940 Vichy became the capital of the collaborationist government under Maréchal Pétain but this did not stop the Resistance Movement operating from the Mont Mouchet area, not all that far from St Flour. With the return of peace came the hydro-electric system and in 1969 Montboudif, in Cantal, celebrated the election of one of its sons, Georges Pompidou, as President of France. This enthusiasm was echoed further north 5 years later by the admirers of Valéry Giscard d'Estaing.

Auvergne is one of the easiest places to get to in the Massif Central. There are daily air services between Clermont-Ferrand and Paris, Lyon, Toulouse, Bordeaux, Marseille and Nice as well as flights linking both Le Puy-en-Velay and Aurillac with Paris. During the season it is also possible to fly from London to Clermont-Ferrand and from Vichy to Nice and Biarritz. Trains from Paris call at Clermont-Ferrand, Moulins, Vichy, Le Puy-en-Velay and Aurillac, all of which have services to Lyon, Bordeaux and Marseille.

Long distance buses do not figure in the French scheme of things but there are a good number of major roads leading to and from the capital, in addition to a couple of shortish *autoroutes*. The secondary roads are numerous and well maintained, providing a comprehensive network between all the different places of interest.

Visitors looking for alternative methods of getting about can hire a bicycle, negotiate the waterways in a kayak or a canoe, set out on horseback or follow one of the many footpaths provided for the purpose. The Parc des Volcans has a cycle track known as the 'Star of the Auvergne Summits' that starts off below St Etienne and continues in a series of wide sweeps all the way down to St Flour.

Thirteen main hiking routes, the *grandes randonnées*, cover some 1,000km (620 miles) — the GR3 following the Loire while the GR4 crosses the Parc des Volcans augmented by, among others, the GR400 round the volcanoes of Cantal, the GR441 round Le Puy, and the GR30 that makes its way to one lake after another. Shorter excursions can be found at regular intervals and, like the *grandes*

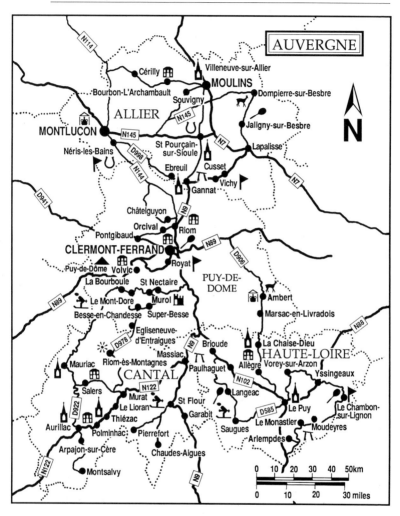

randonnées, are well supplied with *gîtes* and *relais* which provide walkers with a bed for the night.

During the cold weather there is both downhill and cross-country skiing for winter sports enthusiasts. In fact, sports of all descriptions are a feature of holiday life in Auvergne with golf courses, tennis

Hang gliding in Auvergne

courts, swimming and diving, sailing, windsurfing and waterskiing as well as climbing, walking and fishing. For people who want something a little more out of the ordinary, facilities are available for such pursuits as gliding, hang gliding, parachuting and ballooning.

When it comes to accommodation there is plenty of variety, although it is almost impossible to find the out and out extravagance which one expects in Paris or the South of France. However, Clermont-Ferrand, Vichy and Châtelguyon all have some very comfortable establishments with most of the trimmings, closely followed by centres like Le Puy-en-Velay, Moulins, Royat, Aurillac and Le Mont-Dore. There is also an occasional château which takes in paying guests, among them the ancient Château de Boussac at Target-Chantelle and Le Lonzat at Jaligny-sur-Besbre. The Château St Jean, outside Montluçon, describes itself as a private hotel and serves traditional food in its converted twelfth-century chapel.

Most of the smaller towns and larger villages have at least one acceptable *logis* or *auberge*, usually with a handful of private bathrooms and a restaurant. As standards do tend to vary, it is a good idea to have a look round before carting your suitcases upstairs. Jostling each other at the foot of the list are many little inns and taverns which can be cheap, clean and cheerful but may be somewhat lacking in facilities. However, the odd one turns out to be perfectly acceptable, especially if the traveller is tired and hungry and it is getting dark.

In addition to all these there are something like 2,000 *gîtes* and furnished apartments, numerous holiday villages, an occasional youth hostel and a whole variety of camp sites. The latter, apart from falling into the usual categories, determined by the amenities which are available, include seven that are specially equipped for the winter and about twenty others set aside for people who really only enjoy a holiday provided they can take all their clothes off.

Restaurants, like hotels, come in all shapes and sizes. Many of the best-known ones are to be found in centres like Clermont-Ferrand, Moulins and Vichy but there is no shortage of establishments where the food is excellent and it is not necessary to book a table. The simple dishes are often the most memorable, based on traditional recipes and using whatever local produce is in season. Auvergne specialises in *coq-au-vin* and leg of mutton *brayaude*, as well as pork stews and potato cakes cooked with cream.

The fish is delicious, especially salmon and trout, followed by apple pie or whortleberry tart but, as the sweets do not always come up to expectations, the gourmet usually opts for cheese. Familiar varieties can be selected almost at will but there are many others that are every bit as enjoyable, such as *Bleu d'Auvergne*, *Cérilly* which is white and creamy or *Savaron* with a yellowish tinge and somewhat more body to it. Most people try a little of three or four different kinds at a time, working up from the delicate to the more pungent examples, eaten either on their own or with fresh bread but seldom, if ever, with butter. There is a choice of local wines, some good and others better forgotten, and also of *eaux-de-vie* made from sloes, gentian or verbena.

Souvenirs are, as usual, part of the tourist scene and come in styles and prices to suit every taste and pocket. For example, collectors of dolls will find an endless array dressed in more than twenty different regional costumes. Lace and hand-made paper are less obvious but nonetheless most acceptable presents along with semi-precious stones, copper, brass and pewter. Wood carvers provide everything from clogs to little decorative flasks, there are items made from lava which can be either plain or enamelled and anyone in search of pottery will find it almost everywhere.

When it comes to festivals there is a choice between events with religious overtones, which may involve elements of folklore, traditional celebrations such as the extremely colourful Roi de l'Oiseau in Le Puy-en-Velay or Clermont-Ferrand's Court Métrage, along with events like concerts that range from ancient music to Jazz. Less predictable are the countryside contributions which can be ceremonial bread-baking in a community oven, harvest fairs or local fêtes, each bearing the hallmark of its own outlying village. In addition, Aurillac stages a European Festival of Street Theatre, Chilhac concentrates on poetry while here and there a château looks back over its past life with the help of son et lumière.

Puy-de-Dôme

Auvergne is divided up into four *départements* with Allier in the north, Cantal and Haute-Loire sharing the southern part and Puy-de-Dôme sandwiched in between them. It is slightly larger than the others, has a great many extinct volcanoes and is centred on **Clermont-Ferrand**, the provincial capital. The city, the biggest in the Massif Central, follows the twentieth-century conventional pattern with the old town of Clermont in the middle surrounded by suburbs and industrial areas. It is busy without being overbearing, has wide streets, an occasional garden, all the usual assets such as numerous hotels, shops and restaurants and quite a few tourist attractions including the elderly, atmospheric quarter of Montferrand.

For many people, the first place to visit is the cathedral, a splendid Gothic pile dating from the thirteenth century, built of black lava and, despite its impressive silhouette, somewhat tucked away near the Place de la Victoire. Its most outstanding feature is the magnificent stained glass, mostly consisting of reds and blues, which is anything from 500 to 800 years old. The crypt contains a very much older carved, white marble sarcophagus and some original murals while, overhead, the Tour de la Bayette commands a rewarding view of the town.

Another church which should not be missed is Notre-Dame-du-Port, a short walk away. It came into being a shade earlier than the cathedral and has a most imposing south door guarded by statues of saints and angels with scenes from the New Testament such as the Baptism of Christ and the Presentation in the Temple. The interior, not to be outdone, has capitals which are just as intricately carved but tend to be rather less conventional, with demons as well as angels,

Cathedral at Clermont-Ferrand

centaurs, soldiers, minotaurs and mythological birds. There is even a figure of Adam, apparently on his way out of the Garden of Eden, accompanied by an excessively buxom Eve with a great many curls and a large, ornate fig leaf. A small black Virgin, copied from a Byzantine ikon, takes pride of place in the crypt. Other churches of note include the Eglise des Minimes in the moderately spacious

Fontaine d'Amboise, Clermont-Ferrand

Place de Jaude, not far from a large and extremely militant equestrian statue of the Gallic chieftain Vercingétorix.

Clermont is neither short of museums nor of items to put in them. The Musée de Ranquet in the Petite-Rue-St Pierre is barely a stone's throw from the cathedral. It occupies an ancient mansion known as the Maison des Architectes and is largely concerned with local history. There are all sorts of interesting items, ranging from ancient musical instruments and a 300 year old mechanical calculator to carvings, medieval statues, furniture and earthenware produced in Clermont-Ferrand during the eighteenth century.

The Musée Bargoin starts off with archaeology in general, including local prehistoric finds and Gallo-Roman remains in particular, and progresses to paintings, ranging from a highly romantic version of *Jason and the Golden Fleece* to a portrait of Blaise Pascal, the philosopher and mathematician who was born in the city in 1623. In complete contrast, the Musée Lecoq is only interested in natural history, with sections devoted to animals and birds, herbs, flowers and minerals found in the area.

There are one or two fountains dotted about the city including an attractive example in the Place Delille and the much more ornate Fontaine d'Amboise in the Place de la Poterne. It was carved out of lava in the early sixteenth century and rises in tiers to the figure of Hercules, tactfully displaying the arms of the House of Amboise right at the top. However, the strangest fountains are the Fontaines Pétrifiantes de St Alyre where the water in the Grottes du Pérou has the ability to turn everything to stone — or something very like it. The whole place is littered with examples; white figures of men and women in a variety of different costumes have their own allotted places on the grass, along with dogs and other animals, including birds. All manner of different objects are submerged for the three or more months it takes to bring about the transformation. If it was not for the fact that all the 'living' exhibits are so obviously alert, one might be tempted to wonder if every one of them had really started out as a lump of clay, or something similar, before being petrified.

Le Vieux Montferrand, a town in its own right until it joined forces with Clermont, is thought to occupy the site where Caesar set up his main camp during his battles with the local Gauls. This may account for the fact that it is very symmetrical, with the streets at right angles to each other and hardly a curve or a crescent in sight. It is one of those places which should be considered as a whole rather than bit by bit, though anyone walking along its quiet streets lined with ancient houses will find plenty of individual buildings to inspect, but only from the outside. The Maison de l'Annonciation has a statue of St Christopher in the courtyard whereas the Maison de l'Apothicaire sports Tudor-type wood and plaster from the first floor upwards.

The thirteenth-century Maison de l'Eléphant takes its name from the remains of an elderly fresco while one glance is enough to show how the Maison d'Adam et d'Eve got its name. The Hôtel de Fontfreyde and the Hôtel de Lignat are both worth seeing along with many others too numerous to mention. On the other hand, it is possible to view the Fontaine du Lion from almost any angle and step inside the Church of Notre-Dame-de-Prospérité which marks the site of a chapel once attached to the château of the Comtes d'Auvergne.

Those who prefer modern amenities to ancient attractions will find Clermont-Ferrand just as willing to please. There is an opera house and an open-air theatre, a sports complex and a large swimming pool as well as a 9-hole golf course near the Circuit Automobile d'Auvergne, one of France's Grand Prix race tracks.

Another golf course, this time with 18 holes, is only 9km (7 ½ miles) away at Orcines. Art galleries and antique shops, libraries and markets, little theatres and clubs of all descriptions, including three which only play Scrabble, as well as cinemas and discos all appear in the long list of entertainments. The visitor can watch football, practise karate, play tennis, squash or volley-ball, go bowling, ride, cycle, fish or learn to fly at the Aéro Club d'Auvergne. There are three municipal camp sites, *laveries* where you can do your own laundry and garages which will save you the trouble of washing the car.

As far as tourists are concerned, **Royat** is a suburb of Clermont-Ferrand, though the residents might have a different point of view altogether. It is essentially a spa left over from Roman times with nothing to show for it except the thermal springs. When its guests are not fully occupied with improving their circulation and softening up their arteries, they can play golf or tennis, ride or swim, take a few shots at a clay pigeon, go to the cinema or try their luck at the casino. The season lasts from early April to the end of September but it is far from easy to find a local hotel open during the winter.

The main tourist attraction is the Church of St Léger, a construction from the eleventh century which was fortified 200 years later and still looks ready for battle today. There are a couple of grottoes and some pleasant parks to wander about in, one of which has a botanical garden. A workshop specialising in cutting semi-precious stones is open to visitors during working hours and has a shop full of tempting wares like rock crystal, agate and tourmaline. Anyone who feels the need for a breath of fresh, country air can set out on foot for one of the nearby woods, ride or drive up into the volcanic mountains or take the lazy way out by joining an organised excursion to one of the many places of interest in the vicinity.

Looking westwards from Clermont-Ferrand, it is an easy run to **Orcival**, a small village with a large, impressive church that suffered, but not too seriously, during the Revolution. It gives the impression of having been built a section at a time, each little chapel having its own roof joined on to a larger, semi-circular one, the walls punctured by arched windows all the way up to the two-tiered steeple. It is by no means over-decorated, in fact the interior is on the dark and gloomy side, but there are some rather nice sculptures as well as chains discarded by ex-prisoners as votive offerings. A statue of the Virgin carrying a surprisingly adult-looking Child is highly venerated and is carried in solemn procession through the streets on Ascension Day,

PLACES OF INTEREST IN PUY-DE-DOME

Clermont-Ferrand
Bargoin Museum
45 Rue Ballainvilliers. Archaeological museum with many local discoveries. Also paintings and sculptures.

Cathedral
Place de la Victoire. Impressive building with fine stained glass. Ancient crypt and tower with a great many stairs and a good view.

Fontaine d'Amboise
Place de la Poterne. Ancient and decorative large fountain carved out of lava.

Fontaines Pétrifiantes
13 Rue du Pérou. Grottoes and many examples of items petrified by the water.

Lecoq Museum
15 Rue Bardoux. Natural history museum devoted to local flora, fauna and minerals.

Notre-Dame-du-Port
Place Notre-Dame-du-Port. A beautiful church with a superb doorway, many excellent carvings and an ancient crypt.

Ranquet Museum
Petite-Rue-St Pierre. Interesting collection of furniture, sculptures, musical instruments and china, mostly local.

Royat
Taillerie des Pierres Fines
Workshop where semi-precious stones are cut and displayed.

Orcival
Church of Notre-Dame. An imposing building with some good carvings and a much-venerated statue of the Virgin.

Château de Cordès
Near Orcival. Fifteenth-century castle up-dated in the seventeenth century with very formal gardens.

Puy-de-Dôme
An exhibition and information centre at the summit. Some remains of a Roman temple to Mercury. Excellent view.

accompanied by large crowds.

The nearby Château de Cordès is a delightful manor-house-cum-castle, standing at the end of a long tree-lined avenue and surrounded by so much greenery that it is hardly visible from the road. Building was started in the thirteenth century, extensions were added 200 years later and, after the whole place had been re-modelled in the 1600s, it was beautifully decorated and furnished regardless of expense. The château looks out over secluded formal gardens

Volvic
Maison de la Pierre
Passage into a lava flow. Small museum and audio-visual presentation.

Château de Tournoël
Near Volvic. Ruins of ancient fortress with a main courtyard, staircases and fireplaces.

Pontgibaud
Château-Dauphin
Well preserved twelfth-century fortress, restored in the nineteenth century. Contains furniture, pictures and other items of historical interest.

Gorges de la Sioule
Near Pontgibaud.
Picturesque area including a view from Montfermy.

Riom
Hôtel Guimoneau
Rue de l'Horloge. Medieval mansion with a number of statues and an attractive courtyard.

Palais de Justice
Rue St Louis. Contains a four-teenth-century chapel with slightly younger stained glass.

Mandet Museum
Rue d'Hôtel de Ville. Museum of the arts with a wide-ranging and interesting collection.

Auvergne Regional Museum
Rue Delille. Excellent museum full of domestic items, costumes, furniture and other displays concerned with life prior to the Industrial Revolution.

Church of St Amable
Near the Place de la Fédération. Twelfth-century church, much up-dated, with some attractive wood carving in the sacristy.

Church of Notre-Dame-du-Marthuret
Some elderly statues and a lovely one of the Virgin and Child.

Château de Davayat
Near Riom. Seventeenth-century manor-house with furniture, paintings and other contemporary articles.

designed by Le Notre, each one totally surrounded by high, well manicured hedges.

The Puy-de-Dôme, which gives its name to the *département*, is the highest volcano in the Monts Dôme, a once-sacred mountain with a spectacular view over sixty or more extinct volcanoes of assorted shapes and sizes. A winding toll-road climbs almost to the top, having replaced a small steam train that laboured up and down with tourists for the best part of two decades but was pensioned off in 1926.

The Gauls originally chose the site as an ideal place to worship the god Lug and the Romans followed their example with a large, impressive temple to Mercury. After their empire had crumbled, the looters took over, removing whatever treasures had been left behind and reducing the whole place to rubble. The foundations were uncovered in 1872 and have been a popular tourist attraction ever since, especially as local people insist that they are also much favoured by witches and sorcerers. If this is the case, they do not appear to mind sharing their domain with parked cars, television and an information centre.

Small roads wander off in all directions, a couple of them passing quite close to the ruined Château de Tournoël, standing alone on a rocky spur. It is an interesting combination of two different fortresses, one superimposed on the other, that battled through from the tenth century, took part in the Hundred Years War, had a hard time during the Wars of Religion and was then abandoned, although efforts are being made to preserve if not actually to restore it.

Volvic, more or less on the doorstep, has both an old church and an important asset in the Maison de la Pierre. It is here that an ancient quarry leads right into the heart of a lava flow, which makes a change from the usual underground cavern. After burrowing about for a while, visitors are treated to an audio-visual presentation on the subject of volcanoes and the practical use of lava and can look round the small museum. There is also a twelfth-century church and a path up the mountain to the foot of a large statue of Notre-Dame-de-la Garde that watches over the town.

It is also worth making a detour westwards to **Pontgibaud** where the Château-Dauphin, which somehow managed to escape the attention of Cardinal Richelieu, has retained its twelfth-century keep and half a dozen sturdy towers, all in an excellent state of repair. It is open from mid-July to the end of August and is full of antique furniture, pictures, china and various other items of historical interest. The local church is quite attractive and so are the gorges on the River Sioule, 12km (7$\frac{1}{2}$ miles) away. Here there is a ruined mill, a waterfall, a pleasant view from Montfermy and the GR441 close to hand.

Riom, one of the most important towns in Auvergne during the Middle Ages, once belonged to Alphonse de Poitiers, brother of St Louis, the ninth French king of that name, whose main ambition was to capture Jerusalem. It is a rather sedate sort of place with numerous, elderly mansions built of dark volcanic rock but usually sporting red roofs which brighten up the scene considerably. The best of these are judged to be the Hôtel Guimoneau with its attractive courtyard and quartet of statues entitled *Force, Justice, Prudence* and *Temperance*, and the sixteenth-century Maison des Consuls which has the statues of two Roman emperors on display. The most atmospheric area is in the vicinity of the Carrefour des Taules where the two main roads cross each other. They cut the old section into four more-or-less equal portions which are surrounded by wide boulevards.

Within a few blocks of each other are the Palais de Justice, containing a fourteenth-century chapel which was once part of a château belonging to the Duc de Berry, and two very interesting museums. The larger of the two, the Musée Mandet, is devoted mainly to the arts and is well endowed with paintings from the sixteenth to eighteenth centuries and sculptures of a more recent vintage as well as furniture, china and a collection of attractive objets d'art. The Musée Régional d'Auvergne is obviously more concerned with local matters and is the place to see traditional costumes, domestic articles, farm implements, furniture and musical instruments plus a great deal more in similar vein.

The oldest church in town is the Basilique de St Amable, originally constructed in the twelfth century but much restored thereafter, which contains some seventeenth-century woodwork and a reliquary of the saint. However, the smaller Church of Notre-Dame-du-Marthuret is undoubtedly better-known, chiefly on account of the superb statue of *La Vierge à l'Oiseau*, an exceptionally lovely Virgin wearing a diadem and carrying a Child who is looking with a blissful expression at the small bird in His hands. Also worth seeing is the courtyard in the *hôtel de ville* but the fountain of Adam and Eve is rather disappointing.

Riom, with Embraud on the banks of the Allier and Gannat away to the north-east, is acknowledged as an important centre of traditional music which, combined with national costumes, is very much to the fore during the Fête de St Amable in mid-June. There are very few hotels in the town but this is of no consequence as **Châtelguyon**, just next door, has more than enough for both of them.

Châtelguyon is, first and foremost, a spa geared to the needs of patients suffering from a variety of ailments and infections. The medical staff speak English, German and Italian which makes life easier for people who have difficulty in explaining their problems in French. The hotels include one in the top bracket conveniently close to the thermal gardens and the casino, other very comfortable ones

Orcival

A floral welcome to Châtelguyon

and many more with amenities ranging from perfectly acceptable to merely adequate. In addition there are scores of villas and furnished apartments, families who take in paying guests and a couple of camp sites.

The gates of the Château d'Effiat

The local entertainments include concerts, theatre performances, a cinema and a bridge club, while anyone who feels up to it can ride, play tennis or swim, have a game of bowls or mini-golf, take up yoga or go for long walks along the blazed footpaths. It is not, however, an ideal place for people in search of elderly châteaux, interesting churches or even museums. The only tourist attractions are a cross on a hilltop in the centre of the town and the rather ordinary Church of Ste Anne.

Taking a longer view, there are several places to visit in the surrounding area. The Château de Chazeron is a case in point. It was designed originally as a fortress but was converted into a country residence in the seventeenth century when two extra wings were added. It is a rather severe looking building which is hardly surprising when you realise that it was used as a state prison in 1940. The Château de Davayat is much more elegant, standing in its own rather formal park and furnished in the style to which one feels it is accustomed. On the other hand, the Château de la Roche, dating back to the twelfth century, still has its old sentry way, along with a collection of arms and armour, tapestries and furniture, all of which can be seen at specified times throughout the year.

Among the attractions created by nature rather than by man is the Gour de Tazenat, a lake that fills the centre of an extinct volcano, and the extremely viewable Gorges de la Sioule which Puy-de-Dôme shares with the *département* of Allier to the north.

Also on the border, but slightly further east on the road to Vichy, is the Château d'Effiat where a short but excruciatingly bumpy road leads up to the impressive gates. It was the home of Maréchal d'Effiat whose son, Cinq-Mars, double-crossed Cardinal Richelieu and was put to death for his pains. The château is certainly worth seeing on account of its carved woodwork, painted ceilings, beautiful Louis XIV furniture, historic documents and terraced gardens. It is open for guided tours from June to September with a list of times posted up outside and a request to ring the bell. This is a minute version of the type usually seen in a belfry and is activated by means of a strong iron chain. The nearby Château de Denone, built on the site of an ancient castle in the sixteenth century, is also open during the summer.

A choice of minor roads strike out across rather flat and not particularly interesting country to **Châteldon**, an ancient hamlet tucked away in a hollow and surrounded by vines. It has preserved a number of old houses from the fifteenth and sixteenth centuries when they were all part of a fortified village. The most picturesque are those of the winegrowers who had a particular liking for heavy wooden balconies. The scene is dominated by an elderly château of no interest to visitors because it is privately owned and not open to the public. However, there is nothing to stop sightseers inspecting the Church of St Sulpice or admiring the scenery from the *point de vue*.

Still skirting the provincial border, the next place of interest is **Thiers**, an extremely picturesque medieval town with a collection of very viewable houses climbing up the hillside above the River Durolle. In the early days the inhabitants were mostly engaged in making paper but they diversified as time went by and today are kept just as busy producing cutlery. It is, in fact, the centre of the French knife-making industry and has a comprehensive museum in the Maison des Couteliers to emphasise the fact.

The old quarter is another of those atmospheric areas best seen on foot, full of little winding streets lined with decorative buildings. The most outstanding is, without question, the Maison du Pirou, close to a square of the same name. This is a tall, gabled wood and plaster example of medieval domestic architecture at its best. A stone's throw up the hill is the Church of St Genès, a moderately forgettable relic of somewhat uncertain age which, if closed, will be opened up on request. The Terrasse du Rempart, on the main road through the town, provides a splendid view of the Monts Dore and the Monts Dôme.

Although Thiers is on a more or less direct route from Clermont-Ferrand to St Etienne, there is absolutely no need to head straight for either provincial capital. A number of wayward little roads, some apparently designed for carts rather than cars, find their way up into the Monts du Forez and down again onto the Plaine d'Ambert. Others meander off in a westerly direction in search of additional tourist attractions.

The first of these might easily be the extremely functional Château de Vollore. It still belongs to the Lafayette family and holds a great many memories of the famous general and the American War of Independence. The Château d'Aulteribe, built 500 years ago but up-dated at the beginning of the last century, is another possibility. It was once the property of Lord Georges Onslow but is now owned by the State along with his furniture, tapestries, paintings and other works of art.

Ravel, a little further north, is a thirteenth-century castle presented by Philip the Fair to one of his advisers. It is more obviously a museum, basking in trees and terraced gardens, and takes an informed interest in a number of different subjects including natural history. The town of **Billom**, with no château to get excited about, weighs in with some ruins at Mauzun, 8km (5 miles) away, and has a medieval atmosphere. It was a famous university town 700 years ago and parts of it do not seem to have changed very much since then. The Maison du Chapitre turned its back on academic matters to become a prison at the time of the Revolution but, like several other buildings of comparable age and interest, it is firmly closed to visitors. However, the Church of St Cerneuf is a sufficiently good reason for pausing long enough to look inside. Apart from its paintings and sculptures there is a fine twelfth-century grille and one of the oldest crypts in Auvergne with scenes from the life of Ste Marguerite.

As Billom is about on a line with Royat and Orcival, it completes a circuit of the northern section of Puy-de-Dôme and, because it has no hotels to speak of, leaves the motorist with a choice of routes to the south. The decision depends largely on what one intends to see and do and the type of accommodation that is required. One option

The circular hôtel de ville *in Ambert*

would be to head south-east, past the white stone Château des Martinanches, to Ambert.

At the risk of overdoing the list of local châteaux, three others are worth mentioning for the benefit of people who never get tired of inspecting them. The Château de Busséol, once the property of the Stuarts, is the oldest medieval castle in Auvergne and is still occupied. Meanwhile Montmorin, another twelfth-century pile, consists of a keep surrounded by massive protecting walls in a remarkably good state of repair and has an interesting collection of arms and armour. Montfleury is far less militant, being more on the lines of a country house with a couple of towers to give it an air of authority. Its offerings consist of some good furniture and, more unusually, a collection of very viewable carriages.

Ambert is a pleasing little town with a selection of small, rather average *auberges*, a circular *hôtel de ville* and the fifteenth-century Church of St John. It does not exactly put itself out for the benefit of tourists, preferring to leave them to explore the surrounding countryside on their own. One early discovery might easily be a small rural museum with traditional food at the Jasserie du Coq Noir, about 10km

Musée Historique du Papier, Moulin Richard-de-Bas

(6miles) away. Another local attraction is the Parc Zoologique du Bouy, a fairly large area that is home to a wide range of animal and bird life and is open every afternoon from June to September as well as at weekends and on public holidays for the rest of the year.

The Moulin Richard-de-Bas, lies about 5km (3 miles) from Ambert on a small road to the east. It is the site of a totally absorbing Musée Historique du Papier, named after Thomas Richard, a wealthy paper-maker who was murdered in 1793 on his way to Lyon at a place called the Pass of the Dead Man's Cross. In his day the house was occupied by a foreman whereas the last owner to live on the premises was Claude Chantelauze who died in 1934. The first two rooms were the living quarters — a kitchen where everyone gathered for lunch before the staff went off to work in the fields, and the bedroom where parents, grand-parents and children all crowded into two beds with another under the stairs for the apprentice. They are furnished down to the last detail, such as a baby's cot hanging at the foot of its mother's bed and a cushion for lace-making lying on the table.

The history of paper begins in room No 3, named after Tsai-Lun, a Chinese expert who lived near Canton and laid down 105 rules for its production. The Arabs started showing an interest in AD751 after the Battle of Samarkand and built their own paper mills near Damascus. Here they attracted the attention of the Crusaders who, in turn, brought the art back to western Europe. For the next 500 years, paper was made according to the Chinese method but towards the end of the eighteenth century a Frenchman, Louis Nicolas Robert, invented a machine that could make it in rolls. The prototype was sold to British manufacturers who turned out the first working model in 1812.

The fascinating articles on display include everything from 3,000 year old papyrus to a modern version produced in exactly the same way, parchment and vellum from the thirteenth century and books of Tal from India that started out as berries on a palm tree. The visit continues with a tour of the works, showing the whole process step by step until the finished sheets are removed from the drying room. There are even some impregnated with ferns and flower petals, each one different, which can be used for things like lamp shades, invitations, menus and greetings cards. The end products make very superior presents as it is rather a nice feeling to dash off a letter on note-paper produced by hand in exactly the same way as it was 600 years ago.

It is difficult to find a road, large or small, in this area which does not qualify as scenic. They twist and turn, double back on themselves, cross a bridle path or a *randonnée*, keep company with a river or disappear into wooded country in search of a minute village, an isolated hermitage or an unexpected view. One exception to the rule is the straight main road south from Ambert which passes **Marsac-en-Livradois** with its Musée des Pénitents Blancs du Livradois on the way to Arlanc where there is a very fetching hand-made lace museum. Thereafter, the road becomes just as frantic as all the others in an attempt to find a way across the *département* border into Haute-Loire. However, there is still a lot to see in Puy-de-Dôme so, instead of travelling south-east from Billom, there is an alternative route with many similar attractions that leads round the southern outskirts of the capital.

One of the oldest historical sites in the vicinity of Clermont-Ferrand is the Plateau de Gergovie where Caesar was driven back, if only briefly, by the Gauls. Admittedly there is not a lot to see apart from the view but, with the help of a map, it is possible to trace the course of the battle just as it is on the Plateau de Chanturgue where the tactics employed by both sides were vaguely similar.

There is certainly no reason to be at a loss in this part of Puy-de-Dôme. To begin with, there is the Lac d'Aydat which is not especially large but is a good place for fishing, swimming or taking out a canoe, while **St Nectaire** goes a good deal further. This is a spa village strung out along the river where guests can ride or ramble, attend a concert, go to the zoo, a night club or the casino, play tennis, fish and take the waters. There is a dolmen, reached by way of a wandering footpath, and the strange Fontaines Pétrifiantes, similar to the ones in Clermont-Ferrand. Apparently the grotto's ability to petrify anything soaked in the water was first recognised in 1605 and this has now been turned into a cottage industry which does extremely well out of the many tourists who call in every year.

Articles of all descriptions are placed on specially built underground shelves and left until they are properly encrusted and ready to be sold. The permanent display in a small building facing the road includes about 300 different items, from plaques depicting historical events or village scenes of a bygone age to vases, pots and little figures that can be either man or beast. Alongside them are just as many items for sale. It only takes about half an hour to look round any morning or afternoon from April to September but both the shop and the grotto are closed on Mondays at either end of the season.

The Grande Fontaine Pétrifiante is roughly midway between St Nectaire-le-Bas and St Nectaire-le-Haut, the latter dominated by a splendid twelfth-century church standing alone on a kind of island surrounded by grass where there are several places to park the car. It is famous for both the decorative capitals in the nave and a collection of sacred art including a reliquary bust of St Baudime. St Nectaire is also widely known for its cheese but less so for the little rustic museum in the Maison de Sailles and a number of other dolmens scattered about which provided archaeologists with some interesting discoveries towards the end of the last century.

Natural attractions in the vicinity include the Cascade de Saillant in a village of the same name a few kilometres away and the Puy de Châteauneuf involving quite a long walk up to the caves which are thought to have been occupied in prehistoric days. It takes rather less time to reach the summit of the Puy de Mazeyres where there is a good view of the Monts Dore.

The towns of **Issoire** and Murol are also within striking distance, the former being both an industrial centre and home to the extremely decorative Church of St Austremoine. It was originally part of an old

PLACES OF INTEREST IN PUY-DE-DOME — continued

Aigueperse
Château de la Roche
Old fortified building with tapestries, furniture and a collection of armour.

Châtelguyon
Château de Chazeron
Original fortress converted into a country house and used as a prison during World War II.

Gour de Tazenat
North-east of Châtelguyon. A lake inside the crater of an extinct volcano.

Effiat
Château d'Effiat
Very well furnished mansion associated with Maréchal d'Effiat and his son, Cinq-Mars.

Château de Denone
Château on the site of a medieval castle. It was once the home of the financier John Law.

Thiers
Maison des Couteliers
Rue de la Coutellerie. Museum covering all the different aspects of knife-making.

Château de Vollore
House associated with General Lafayette and, through him, the American War of Independence.

Château d'Aulteribe
Old castle containing furniture, pictures and other works of art that belonged to Lord Georges Onslow who once lived there.

Château de Ravel
Near Lezoux. Thirteenth-century castle with attractive terraced gardens and a museum.

Billom
Church of St Cerneuf
Atmospheric church with murals and statues. The crypt is one of the oldest in Auvergne.

Ruins of the Château de Mauzun
Near Billom. Reached only on foot but worth it for the view.

Château des Martinanches
Near Billom. Moated château with Louis XV and Louis XVI furniture.

Château de Montmorin
Very well preserved twelfth-century castle with interesting collection of arms and armour.

Vic-le-Comte
Château de Busséol
Near Vic-le-Comte. Oldest medieval castle in Auvergne which once belonged to the Stuarts.

Château de Montfleury
Near Vic-le-Comte. Typical old country mansion housing a collection of carriages.

Ambert
Parc Zoologique du Bouy
Near Ambert. Quite extensive
wildlife park with about 300 animals.

Moulin Richard-de-Bas
Near Ambert. Extremely interesting
paper museum with exhibits going
back 3,000 years and a factory in
operation.

Marsac-en-Livradois
Museum of the White Penitents
A small museum of items linked with
the Order and its history — the explanation is accompanied by
religious music.

Arlanc
Lace Museum
Some attractive examples of hand-
made lace of various types and
ages.

Plateau de Gergovie
Two sites, on either side of Clermont-Ferrand, where the ancient
Gauls had some success against
Julius Caesar. Some remnants of
that time at L'Oppidum des Côtes
de Clermont, reached only on foot.

St Nectaire
Fontaines Pétrifiantes
Grottoes with petrifying water, a
small exhibition and a shop.

Church of St Nectaire
Well known for its stone carvings
and a reliquary bust of one of the
saint's companions.

Murol
Castle Ruins
Typical example of early military
architecture.

Moulin-Neuf
Grottes de Jonas
Prehistoric caves described locally
as a troglodyte fortress. Also a
small medieval chapel.

Besse-en-Chandesse
Church of St André
Rather dark with some carved
stalls and capitals.

Chapelle de Vassivière
Near Besse-en-Chandesse.
Modest little chapel where the
Virgin from the Eglise St André
spends the summer.

Puy-de-Sancy
Highest peak in the Massif Central.
Cable car up to the summit.
Splendid view.

Egliseneuve-d'Entraigues
House of the Auvergne Cheeses
A cheese-making museum with
traditional equipment, an audio-
visual presentation and samples
offered with wine.

abbey and, although rather dark inside, is worth a short visit which should, if possible, include the crypt. There are one or two unremarkable little hotels, a camp site, a heated swimming pool, bicycles for hire and facilities for riding, fishing and playing tennis.

Murol is smaller, closer to St Nectaire and the proud possessor of some ancient ruins left over from a typical thirteenth-century military fortification. Tours are laid on from April to mid-October, on public holidays and on request at other times of the year. There are a few hotels, one with tennis and swimming on the premises, bicycles and pedalos for hire, bathing and fishing in the river and plenty of opportunities to walk. The Lac Chambon, the prehistoric Grottes de Jonas and a little country museum at Moulin-Neuf are all worth visiting.

An attractive secondary road connects Murol with **Besse-en-Chandesse**, a rather more sophisticated but just as elderly hilltop town which was fortified during the Middle Ages. It is full of picturesque old houses built of lava, particularly in the Rue de la Boucherie where the Maison de la Reine Margot is described by local people as the home of Marguerite de Valois, the wife of Henry IV. Other time-honoured attractions include the old Porte de Ville, the Tour de la Prison where the railway line runs alongside all that remains of the ramparts and the twelfth-century Church of St André. It is a bit dark and gloomy but has some medieval choir stalls and a highly-respected statue of Notre-Dame de Vassivière.

Every July a procession of cowherds and cattle escorts the Black Virgin up to a small chapel in the mountains which was built for her in 1555 by Catherine de Médici. There are songs and dances, colourful traditional costumes, lots of fireworks and heartfelt prayers beseeching her to keep an eye on the upland pastures for the next three months or so. Then, in late September, she is conducted down in a similar manner to take up her winter quarters in the church.

On the other hand, Besse-en-Chandesse has a very modern side to it, particularly taken in conjunction with Super-Besse, roughly 7km (4 miles) away. It is a popular resort for holidaymakers in the summer and skiers in the winter, has a Musée de Ski and supplies information on local flora and fauna to the Faculté des Sciences in Clermont-Ferrand. There are two quite large and very comfortable hotels and several somewhat smaller ones, all of which stagger their opening and closing times to meet the needs of both summer and winter visitors.

Lac Pavin, a short distance through the forest, claims to be one of the loveliest in Auvergne and keeps itself that way by not cluttering up the shoreline with facilities for bathing and other water sports, including fishing. However, the town provides tennis and river fishing and supplies bicycles for hire, which is hardly surprising as it is on the Star of the Auvergne Summits cycle route. Long distance hikers have a choice of two *grandes randonnées*, the GR30 round the lakes and the GR4 linking St Flour with Aubusson, of tapestry fame, in the *département* of Creuse. Besse-en-Chandesse is also plumb in the middle of the Parc des Volcans d'Auvergne.

Le Mont-Dore, 25km (15$^1/_2$ miles) to the west, is both a winter sports centre and a spa. It is a busy place with no old buildings worth mentioning, a total lack of museums but plenty of entertainments to keep its guests occupied. There are cinemas and night clubs, a 9-hole golf course, a casino and even a club which interests itself in biology and geology. There are plenty of hotels, none of them in any way outstanding, and ample opportunities for tennis, riding and especially walking.

The **Puy-de-Sancy**, which is the source of the Dordogne, is a pleasant, scenic drive away. A cable car runs up to the summit from a large parking space with a restaurant in attendance and a Swiss chalet type of hotel in the background. Cows graze in the surrounding pastures and, in the late spring, children come down from the top with their arms full of wild daffodils. However, most people make the trip up for the view which is nothing short of magnificent, especially when the weather is clear.

La Bourboule is a cheerful little spa further down the Dordogne with a collection of rather forgettable hotels, several colourful bridges spanning the river and a general air of wellbeing. It has parks full of trees and flowers, a cable car up to the Plateau de Charlannes, a couple of attractive waterfalls a fairly brisk walk away and a comprehensive programme of events. Folklore plays a major role during the season, along with fêtes and concerts. Guests can swim or ride, play tennis, mini-golf or *boules* and go for a gentle stroll through the town in the absence of blazed footpaths.

The baths are open to children as well as adults and if it is true that the water has the highest arsenic content in Europe at least the people who knock it back by the glassful do not appear to suffer any disasterous after effects. The town is totally lacking in buildings of historic interest which is a trifle strange because it was an accepted

Skiing in the Monts Dore

La Bourboule with its bridges over the river

A game of boules in the main park of La Bourboule

spa as long ago as 1463. The baths were considerably modernised 400 years later and then reconstructed in 1976 along the lines suggested by Corbusier. However, this lack of antiquity does not matter in the very least because it is the scenery rather than the architecture which makes the most lasting impression.

The Monts Dore have been around a good deal longer than the Monts Dôme and as a result are a bit more weather-beaten. They came into being around 3 million years ago, only to be eroded by glaciers which covered the whole area with an icy blanket, creating deep gullies separated by spines that look as if they could have been cut with a knife. A good place to get the overall effect is in the Vallée de Chaudefour between Super-Besse and the Puy de Sancy. It is a jumble of granite and lava with rather bare peaks, trees struggling up the hillsides from the valley and an outstanding array of alpine plants.

Small roads make a determined attempt to explore the area but anyone walking or riding will undoubtedly get a much more intimate view. The Parc des Volcans as a whole supports animals such as wild boar, stags, chamois and badgers. There are birds ranging from royal kites to owls, fish which can be caught provided one has a licence, and literally hundreds of different kinds of wild flowers, not all of which may be picked.

Both the road and the *randonnée* to the south call in at **Eglise-neuve-d'Entraigues** where there is a modest *auberge* and also the House of the Auvergne Cheeses. The latter is open from mid-June to the end of September, has an exhibition of traditional tools used in cheese production, an audio-visual programme showing how it is made and invites passers-by to sample the end product with a glass of wine. It is also the last port of call before crossing the *département* border into Cantal.

Cantal

The *département* of Cantal has just as many and varied a collection of attractions as Puy-de-Dôme, grouped together behind the thresholds of Corrèze, Lot, Aveyron and Lozère with Haute-Loire on its eastern boundary. A large proportion lies in the Parc Naturel Régional des Volcans d'Auvergne where the Monts du Cantal were about 17 million years old when the Monts Dore were thrown up to join them. There are a dozen different valleys round the Puy Mary, a granite tableland etched by ancient glaciers and covered with forests, peat bogs, bare peaks and lush pastures, as well as wild flowers in profusion and plenty of animal life. The area is dotted with historic towns, forgotten villages and châteaux in various stages of repair. There are byways as well as the occasional highway, bridle paths, cycle routes and *randonnées* for determined hikers.

A good base from which to explore the north-western corner of the *département* is the old hill village of **Salers**, full of black lava houses with the scanty remains of its original fortifications and a few small hotels. It is an extremely photogenic little town with most of its main attractions overlooking the Grande-Place or just a step away down a narrow, cobbled street. It is also very tourist conscious; there are shops crammed to the gunwales with every type of souvenir and even some items that it might be difficult to find elsewhere. In one instance the focal point of a display is a glass vessel containing *'Eau-de-vie de Serpent'* with a large snake curled up in a jar and a small one preserved in the bulbous stopper to keep it company. Glass engravers invite passers-by to inspect their work and most of the historic buildings are open to visitors during the season.

The church, which is slightly out on a limb at the foot of the Rue de Beffroi, was consecrated in 1552 and is well worth a visit. It is only a short amble up the steepish pedestrian alley to the Grande-Place where a fountain and a comparatively recent monument are watched over by a couple of elderly mansions and the fifteenth-century *hôtel de ville*. The Maison de Bargues, about a block away, shows off some well-furnished rooms with the accent on the seventeenth century while the Maison des Templiers, with its heavy wooden door, concentrates on local folklore and the history of the town. The Avenue de Barrouze leads straight up to an esplanade of the same name which combines a pleasant garden with an excellent view of three separate valleys and the Puy Violent. There is not much in the way of organised entertainment in Salers but the pilgrimage to Notre-Dame-de-Lorette on Trinity Sunday is an extremely colourful affair.

Mauriac, slightly to the north-west, also has a special pilgrimage, this time in honour of Notre-Dame-des-Miracles, in early May. It is primarily an agricultural centre with three modest *auberges* providing some rooms with baths en suite and good home cooking. There is also a delightfully understated church built in the twelfth century. The Gorges d'Auze are only about 3km (2 miles) away and it is possible to see the Cascade de Salins without even getting out of the car.

There are three châteaux of interest in the vicinity, the nearest being the Château de la Vigne in the neighbourhood of Pleaux. Although it is not the most picturesque of country houses, it does occupy the site of an ancient fortress which means that it has a comprehensive view of the surrounding area. Inside there are several rooms full of period furniture, eighteenth-century wood carving and Aubusson tapestries, in addition to which there are frescoes depicting the life of St Hubert in the Salle de Justice. Another good place for tapestries is the Château de la Trémolière in the little village of Anglards de Salers. A collection of ten of these date from the end of the sixteenth century and incorporate some imaginative birds and animals, including a spirited unicorn.

The last of this antiquated trio is the very functional Château d'Auzers which started life as a fortress during the Hundred Years War. It had to be patched up a bit when the fighting ended but very little has changed during the last 500 years, despite the fact that it is still occupied. From the outside it looks a trifle forbidding with its rough stone walls and turrets interspersed with an occasional chimney but inside there is a beautifully decorated oratory and some fine Louis XV furniture.

Anyone who prefers forests to furniture and pictures would be better advised to make for the Gorges de la Rhue, slightly to the north of **Riom-ès-Montagnes**. This popular little holiday resort has nothing much in the way of hotels though it does provide furnished accommodation and space for tents and caravans. Visitors can swim, fish, play tennis and wander along blazed footpaths. For horticulturists an obvious choice would be the Maison de la Gentiane et de la Flore with its display of medicinal plants, audio-visual presentation and a botanical garden full of local vegetation.

The village started life as a Gallo-Roman settlement, has a dolmen of sorts and an interesting eleventh-century church that was once attached to a Cistercian abbey. Apart from the Gorges de la Rhue and the nearby Cascade de Cornillou, reached by way of a rather neglected cart track quite unsuitable for cars, the main places of interest lie to the south.

Apchon is a case in point, a hamlet built of volcanic rock with the ruins of an ancient fortress some 20 minutes' walk away. It is certainly one to add to the collection, apart from which it has a memorable view. Slightly further afield, the little Chapelle de la Font-Sainte is the focal point of a pilgrimage towards the end of August when the villagers combine a religious procession with a kind of glorified picnic that rounds off the celebration very nicely. Cheylade, about the same distance away down an almost parallel minor road, is well known to fishermen, collectors of extremely elderly churches and winter sports enthusiasts. As far as waterfalls are concerned, there are two for the price of one practically on the doorstep, namely the Cascade du Sartre and the neighbouring Cascade de la Roche.

The route over the Pas de Payrol provides some outstanding views and also takes in the Puy Mary, a famous peak which only misses being the highest point in the Monts du Cantal by 70m (230ft). The road up is winding, steep and narrow, painfully so in places, but there is room for two cars to edge past each other and several spots where one can pull off to admire the scenery or avoid a confrontation with an oncoming coach or lorry. The verges are a delight at close quarters with tiny waterfalls and hundreds of wild flowers that look like forget-me-nots, variegated daisies, purplish foxgloves and many others less easy to define.

An *auberge* near the top has a curio shop in close attendance and a view across to the slightly higher Plomb du Cantal; the only thing lacking is a direct road connecting the two. It is here that hikers have the advantage over motorists because the GR400 bridges the gap quite easily whereas the driver has to choose between two minor shortcuts leading off the road to Aurillac, or press on to the town and then double back. Long distance walkers maintain that it takes a week to inspect the Monts du Cantal properly, covering about 20km (12$^1/_2$ miles) a day and spending the nights at a small *auberge* or a conveniently placed mountain refuge.

The motorist, however, can visit several outlying places. The Route des Crêtes produces little villages like Fontanges with the ruined Château de Cropières where Mademoiselle de Fontanges, one of Louis XIV's light-of-loves, was born. It also has some very splendid views.

Apart from this, a great many small, scenic byways criss-cross the area, discovering attractive little hamlets or an impressive mountain fortress such as the Château d'Anjony at Tournemire. This is a strange sort of place, resembling nothing so much as a bunch of rockets with a large, fat one in the middle and even taller, slimmer ones at each corner pointing their roofs to the sky. This ancient complex completely dominates the somewhat barn-like buildings which complete the picture, surrounded by some grass and a great many trees. The fortress itself took 10 years to build, from 1439 to 1449, and was the property of a nobleman who fought alongside Joan of Arc and whose family have lived there ever since. It is well worth seeing for its frescoes, tapestries, furniture and objets d'art and is open to visitors from Palm Sunday until the end of October.

Aurillac has just as much to recommend it whether your interests lie in the past or in the present. It is an elderly town on the River Jordanne which gave the Christians their first French pope in AD999. Gerbert, or Sylvestre II as he was later known, was both a doctor and mathematician who received much of his training in Spanish universities at the height of the Moorish occupation. As a result, his theories were regarded as unconventional by some people whereas others were convinced that they smacked of sorcery. Pretty soon this viewpoint resulted in a whole crop of legends that gave the Church some cause for concern over the next few hundred years.

A statue of the Pope stands in a rather uninteresting garden beside the Pont Rouge, overlooked by some old houses including the Musée de Cire which traces the history of the town. Quite apart from this, Aurillac is by no means short of museums. The Musée Jean-Baptiste Rames is concerned with archaeology and keeps an eye on the remains of the Temple de Lescudiliers which was unearthed locally in 1977. The Musée Hippolyte-de-Parieu houses paintings and sculptures while arts and crafts produced in the area since Roman times find their way into the Musée du Vieil Aurillac. However, the most outstanding of all is the Maison des Volcans, in the thirteenth-century Château St Etienne, where visitors can study the subject of volcanoes in general and those of Cantal in particular.

The town also has its full compliment of churches starting with the Eglise St Géraud, originally part of a Benedictine abbey founded by the Comte Géraud in AD916 and up-dated at regular intervals ever since. The Church of Notre-Dame-aux-Neiges was once attached to the ancient Convent of Cordeliers which, like so many others, failed to survive the Revolution. Both are equally well worth seeing, whereas people who know very little about medieval architecture, and care less, would probably prefer the Eglise du Sacré-Coeur, a comparatively new addition having been built from scratch just before the outbreak of World War II.

The Maison Consulaire, home to the Musée du Vieil Aurillac, is one of the most eye-catching of all the ancient buildings with a great deal of embellishment round and above the main door in the Rue de la Coste. However, there are plenty of others tucked away in the narrow, winding streets near the Palais de Justice which, incidentally, has its own collection of tapestries dating from the seventeenth century.

Anyone who decides to make their holiday headquarters in Aurillac will find two reasonably priced hotels in the upper bracket, one of them only a short walk from all the main attractions, a choice of several smaller ones and a sports complex with both an open-air and a covered swimming pool. Souvenir hunters are confronted by everything from cowbells to brassware, tripe cooked with sheeps trotters known as *tripoux* to cured hams and local cheeses.

It is also a good place to ask for advice on a whole host of different subjects. For instance, the Haras d'Aurillac will assist hopeful riders, the Association de Randonnée Pedestre du Cantal points ramblers in the right direction, Les Ailes du Plomb du Cantal helps them to get airborne while M. le Chef d'Agence S.N.C.F. has all the details of a special train journey round the *département* which takes about 12 hours. There are local craftsmen who are prepared to welcome visitors to their premises, an area for tents and caravans, *gîtes* for rent and bicycles and canoes for hire.

Before heading north again it might be an idea to explore this south-western corner of Auvergne and there can be few better places to begin than at the Château de Conros near Arpajon-sur-Cère. It began as a fortress in feudal days when it belonged to the Astorg family, who were the seigneurs of Aurillac towards the end of the Middle Ages. Not long afterwards, someone had the bright idea of turning it into a desirable country residence without destroying either the chapel or the old guardroom. It was restored again quite recently and is now an interesting place to visit, partly on account of its contents and partly because special exhibitions are held there during the summer.

Somewhat further to the west is **Laroquebrou**, an agreeable, if small, medieval village guarding the entrance to the gorges of the Cère. It has most of the necessary attributes — a viewable little church filled with the tombs of the Montal family, the remains of a rather uninspiring château and a number of country roads that thread their way past the Barrage de St Etienne-Cantalès, cross the main route to Maurs and, by one means or another, arrive eventually at **Montsalvy**. This typical holiday hamlet stands on the wooded plateau of La Châtaigneraie. It has a delightful *auberge* that runs to showers but not private baths, a hint of ancient ramparts, a pleasing eleventh-century church and a view from the nearby Puy de l'Arbre across the Massif du Cantal. It is also a good base from which to set off for the Gorges de la Truyère across the border in Aveyron.

A main road leads north from Montsalvy back to Aurillac where, instead of following the more attractive Route des Crêtes, it is necessary to head for Murat in order to inspect the Château de Pesteils at **Polminhac** and see the Plomb du Cantal. The château is quite impressive, consisting of an extremely tall keep left over from the thirteenth century with a 300 year old manor house attached. This was extended still further in comparatively recent times and made its film debut in a production called *L'Eternel Retour*. The house is known for its painted ceilings, Aubusson tapestries, pictures and furniture, leaving the keep to contribute some fourteenth-century frescoes.

There are two other châteaux in the area, neither of which seems to be in favour of visitors, and a brace of modest *auberges* in Polminhac, giving it a slight edge over Vic-sur-Cère, 5km (3 miles) up

PLACES OF INTEREST IN CANTAL

Salers
Church of St Martin
An attractive church containing many interesting items including the *mise au tombeau* and five tapestries.

Maison de Bargues
A furnished, fifteenth-century mansion.

Maison des Templiers
A display of items associated with the town.

Ancien Bailliage
A Renaissance mansion complete with a tower.

Mauriac
Notre-Dame-des-Miracles
One of the best examples of its kind in the area with some viewable contents including the statue of the Virgin.

Château de la Vigne
Ally, Near Pleaux. Period furniture, tapestries and a good view.

Château de la Trémolière
Anglards de Salers. Collection of fine, sixteenth-century Aubusson tapestries.

Château d'Auzers
Auzers, near Saignes. Rather austere fortress with paintings and furniture.

Riom-ès-Montagnes
Maison de la Gentiane et de la Flore
Horticultural centre with a botanical garden, displays of plants and an audio-visual presentation.

Apchon
Typical village with ruined fortress about 20 minutes walk away. Panoramic view.

Cascade du Sartre
Impressive waterfalls except in very dry weather.

Puy Mary
Second highest peak in the Monts du Cantal. About 1 hour's walk from the Pas de Payrol to the summit where there is a magnificent view.

Route des Crêtes
A scenic route between Puy Mary and Aurillac with an occasional village and beautiful scenery.

Tournemire
Château d'Anjony
A fifteenth-century fortress with very viewable frescoes, which are profane as well as sacred, good furniture and old tapestries.

Aurillac
Musée de Cire
Place Gerbert. A museum concerned mainly with local personalities and local history.

Musée Jean-Baptiste Rames
Sections devoted to archaeology and natural history with reconstructed interior of old farmhouse.

Musée Hippolyte-de-Parieu
Fine arts museum.

Musée de Vieil Aurillac
In the Maison Consulaire. Exhibits of various kinds found in the city and examples of local arts and crafts.

Maison des Volcans
In the Château St Etienne. Concerned exclusively with volcanic matters on a local as well as a world-wide basis.

Eglise St Géraud
Frequently restored church, moderately decorated inside.

Notre-Dame-aux-Neiges
Old chapel with an elegant interior and a much revered statue of the Virgin.

Palais de Justice
Seventeenth-century tapestries in the Court of Assizes.

Château de Conros
Near Arpajon-sur-Cère. Ancient fortress-cum-country house. Chapel, guardroom and objets d'art. Exhibitions during the summer.

Polminhac
Château de Pesteils
Painted ceilings, frescoes, tapestries, pictures and furniture.

Thiézac
Chapelle de Notre-Dame-de-Consolation
An attractive, rustic chapel pleasantly decorated inside.

Etablissement de Pisciculture
Near Thiézac. Fish farm producing trout to stock the local rivers.

Plomb du Cantal
Highest peak of the Monts du Cantal. Splendid view. Reached on foot or by cable car from Super-Lioran.

Puy Griou
A difficult mountain to climb near Super Lioran. Allow at least 4 hours. Exceptional view from the summit.

Laveissière
The Buronnier's House
Reconstructed, characteristic farmhouse with audio-visual presentation.

Albepierre-Bredons
Church of St Peter and St Paul
Famous little fortified church consecrated in 1095.

St Flour
Cathedral of St Pierre
An impressive, understated church with some interesting contents.

Musée de la Haute-Auvergne
Adjoining the cathedral. Sections for archaeology, sacred art, manuscripts and other matters pertaining to the city.

Alfred Douet Museum
In the Maison Consulaire. An attractive old mansion with numerous exhibits not necessarily connected with the area.

Viaduc de Garabit
Construction by Gustave Eiffel, built between 1882 to 1884, which pre-dates the Eiffel Tower by about 5 years.

Château d'Alluze
Ruins of an ancient fortress near the Lac de Grandval.

Oradour
Château de Rochebrune
Fifteenth-century château over-looking the valley with contents including paintings and items of local interest.

Brezons
La Bohal
Well preserved keep from the thirteenth century and an excellent example of medieval military architecture.

Massiac
Church of St André
Small church with interesting statues.

Plateau St Victor
Near Massiac. Prehistoric area with later ruins. Derelict, hilltop chapels and one in a good state of repair.

the road. This is an entirely forgettable but useful place with several small hotels, a house that once belonged to the princes of Monaco and a small church. The town forms part of a popular holiday area with **Thiézac**, another 6km (4 miles) further on.

The local church at Thiézac has one or two interesting items but not a great many more visitors than the Chapelle de Notre-Dame-de-Consolation, built on the orders of Anne of Austria when she was afraid that she would never be able to have any children. Her prayers were answered, her son grew up to be Louis XIV and ever since then there has been an August pilgrimage to the chapel in honour of the Virgin of Miracles. Fertility is obviously no problem on the local fish farm, which is open every afternoon to visitors and produces something like 2 million trout a year. The GR400 runs past the village up to the **Plomb du Cantal** and there is also a cable car up to the summit from Super Lioran.

When it comes to winter sports, **Super Lioran** pulls out all the stops, providing its guests with a wide range of accommodation from a large, modern hotel to special stopping places for cross country skiers who plan to be away for the night. The centre is just as popular during the summer but tends to take its own holidays in the spring and autumn when most of the hotels are closed. This leaves the *auberge* in **Le Lioran** to cope all on its own. The parent village is another unremarkable little place, surrounded by magnificent pine forests and the proud possessor of two long tunnels which are invaluable when the nearby passes are deep in snow.

Unlike the volcanic areas to the north, the Monts du Cantal were created by a single volcano, about 70km (44 miles) in diameter, with a whole host of little craters and chimneys that bubbled away merrily until it became extinct. There is a certain fascination in looking down on a wide plain, pimpled with grass-covered hills and small rocky outcrops, which stretches away to the distant ridge and trying to visualise what it must have been like millions of years ago.

Returning to Le Lioran and the present day, there is an opportunity to visit a typical farmhouse, or *buron,* at **Laveissière**, on the road to Murat. It has been turned into a kind of museum with all the appropriate atmosphere and an audio-visual presentation on the art of making cheese. **Murat** itself looks on cheese production as one of its major occupations, along with wood and tourism. It lost its château on the instructions of Cardinal Richelieu but even he could not spoil the view from the site, known as the Rocher de Bonnevie, now presided over by a statue of Notre-Dame-de la Haute-Auvergne.

The old town, with its narrow streets and old-world houses protected by heavy tiles made from lava, clusters round the Eglise Notre-Dame des Oliviers which is only mildly viewable. However, the little fortified church in **Albepierre-Bredons**, once part of a medieval priory, more than makes up for it, especially as it is only 2km (1 mile) away and has some ancient rock dwellings close by. Murat has a clutch of modest hotels, a camp site and facilities for tennis and fishing but nothing else of any consequence.

The same cannot be said of **St Flour** — a town built of granite on granite with some delightful hotels and plenty of things to see and do, which makes it a good base for exploring the area. Foremost among its local attractions is the decidedly sombre Cathedral of St Pierre, occupying the site of an ancient priory and including in its treasures a wooden statue of Christ known as *Bon Dieu Noir* and a bronze reliquary containing the remains of St Flour. He was one of the men who preached Christianity in Auvergne during the fourth century and the town grew up round his tomb.

The Musée de la Haute-Auvergne, adjoining the cathedral in one wing of a seventeenth-century palace which it shares with the *hôtel de ville*, covers a wide range of subjects. The section devoted to sacred art includes a twelfth-century statue of St Pierre from the church at Albepierre-Bredons. He is seated in a tightly-fitting, wrap-around chair with a slightly glazed look in his eyes and two extremely long fingers raised in blessing. Other rooms are given over to archaeology and items of everyday life in the history of the province, culminating in a tribute to the members of the Resistance Movement in Cantal during World War II. On the other side of the Place d'Armes is the ancient Maison Consulaire, housing the Alfred Douet Museum. Apart from the building itself, which has a splendid fireplace in the Salle des Gardes, there is a collection of old weapons, tapestries from Aubusson, enamels from Limoges, French and Dutch paintings and much else besides.

The Terrasse des Roches has taken the place of the original ramparts and in doing so has inherited a view across the modern suburbs down below to the Landes Valley, with its picturesque gorges, and the mountains of La Margeride. The streets of the old town, some barely the width of a car, are lined with antiquated houses, few if any of which are open to view.

If history becomes a trifle overpowering, outdoor enthusiasts

Cable car at Super Lioran

have several other options open to them. There are horses to ride, fish to catch, opportunities for swimming or playing tennis, footpaths to follow in summer and places to ski in winter. Anyone whose idea of a good holiday includes catering for the family can settle into furnished accommodation, pitch a tent or park a caravan.

The countryside around St Flour is by no means over-populated. The villages, like so many of the roads, are inclined to be small, sheep as well as cattle wear bells that tinkle incessantly and the mountains echo to the voices of shepherds as they shout instructions to the dogs watching over their flocks. Buzzards drift majestically overhead while jays, wagtails, hoopees, yellow hammers and others of their ilk carry on endless conversations among themselves.

The main roads have their quota of modern houses, some painted and some in natural stone and there can be a lot of traffic on the route to **Garabit**, 12km ($7\frac{1}{2}$ miles) to the south-east. The village comes complete with a handful of small hotels but the main attraction is undoubtedly the viaduct, built by Gustave Eiffel a little over 100 years ago and the first major steel construction in France. From here it is wise to have a reliable map in order to find the best way round the Lac

Ruined Château d'Alluze, near Garabit

de Grandval to the ruined Château d'Alluze, isolated on a hilltop and looking rather the worse for wear. A road runs up to the fortress with its large keep supported by four round towers which proved their worth during the Hundred Years War.

The lake, formed by a barrage on the River Truyère, spreads itself over a large area with attractive little bays and fir trees lining the shore, creating a scene that could just as easily be Finnish as French. Motor launches are available for trips in the summer, holidaymakers can waterski, windsurf or sail, while a short, sharp trot up the Belvédère de Mallet is worth attempting for its view over the water.

Chaudes-Aigues, the only spa in Cantal, is just a short drive away. It is fairly small and compact with no casino or up-market hotels but a reputation for having the hottest thermal springs in Europe. In fact, the residents have been piping hot water round the village and into their homes for centuries and, as a result, they cannot see anything particularly modern about central heating.

The Romans were the first to enjoy splashing about in temperatures up to 28°C (82°F) but for some reason they do not seem to have left any traces of their occupation. It was not until 1964 that Chaudes-

Aigues took its place as one of the ten recognised spas in Auvergne. Visitors can also swim, fish, play tennis, walk in the woods and take part in local fêtes and festivals which have a decidedly traditional air about them.

In addition to all this, there are two châteaux in the vicinity — one ancient and the other a relative newcomer at Faverolles, within easy reach of both the Viaduc de Garabit and the Barrage de Grandval. The Château de Rochebrune at Oradour, just off the main road to the north, once formed part of a line of defences protecting the southern approaches to St Flour. It is an atmospheric fifteenth-century fortress that rose up from the ruins of an ancient castle surrounded by trees and terraces. Despite being somebody's home these days, it is open regularly to visitors, providing they make the necessary arrangements when out of season. The building is fully furnished and provides a home for a collection of pictures and a display of various examples of Auvergnat folklore.

A pleasant, small road cuts across country to Pierrefort and on to **Brezons** where students of military history will find plenty to interest them in La Bohal. It was an outstanding thirteenth-century fortress that incurred the displeasure of Cardinal Richelieu who, characteristically, had everything removed except the keep. This has been extremely well restored and maintained and can be seen at almost any time during August and September, though only after making an appointment. Alternatively, a maze of little roads wander northwards from Pierrefort, some of them coming to an abrupt end after a few kilometres, whereas others soldier on towards **Roffiac** where there is a typical little church dating from the beginning of the twelfth century and just the vestige of a slightly younger château.

Depending on time and inclination, one can either visit the Cascade du Sailhant, which involves walking for about a quarter of an hour, return to St Flour or press on to **Massiac**. This is an attractive little place in the shadow of rocky cliffs, providing some interesting statues in the Church of St André and two *auberges* which are fully modernised for anybody who wants to stop for a while.

The surrounding area, particularly the Plateau St Victor, was inhabited before and during the Bronze Age and is a happy hunting ground for archaeologists. There are also bits and pieces that were left behind during the Middle Ages but the only chapel still intact is a small stone building, rather like an elderly cottage with a tiny belfry, which is dedicated to Ste Madeleine. There is no road up to it, which is a pity for anyone who dislikes walking because it is a charming little relic with a view over the town and across the border into the adjoining *département* of Haute-Loire.

Haute-Loire

Haute-Loire is most things to most visitors. It shares the south of Auvergne with Cantal, the Parc Régional du Livradois-Forez with Puy-de-Dôme and common boundaries with Lozère, Ardèche and Loire. It is an area of infinite variety with the pointed remains of ancient volcanoes, wooded valleys, extensive grasslands, memorable villages and historic towns. It can be very hot in summer and quite cold in winter, delicately coloured with carpets of wild flowers in the spring or set ablaze by autumn leaves but one thing is certain, it is never boring.

The most striking town in the *département* is **Le Puy-en-Velay**, very dramatic if seen for the first time from the north but softer and tinged with pink when approached along the main road from Lozère or Ardèche. In bygone days it was a famous place of pilgrimage and though this has diminished down the centuries, it is still every bit as crowded during the high season. Nowadays, however, guide books have taken the place of rosaries and the obligatory garb appears to be sensible shoes and a determined expression. It must be admitted that a certain degree of determination is necessary in Le Puy-en-Velay because some of the outstanding attractions can only be reached with a good deal of effort. The Chapelle St Michel d'Aiguilhe is a perfect example, perched on a rocky pinnacle with 268 steps to climb in order to inspect it properly.

According to some people, the site was chosen originally by the Romans for their temple to Mercury, the messenger of the gods, who perhaps needed a high take-off point to cut down flying time. The present eleventh-century structure has more than a hint of Moorish influence about it. Beyond the single doorway, flanked by columns and smothered overhead in black, white and grey mosaics, the interior is dark and unconventional. It follows the contours of the rock with short, slender pillars, some almost invisible murals and a lonely stained glass window.

It is possible to get much closer to the Cathedral of Notre-Dame before having to tackle another flight of steps that are steep but not unbearably so. It is a large, rather formidable building with the west façade protruding from the hillside on a giant platform, adding to its

Viaduc de Garabit

imposing appearance. Time is needed to inspect all the different chapels, some of which are decorated with frescoes, and climb up and down stairways to the ancient vaults. One can also wander round the cloister, with its low hedges and two-toned archways which are younger, much more subdued and yet vaguely reminiscent of those at Cordoba. On one side is the Chapelle des Morts and on the other the Chapelle des Reliques et Trésor d'Art Religieux which closely resembles a small museum.

The Maison du Prieur, forming part of the same complex, has a permanent exhibition of local crafts, farm implements, domestic appliances and regional costumes but the main treasure is kept in the sacristy. This includes the famous Bible of Théodulfe which dates from the time of Charlemagne. From behind the cathedral another daunting pathway leads up to the gigantic statue of Notre-Dame-de-France on the peak of the Rocher Corneille. It was cast in 1860 from more than 200 Russian cannons captured at Sebastopol during the Crimean War and has a narrow iron ladder inside so that anyone with sufficient energy left can clamber up to admire the view from inside the Virgin's coronet.

Ancient church at Roffiac

Back at ground level, the second most popular local attraction is the Musée Crozatier in the attractive Jardin Henri Vinay, a fair distance away, beyond the encircling boulevards of St Louis and Maréchal Fayolle. Although there is a section devoted to Roman and Gothic art along with other exhibits of various kinds, it is usually referred to as the Lace Museum because of its fascinating collection spanning more than 400 years. The old heart of the city is full of winding streets, pedestrian walkways, elderly churches and some decorative houses, most of these to be found in the Rue Pannessac. The small shops can be either quaint or contemporary and there is a Saturday market in the area round the cathedral where, at one time, medieval vendors displayed their wares for the benefit of pilgrims and soldiers home from the crusades.

Le Puy celebrates in style, particularly during the Roi de l'Oiseau festival in September. It is the time when archers parade with their bows at the ready, accompanied by the odd cannon or two and townspeople in sumptuous costumes. Small groups of appropriately dressed musicians are kept busy reproducing medieval serenades on instruments that are just as traditional as the melodies. There are also a number of religious events, including the torchlit Procession of Penitents and the Procession of Notre-Dame-du-Puy in August.

Anybody who decides to spend a few days in town will find two comfortable hotels, a handful of smaller establishments, a youth hostel and a camp site which is invariably crowded during the season. There is a large underground car park that comes in handy, swimming pools for all seasons and facilities for riding, cycling, fishing, playing tennis and walking. Places of interest in the immediate vicinity include the Rocher St Joseph whose large statue of the saint has a panoramic view over the city.

Polignac, on the other hand, is dominated by an ancient fortress which, in its time, housed an army of 800 men along with their families and a considerable number of retainers. There is also a small church dating from the twelfth century with statues of leading members of the ruling family including Héracle who was killed at Antioch. The Maison de l'Artisanat de Bilhac-Polignac exists in order to keep the traditional arts and crafts of the region alive by holding exhibitions and running courses in such things as making lace. The nearby Château de St Vidal was a feudal mansion and offers an occasional glimpse of the original building which fortunately escaped the extensive reconstruction carried out in the fifteenth and sixteenth centuries.

Following the Loire southwards from Le Puy-en-Velay makes a pleasant outing but hardly a demanding one. There are not a great many places of special interest before the provincial border despite the wealth of small, scenic byways and the occasional view. However, provided time is no object, the area is worth exploring in order to call in at **Arlempdes**, an extremely atmospheric hamlet poised on a hilltop above the river. It has a local inn, the remains of a splendid castle, a twelfth-century chapel and a gateway through the surrounding walls which, according to a strategically placed white plaque, date from 1066 'and all that'.

Its moments of grandeur passed their peak in the Middle Ages, long after the Gallo-Roman Villa des Souils had been destroyed. This was apparently quite an important place in its day but depressingly little remains apart from a few foundations which have been tidied up very efficiently by archaeologists. At this stage, the Loire is small and smooth with a fishermen's rest beside the water, a well maintained road and some modest gorges on the Mejanne River at the point where it crosses into Ardèche.

Le Monastier-sur-Gazeille, to the north-west, managed to restore a portion of its ancient abbey after the Hundred Years War, along with part of the château which was once the home of the local abbot. Exhibitions are held there in the summer to draw attention to prehistoric events that took place in the valley of the Loire. **Pradelles**, about the same distance away in the opposite direction, overlooks the Allier, has the remains of its original fortifications and an old market place partly surrounded by arcades.

Visitors can find a bed for the night, a whole range of outdoor activities and a good many picnic spots in the surrounding woods but nothing in the way of dolmens or antiquated ruins. Another alternative for anyone not heading south to Aubenas, in Ardèche, would be to turn north again to the Lac du Bouchet. This is a large, circular pocket of water, neatly contained in a volcanic crater, with fir trees all round and opportunities for canoeing and fishing but not swimming.

At this point, motorists have to decide whether to inspect the Allier at close quarters, slightly to the west, and carry on up the gorges or follow a convoluted secondary road to **Sauges**. Apart from its Tour des Anglais and an eleventh-century church containing the reliquary of St Benilde, the village is known principally for its time-honoured Procession of Penitents. It is also a minor holiday resort, short on hotels but offering all the usual summer activities while insisting that it usually has enough snow for skiing in winter.

The same road, now of no particular merit, continues on towards **Mont-Mouchet**, the operational headquarters of the local Resistance Movement during World War II. There is a national monument in **Auvers** to the members of the Maquis and a museum opposite with a collection of relevant documents, letters and photographs which is open from May until mid-October.

The country hereabouts is hilly rather than mountainous, with roads winding in and out of the valleys somewhat lethargically. At least one village adds to its quota of wild flowers by tossing garden varieties, such as sweetpeas, on to a minute traffic island until it looks like an advertisement from an expensive seed catalogue. Lines of mature trees stand like sentries along the roadsides and practically every stream has its own solid stone bridge. Some of them may only have been built quite recently but they all give the impression of having been in existence for hundreds of years.

It hardly matters whether one opts for the road along the gorges or the route to Sauges because they meet up eventually at **Langeac**, a village with a certain amount to offer in addition to an attractive little

PLACES OF INTEREST IN HAUTE-LOIRE

Le Puy-en-Velay
Chapelle St Michel d'Aiguilhe
An unusual, impressive church on a rock pinnacle, reached only after a long climb.

Cathedral of Notre-Dame
A large, imposing building with a great deal to see including several chapels, the cloister, a collection of sacred art, a smallish museum and the cathedral treasures.

Statue of Notre-Dame-de-France
On the peak of the Rocher Corneille, above the cathedral. A long walk up and an iron ladder to climb inside the statue to the top.

Musée Crozatier
In the Jardin Henri Vinay. Various exhibits but principally a superb collection of lace.

Eglise St Laurent
Avenue d'Aiguilhe. Viewable old church. Closed at the time of writing.

Rocher St Joseph
On the road to St Flour. Large statue on a rock pinnacle, complementing the statue of Notre-Dame-de-France.

Polignac
Ancient Fortress
Large building on a flat-topped hill. Small but interesting associated church nearby.

Maison de l'Artisanat de Bilhac-Polignac
Craft centre with exhibitions and classes.

Château de St Vidal
Feudal mansion somewhat updated in the sixteenth century.

Arlempdes
Hilltop village in the Loire with castle ruins, high walls and a small chapel. Remains of Gallo-Roman villa close by.

Le Monastier-sur-Gazeille
Abbey and Château
Somewhat battered remains from the Middle Ages. Archaeological exhibitions during the summer. The starting point for Robert Louis Stevenson's *Travels with a Donkey*.

Pradelles
Old fortified village. L'Oustalou reconstructs past village life.

Lac du Bouchet
A completely circular lake in an extinct volcanic crater surrounded by trees.

Gorges de l'Allier
Very attractive drive from Chapeauroux to Brioude with several small villages en route.

Sauges
Tour des Anglais and small church Village known mainly for its Procession of Penitents.

Mont-Mouchet
Headquarters of the local Resistance Movement in World War II.

Auvers
Near Mont-Mouchet. Monument

and museum centred on the members of the Maquis.

Chavaniac-Lafayette
Birthplace of the eighteenth-century soldier and statesman. Beautifully furnished château. Articles associated with the life of Lafayette, the American War of Independence and World War I. Park and rosegarden.

Blassac
Church
Small building with fourteenth-century frescoes.

St Ilpize
Ruins and Rock Cellars
Medieval site on the Gorges de l'Allier.

Brioude
Basilique St Julien
A large and very impressive cathedral, well worth seeing for its chapels and decorations.

Blesle
Church of St Pierre
Part of a ninth-century abbey. Old choir stalls, stone carving and sacred treasures.

Auzon
Old, once fortified village with the remains of a château and ramparts and an elderly church. Several viewable statues including the one of Notre-Dame-de-Portail.

Lavaudieu
St André de Comps
Eleventh-century Benedictine abbey with frescoes and small museum in a delightful rural village.

Château de Domeyrat
Quite impressive ruins and a small church of comparable antiquity.

La Chaise-Dieu
Abbaye St Robert
Large and very impressive church with a number of outstanding features including the tomb of Pope Clément VI, the *Danse Macabre* mural and some fine Flemish tapestries. Also the Salle de l'Echo.

Historial de la Chaise-Dieu
Small museum tracing the history of the abbey.

Signal de St Claude
Panoramic view.

Allègre
Ruins
Improbable remains of a substantial medieval fortress and view of the Monts du Forez, Le Mézenc and Le Velay.

Château de la Rochelambert
Splendid château, beautifully furnished which featured in George Sand's *Jean de la Roche*. Prehistoric caves nearby.

St Paulien
Church
Viewable interior.

Le Chambon-sur-Lignon
Holiday centre with golf, archery, riding etc. Small arts and crafts museum. Thatched houses at Moudeyres in the vicinity.

church. The hotel accommodation is limited and somewhat on the basic side but there are some furnished, self-catering alternatives as well as a camp site. Local activities include tennis, swimming, riding and fishing. There are also marked footpaths through the woods, canoeing on the river and opportunities to study folklore at first hand.

In many respects, Langeac differs very little from the majority of villages along the way but it scores over the others in one important respect — it has a direct line to Chavaniac-Lafayette, the birthplace of the famous general so dear to the hearts of Americans. The present château, flanked by two sturdy round towers, was built in the seventeenth century on the site of an ancient fort. Apart from a large park and a fragrant rose garden, it has a wax museum and a great many reminders of the American War of Independence and World War I. A conducted tour lasts about 1 hour and includes the guard-room, the *grand salon*, the Louis XIII dining hall and the room where the future Marquis de Lafayette was born in September 1757. A special section is concerned with the main events in the life of this eminent soldier-statesman. He led the National Guard to Versailles at the beginning of the Revolution, fled to Lièges when he was officially declared to be a traitor to the Republic, but returned 7 years later and subsequently took his place in the Chamber of Deputies.

Provided one is prepared to dart about a little, there are plenty of attractions to be seen in this area. The main gorges of the Allier, which account for some 30km ($18^1/_2$ miles) in all, pass close to Blassac where the fourteenth-century frescoes adorning the local church will be shown to anyone who asks to look at them. **St Ilpize**, with its cellars cut out of the rock, is slightly further up on the opposite bank, calling for a short deviation from the main route. It was an important stronghold during the Middle Ages but got caught up in the Hundred Years War and was extremely lucky to escape with its little chapel and the ruins of a château, now all of 600 years old.

A few kilometres further on, the road joins the main route from Clermont-Ferrand to Aubenas just short of **Brioude**. This is an old town, steeped in legends centred mainly on St Julien, a Roman soldier who took refuge there after being converted to Christianity. He was unfortunate enough to be discovered and died the death of a martyr in AD304. The Basilique St Julien is a very grand affair and prides itself on being the largest Romanesque church in Auvergne. It is much decorated both inside and out.

Building started in the eleventh century and continued for more than 200 years with a certain amount of refurbishing thereafter. The porches and chapels are especially memorable in themselves as well as for the paintings and sculptures which adorn them. The old town was built in the form of an amphitheatre and still has a number of ancient houses, particularly in the little winding streets near the cathedral. Meanwhile, the *hôtel de ville* occupies the site of an original château and has an excellent view across to the mountains of Livradois.

To the west and north of Brioude the most interesting villages are **Blesle** and **Auzon**. The former is a curious little place founded by the Benedictines in the ninth century and still clustered round its rural-looking Church of St Pierre. At one time this was part of the wealthy monastery and, as such, was treated to some imaginative stone carving, old choir stalls and a small collection of treasures. Time appears to have had very little effect on what is, in essence, a market hamlet with a few modest reminders of its distant past.

Auzon falls roughly into the same category and clings just as tenaciously to everything it has managed to preserve since the Middle Ages. The list is really quite short, due partly to Richelieu who tried his best to destroy the château and its ramparts but left the church more or less intact. Inside, among a number of other statues, is the elegant Notre-Dame-du-Portail, dating from the end of the fifteenth century.

A third village with comparable attractions is **Lavaudieu**, some 10km (6 miles) to the south-east of Brioude but more or less isolated because of the shortage of roads. It comprises hardly more than a few farmhouses on the banks of the River Senouire with the remains of a Benedictine abbey founded nearly 1,000 years ago. The outstanding features are a number of noteworthy frescoes which were only brought to light in 1967, a wholly delightful cloister and a small local museum. A bridge over the river is a favourite meeting place for local worthies of uncertain age who are quick to direct visitors up the steep alleys leading to the church but less inclined to help motorists trapped in a herd of cattle who have plenty of time in hand and nothing much to do with it.

Both the road and a long distance footpath keep company with the river as far as the ruined Château de Domeyrat where they part company. The ramblers make for Paulhaguet whereas drivers have a choice of byways through the forest to La Chaise-Dieu. Whichever route is chosen, it is bound to wander to a certain extent, shaded by

Arlempdes

oaks, pines and some beech trees. There are little, unexpected touches like a sign that reads 'Poterie 2km' or another for a 'Château' which turns out to be a small ruin.

Although **La Chaise-Dieu** is relatively modest as towns go, it is home to the very large, somewhat dour and justly famous Abbaye St Robert. The church was built in the fourteenth century at the instigation of Pope Clément VI so it is hardly surprising that it presents a severe, no-nonsense face to the world. The lofty interior, described with perfect accuracy by one visitor as 'haughty', is filled with treasures including a splendid organ which is played in the annual music festival. The tomb of Clément VI stands exactly in the centre of the church, surrounded on three sides by most impressive stalls and watched over by the statues of more than forty members of his family. Beyond them, on the left, is the famous mural, measuring 26m by 2m (85ft by 6$\frac{1}{2}$ ft) and christened *Danse Macabre*. The theme is a medieval celebration with guests from every walk of life, most of whom have a skeleton in attendance.

On the opposite side of the church are some exceptionally fine tapestries woven in Flanders during the sixteenth century. The

Lavaudieu

cloister is nearly as dramatic as the church with heavy vaulting, no decoration to speak of and a low fence round the lawn in the middle which effectively keeps people off the grass. The Tour Clémentine, square and militant, overlooks the Place de l'Echo. This takes its name from the Salle de l'Echo which was designed so that anyone talking softly could be heard quite easily in the nearby room. In this way it was possible for priests to hear the confessions of lepers in perfect safety during the Middle Ages. The Historial de La Chaise-Dieu, with its little museum tracing the history of the abbey, is almost next door. The only other local attraction is the Signal de St Claude, with a panoramic view that takes in everything from the Cévennes to the Monts Dore.

Naturally, La Chaise-Dieu keeps one eye on the tourist trade. There are four small, quite modest hotels, all with restaurants and three with car parks, as well as furnished accommodation and space for tents and caravans. Guests can swim, play tennis, ride and fish, try out a kayak for the day, walk in the forest and ski during the winter. The residents take an informed interest in both folklore and ancient music which figures prominently during the music festival in August and early September.

As far as excursions are concerned, there are several places of interest within easy reach on the way down to Le Puy-en-Velay. The **Lac de Malaguet** is a good place for fishing, **Allègre**, nearby, has some rather peculiar remains of an old fortress that look as if they would topple over at the slightest provocation, whereas the feudal Château de la Rochelambert is both well maintained and very substantial, despite suffering a great deal during the Wars of Religion. George Sand was a frequent visitor and liked it so much that she included it, turrets and all, in *Jean de la Roche*. The rooms are beautifully furnished and, like the chapel, are well worth visiting. It would also be a pity to miss the collection of prehistoric caves which have Celtic links and are only a short walk away. There are several of them at different levels, inter-connected to the extent that they take on the appearance of an underground home with a useful view over the valley.

St Paulien, practically next door, was an important centre in bygone days, when it was known to the Romans as *Ruessium*. It has an elderly church, much restored and refurbished about 300 years ago. There is no direct road from St Paulien to **Vorey-sur-Arzon**, which is known purely on account of its aquatic leisure park. However, it is worth discovering a way round the back in order to join the scenic route along the Loire as far as **Retournac**. This has a little twelfth-century church, a ruined chapel and the Château du Chabanoles, housing a few bits and pieces from the reign of Louis XV.

From here one should branch off in a south-easterly direction for **Yssingeaux**, a small place surrounded by cone-shaped volcanoes which has every intention of becoming a popular holiday resort. It already has a couple of basic hotels, furnished rooms and a camp site. All the usual sports facilities are close to hand, including footpaths through the most attractive countryside all round and, by way of a change, there is an elderly town hall and the Chapel of the Penitents. However, it has quite a long way to go in order to catch up with **Le Chambon-sur-Lignon**, almost on the border with Ardèche.

Although this thriving holiday centre has nothing in the way of historic attractions, it makes its mark in several other respects. To start with, it has enough hotel beds for 300 visitors, with at least two of the establishments listing tennis and swimming among their facilities. The sports centre has opened one of the few golf courses to be found in this part of the world and will also give tennis lessons.

The river is stocked with trout to keep the fisherfolk happy, there are archery butts for anyone who fancies becoming a latter day Robin Hood while the riding stables are ready to handle anything from a short lesson to an organised pony trek.

In addition, there is a small museum concentrating on the arts and crafts of the Massif Central and a folklore group which is prepared to share its knowledge with visitors. Motorists who would like a day out in the country can visit the little volcanic Lac de St Front, discover some traditional thatched houses in Moudeyres and inspect the winter sports facilities at Les Estables before crossing the provincial border to pinpoint the source of the Loire.

Allier

The *département* of Allier, in the north of Auvergne, is much less dramatic from the scenic point of view than the other areas further south. There is little evidence of volcanic action; in fact the land is green and fertile with large tracts given over to the cultivation of sunflowers and cereals. Herds of cattle add to the pleasant rural atmosphere, having an occasional vineyard and a scattering of woodlands for company. Although definitely part of the Massif Central, it does not really give that impression, making it difficult for the ordinary visitor to decide where the region actually begins. There are not nearly as many lakes as elsewhere and, on the whole, the rivers are either placid and well used, like the Allier, the Besbre and the Sioule, or small and self-effacing with hardly a gorge in sight. Aside from this, there are towns, both ancient and modern, some worthwhile châteaux, leisure parks and a good many other attractions.

Vichy is, without a doubt, the most famous town in Allier, with all the slightly faded elegance that clings like a mist to so many rich holiday playgrounds of the last century. However, the story did not begin then. The Romans were among the first to take the waters but more than a 1,000 years went by before any serious attempts were made to turn the little fortified village into a thriving spa. Madame de Sévigné found it an ideal place to write her letters and diaries but it was not until the eighteenth century that Louis XV's daughters, Adelaide and Victoire, added their royal seal of approval. After that there was no stopping Vichy. Bonapartes arrived in droves, Frenchmen and foreigners alike brought their ailments to be cured and, as recently as 1940, Maréchal Pétain and his collaborationist govern-

Ruined Château de Domeyrat

ment were based there while the Germans held the reins in Paris.

At the end of World War II, Vichy returned to the serious business of coping with everything from rheumatism to indigestion, at the same time exporting its slightly fizzy mineral water for those who could not make the trip to collect it for themselves. There are well over a hundred doctors in the town, many of them fluent in English, some of the best hotels and restaurants in Auvergne, seventy or more smaller establishments offering varying degrees of comfort and nearly a thousand villas, furnished apartments and *pensions* as well as three camp sites.

On the entertainment front, two casinos, a dozen cinemas, a handful of theatres and an opera house vie for attention with open-air concerts, festivals and the local culture centre. Shopping is easy, enjoyable and frequently expensive, a complaint which is echoed by the usual crop of unsuccessful punters after a visit to the races. There are tennis courts, swimming pools, riding stables and an 18-hole golf course which will provide lessons.

The town has also made its mark in the boating world with a yacht club, a number of organised nautical events during the season and

Lace-making

plenty of opportunities for pushing the boat out, both literally and figuratively. Only a minute proportion of the 400 springs are pressed into service, at least one of which is equipped with a series of taps so that passers-by can fill their own bottles without being interrupted.

Architecturally, Vichy is completely conventional, having well-kept gardens and promenades along the river's edge, and a large tree-filled Parc des Sources, totally surrounded by covered walk-ways, where bands play and crowds gather in all but the very coldest weather. It is a trifle odd that such an elderly spa should be so lacking in historic buildings. There is just a trace of the old convent at the Sources des Célestines which perpetuates the name and stands in its own grounds full of rare conifers, the Tour de l'Horloge, left over from a fifteenth-century fort, and the Maison du Bailliage, also known as the Castel-Franc. This is a small museum with a collection of souvenirs calling to mind a number of visitors from the days of the Romans to those of the Second Empire.

The Maison du Missionnaire claims to be a fraction more exotic whereas the Centre des Recherches Archéologiques delves into the past history of the area and does not appear to be particularly anxious to share its findings with casual visitors. Madame de Sévigné's old home has been turned into a plush hotel while the town gardens, laid out on the orders of Napoleon III, are full of birds and children. Churches are conspicuous by their absence, the only one of any note being the Eglise St Blaise whose Virgin — inevitably Notre-Dame-des-Malades — is honoured with a torchlit procession in August.

The immediate surroundings, referred to as the Agglomération Vichyssoise — which promptly calls to mind a delicious potato soup — includes the Site des Hurlevents, complete with an orientation table and an extensive view, and Bellerive, home of Vichy's Sporting Club. The outlying suburb of **Cusset** is an old town with royal connections, a medieval tower and some moderately attractive fifteenth-century houses in the Place Victor Hugo. The church is totally forgettable, unlike the one at **Châtel-Montagne**, away to the east. This large, workmanlike construction completely dwarfs the houses all round and, probably because it is built of granite and decorations have been kept to a minimum, it is considered to be one of the finest examples of its kind.

The nearest hotel, and a very basic one at that, is at **Le Mayet-de-Montagne** where L'Association des Amis de la Montagne Bourbonnaise keeps alive a whole range of traditional crafts and where local publicity claims, without much obvious justification, that the village is a good place to ski. All in all, this corner of Allier is more likely to appeal to hikers than to motorists because the GR 3 runs through the wooded hillsides, taking in an occasional viewpoint like the Rocher St Vincent on its way south.

Most people would probably find more to interest them in **Gannat**, to the west of Vichy. This is an ancient village with two small churches and a medieval château that has served both as a home and as a prison. Nowadays it gives houseroom to the Musée des Trésors des Portes Occitanes which has accumulated a varied collection of items including the local archives, religious relics and sundry exhibits that were once commonplace articles in the homes and workshops of the Bourbonnais. Gannat is also recognised as an important traditional music centre and dresses up the ancient melodies with folklore whenever it decides to hold a world festival. There do not appear to be any specific dates for these events but anyone who is really interested can get the details by telephoning 70.90.12.67

Ebreuil, a lake side village some 10km (6 miles) further west, has a good deal in common with Gannat. They are both close to the border with Puy-de-Dôme, have a few hotel rooms, furnished accommodation and camp sites, as well as all the usual sporting facilities. There is also a canoe club which organises trips along the river with places to stop overnight.

Ebreuil, however, is known principally for the Church of St Léger which first saw the light of day in the tenth century as part of a Benedictine monastery. It has some very worthwhile murals, one depicting the death of St Valéry that calls to mind the murder of Thomas Becket at Canterbury, and an ornate sixteenth-century reliquary of St Léger. It is within easy reach of the Gorges de Chouvigny, the Forêt des Colettes and **Charroux** which is still protected by a rather unattractive but very substantial gateway in ramparts which have all but disappeared. It boasts a twelfth-century fortified church and some picturesque old houses in the Rue de la Poulaillerie.

Continuing in a circle round Vichy, the next place of interest is **Billy** which has a twelfth-century fortress built by the Sire de Bourbon to watch over the Vallée de l'Allier. The whole place was enclosed in a series of walls and ramparts, making it the largest defensive fortification in the Duchy. From here a small road carries on through St Félix and Magnet before joining up with the main route to **Lapalisse**, a pleasing town completely dominated by an enormous château.

It is a splendid place, originating in the twelfth century but considerably enlarged more than 300 years later by Jacques de Chabannes, a marshal of France who died after the Battle of Pavie in 1525, before his home was completed. A guided tour includes the private chapel where members of the family are buried in the crypt, a spacious dining hall, the library and a number of reception rooms, among them the magnificent Salon Doré. There are some exceptionally fine tapestries, beautiful furniture, golden caskets, portraits and other memorabilia.

During the summer, history is re-enacted on the premises with a production called *La Memoire du Temps* that starts after nightfall on Friday and Saturday evenings. Lapalisse does not exactly bend over backwards to attract visitors. There is nothing out of the ordinary about its little hotels but, somewhat surprisingly, it has a parachute centre and an aero club. It also arranges long distance rambles if required.

St Pourçain-sur-Sioule, about 30km (18$^1/_2$ miles) away, is a bit more tourist conscious, perhaps because it is a recognised holiday

*Château de la
Rochelambert*

centre on the main road north from Clermont-Ferrand through Moulins to Paris. It is a great place for fishing, country walks and other outdoor activities such as tennis, riding, swimming and canoeing.

It is possible to get a room with a private bath, admire the surrounding vineyards and taste the end products — red, white and rosé — at the Maison du St Pourçain which acts as a shop window for the local co-operative. The town was once the site of the ancient Abbaye Ste Croix which came to a sticky end at the time of the Revolution. By some means or other, the church managed to survive and it takes about half an hour to look round, inspect the fifteenth-century stalls, pay one's respects to a rather mutilated Pietà in the sacristy and examine the sparse remains of the monastery.

For a complete change of scene, families could do far worse than opt for a day out at the Parc des Gouttes near **Jaligny-sur-Besbre**. There are plenty of places to picnic on the grass, under the trees or

Fishermen's Rest on the Loire

overlooking the water. Fishermen can pass the time beside a well stocked lake with a reasonable chance of catching something. Others can play mini-golf, practise with a bow and arrow, hire a pedalo or, in the case of children, set out for a ride on a pony. The attendant zoo is inhabited by some 300 birds and animals and there are exactly the same number of seats in the restaurant for people who do not like picnics.

St Pourçain-sur-Besbre, not to be confused with its namesake on the Sioule, is a great deal smaller, less geared to the needs of holidaymakers and has nothing to show for its long life apart from a small church. However, there are two châteaux close by though one of them, the Château de Beauvoir, only allows visitors into the grounds. The Château de Toury is much more amiable and lays on conducted tours between April and October.

It is a fairytale sort of castle, all towers and turrets, which, according to legend, was built in one night and is guarded by a ferocious red dragon. He must be exceptionally well trained because he has not eaten a single tourist so far and keeps well out of sight when people arrive to inspect his domain! According to its small museum, the fortress was built in the twelfth century, was refurbished 200 years later and played an important part in both the Hundred Years War and the Wars of Religion.

Slightly further up the road from the Château de Toury, and a trifle difficult to locate because the signposts have a habit of disappearing into the hedges, is the Zoo du Pal. It has fewer sporting facilities than the Parc des Gouttes, about twice as many animals and totally different ideas when it comes to entertaining its younger visitors.

To start with, no cars are allowed inside the entrance where a small train waits to transport its passengers through the undergrowth to a siding a few minutes' ride away. Once there, the zoo is laid out on the right-hand side beyond the restaurant whereas the so-called Parc d'Attractions is all too obvious on the left. Stairs lead up to a mono-rail, which is claimed to be unique in France, and, when all the passengers have taken their seats in the open carriages, it sets off over the heads of lions and tigers for extremely distant parts. 'King Kong' is the first hazard, to be followed by an 'Enchanted Forest', an 'Avalanche', a 'Space Station' and other such unlikely destinations, each greeted with screams of childish glee.

After all the excitement, **Dompierre-sur-Besbre**, a bare 5km (3 miles) away, seems unnaturally quiet and none the worse for that. It has no obvious tourist attractions and nothing startling in the way of hotels but it is well placed for the valleys of the Besbre and the Loire, which marks the provincial border at this point, as well as having Moulins 30km (18$\frac{1}{2}$ miles) to its west.

Moulins is situated right on the edge of the Massif Central and was originally the capital of the Ducs de Bourbon. These days it combines all the attractions of an old market town with the undoubted advantages of modern commerce and industry, while still retaining enough reminders of the past to qualify as a popular tourist spot. The historic centre, as usual, is cocooned in the middle with very ordinary suburbs all round, and the Allier flowing past a few blocks away.

The most obvious landmark is the flamboyant Cathedral of Notre-Dame, parts of which date back to the fifteenth century. It is extremely decorative inside with some fine stained glass, paintings, statues and a treasure house containing a magnificent triptych by the Maître de Moulins. The centre panel shows the Virgin and Child surrounded by more than a dozen small figures, at least two of which are angels. On the right, Pierre II in his ducal robes is being presented by St Peter, while on the opposite side Ste Anne performs the same service for an equally richly attired Anne de Beaujeu and her daughter Suzanne.

There are three museums in town which just manage to avoid stepping on each other's toes. The Museum of Art and Archaeology in the old royal residence goes in mainly for sculptures, paintings and pottery along with various antiquities discovered in the area. The Musée du Folklore et du Vieux Moulins has less palatial quarters in a fifteenth-century mansion overlooked by the Jacquemart. This is a curious, free-standing bell-tower whose four small figures — a mother, father and two children — take turns to draw attention to the time every quarter of an hour. The museum is full of costumes, dolls, cooking utensils and old farm implements, along with a facsimile of a nineteenth-century home. Finally, the Musée Historique du Bourbonnais which is in Yzeure, on the outskirts, fills in all the missing details with the help of documents, maps and photographs.

Other places to see, but only from the outside, are the fifteenth-century Vieux Château, facing the cathedral, and the Palais de Justice which has taken over an ancient college that used to belong to the Jesuits. A stone's throw down the road, the Duc de Montmorency, who fell foul of Cardinal Richelieu and was decapitated in Toulouse in 1632, has a mausoleum to himself in the Chapelle du Lycée Banville which can be visited by simply asking for an order to view from the tourist office.

There are several hotels in Moulins including one charming, if slightly expensive, establishment with a most inventive chef. The dining room is small and frequently crowded with people anxious to try such unusual dishes as *foie gras* with mushroom and banana sauce or snails flavoured with walnuts. Local sports and pastimes range from flying facilities at the aerodrome to organised walks and outings on horseback or bicycle.

North of Moulins is **Villeneuve-sur-Allier** which has little in the way of creature comforts but two undoubted attractions as far as visitors are concerned. The first, in order of appearance, is Le Riau, an ancient fort with a roadway through the middle and a couple of tall, slender towers. The fifteenth-century manor house that goes with it is typical of its time with wide moats and a half-timbered barn added in 1584. On the other hand, Balaine only came on the scene in 1804. The large château is surrounded by a botanical garden which is said to contain more than 1,200 different types of shrubs and trees. It is the oldest private arboretum in France and, although it looks its best

Lapalisse

in spring and summer when all the flowers are out, visits can also be arranged at other times of the year.

Further to the west, and still hugging the provincial border, is the Château de St Augustin with its large animal reserve. It is a very attractive place where a host of different species such as elephants, tigers, yaks, bison and buffalo live together in apparent harmony with other creatures which are common to the region. Naturally, the more dangerous inmates can only be admired from a car but there are plenty of more friendly specimens in the park as well as hunting trophies adorning the hall of the château which has been there for some 200 years.

Another place that should not to be missed is the splendid **Forêt de Tronçais** which was the pride and joy of the Ducs de Bourbon until it was confiscated along with all their other possessions in 1527. These days it pays its way by providing wood for various industries and manufacturers. At the same time it is home to a great many deer and is a constant delight to anyone looking for mushrooms who knows which to take and which to leave well alone. However, the jewel in its crown is the oak grove, said to be the finest in the country,

Château de Toury

with trees that were fully grown before Joan of Arc was born. Guided tours are arranged during the summer by the Forestry Department in Moulins but anyone who simply wants a tourist's eye view of the main attractions provided for them need only contact the appropriate association in Cérilly, a small town on the outskirts.

A touch to the south-east of the Forêt de Tronçais is **Bourbon-l'Archambault**, a popular little spa where Talleyrand used to go to sort out his problems and try to cure his rheumatism. It offers hotels, furnished apartments and villas, as well as a camp site. There are facilities for swimming, playing tennis, *boules* and mini-golf, walking and fishing. The local château is worth a quick visit, despite the fact that most of it disappeared a long time ago, and so is the Church of St Georges, but there is nothing much one can do about the large, round Tour Quiquegrogne except stand outside and look at it. The only other distractions are the Musée Augustin-Bernard in the Place des Thermes with its reproduction of a typical home, national costumes and associated displays, and a view from a park at the top of the Allées Montespan which takes in the whole of the spa.

Motorists who feel like a day out usually head straight for

Souvigny, mainly on account of the extremely viewable Priory Church of St Pierre. It was consecrated in 1064 but needed a good deal of restoring in the fifteenth and eighteenth centuries. Apart from the ancient tombs of St Mayeul and, it is thought, St Odilon, two Ducs de Bourbon are buried there with their wives in marble splendour. Of equal interest is the beautifully carved *Calendrier*, divided up into months, each one pinpointing the appropriate seasonal activity such as treading the grapes in autumn or thawing out in front of a blazing fire in mid-winter. It can be seen in the Eglise-Musée St Marc with other items of local history.

It is no good hammering on the gates of the somewhat unusual Château du Plessis nearby because tourists are definitely not admitted. It is better to explore the Forêt de Gros-Bois surrounding the remains of the ancient Abbaye de Grammont and then drive on to **Ygrande** with its attractive church and rustic museum.

Due south of the Forêt de Tronçais is **Hérisson**, a small fortified village with the ruins of a thirteenth-century castle. It stands four square with **Chasteloy** which contributes a characteristic church (this is closed on Friday mornings), a few murals and an annual music festival in August. Most of the little villages hereabouts have something to offer. **Huriel**, for example, weighs in with a twelfth-century keep known as La Toque and the obligatory church while **Domérat** relies on Bacchus to emphasise the importance of wine in days gone by, adding its own church with an eleventh-century crypt and a statue of Notre-Dame-de-la-Râche to counteract any false impressions.

The last major centre to be visited in Auvergne is **Montluçon**, which takes itself very seriously. Apart from a small, circular area in the middle, huddled in the shadow of a fortress built by Louis II during the Hundred Years War, it shows considerably more interest in the present than in the past. However, there are guided tours of the old town including a visit to the Church of Notre-Dame, which is slightly disappointing, and the museums housed in the château which are not. The Musée Folklorique is mainly interested in things like geology, the development of local industry and ceramics. The Musée International de la Vielle, on the other hand, has a fascinating collection of ancient musical instruments, some of which are local while others come from different parts of France or Italy.

There are ample opportunities for joining a training course in Montluçon, with the emphasis on archaeology, ornithology and arts and crafts but it is necessary to look further afield in order to improve one's riding, diving or expertise in a canoe. The hotels are hardly more than adequate and the only publicised celebration is a fête in early September with a procession in honour of the Virgin.

There is no particular reason to stop in Montluçon, with **Néris-les-Bains** only 8km (5 miles) distant. It has one first class hotel, at least a dozen other options, various furnished accommodation and a reasonable camp site. Nor is there any shortage of entertainments. The 18-hole golf course is open to visitors, tennis and swimming are both available and it is a simple matter to find a horse or a kayak, spend the day fishing or follow a marked footpath into the woods and across open country. Of course, Néris-les-Bains is primarily a spa and, as such, entertains its guests with fêtes, theatre performances and concerts not to mention a lively disco and a casino.

The Romans built all sorts of aids to gracious living here as well as the baths. There was an amphitheatre on the site now called the Parc des Arènes, a temple or two and quite a few villas which have all disappeared, leaving nothing but a few mosaics behind. These and other local discoveries are preserved in the Musée Rieckotter which is open throughout the summer. A large burial ground near the church provided archaeologists with more than a sarcophagus or two when they started digging in the area in the mid-1960s.

The church itself grew up in stages, beginning with a fourth-century monument and progressing to a primitive building at the time of St Patrocle, who was instrumental in replacing paganism with Christianity. It is a bit dull and dismal as elderly churches go, with hardly a redeeming feature apart from a touch of Roman brickwork near the north door. The spa is tucked away in the south-west corner of Allier and is conveniently placed for a trip back down to Clermont-Ferrand or across the border into Limousin.

PLACES OF INTEREST IN ALLIER

Vichy
Maison du Bailliage
Boulevard Président John Kennedy. Small museum. Partly archaeological and partly nostalgic.

Centre des Recherches Archéologiques de Vichy
Rue Masset
Exhibitions of investigations carried out at the centre.

Châtel-Montagne
Church
Large, rather severe church and a good example of its type.

Gannat
Musée des Trésors des Portes Occitanes
In the château. Museum includes both religious items and local articles of interest.

Ebreuil
Church of St Léger
Ancient church somewhat restored with twelfth-century frescoes and a reliquary of the saint.

Billy
Old fortified town with twelfth-century fortress.

Lapalisse
Château de La Palice
Large, fifteenth-century château with fine tapestries, furniture and a Gothic chapel.

St Pourçain-sur-Sioule
Maison du St Pourçain
Wine tasting.

Abbey Church of Ste Croix
Viewable small church and remains of the original abbey.

Jaligny-sur-Besbre
Parc des Gouttes
Thionne, near Jaligny-sur-Besbre. Leisure centre and zoo.

St Pourçain-sur-Besbre
Château de Beauvoir
Near St Pourçain-sur-Besbre. Elderly fortified château with only the grounds open to the public.

Château de Toury
Near St Pourçain-sur-Besbre. Fortified castle with a long history, a small museum and a legend.

Dompierre-sur-Besbre
Zoo du Pal
Fairly large zoo with small trains and an amusement park.

Moulins
Cathedral of Notre-Dame
Fifteenth-century church extended in the seventeenth century with some fine stained glass windows, decorated chapels and a treasure including an outstanding triptych by the Maître de Moulins.

Museum of Art and Archaeology
In the residence of Anne de Beaujeu. Items from the Bronze

Age, Roman times etc. Sculptures, ceramics and some pictures and tapestries.

Musée du Folklore et du Vieux Moulins
Rue des Orfèvres. A local-interest museum with a memorable collection of dolls, costumes, rustic items and a reconstructed nineteenth-century home.

Mausolée du Duc de Montmorency
In the Chapelle du Lycée Banville. Rue de Paris. A marble sarcophagus and some decoration.

Yzeure
Musée Historique du Bourbonnais
A museum devoted to the history of the province up to the end of the nineteenth century.

Villeneuve-sur-Allier
Le Riau
An ancient fort with a medieval manor house, pleasantly decorated and furnished.

Balaine
Near Villeneuve-sur-Allier. Nineteenth-century house and botanical garden with an exceptional collection of trees and shrubs from all over the world.

Château de St Augustin
Near Le Veurdre. An eighteenth-century château with a large game park and a wide selection of animals.

Forêt de Tronçais
Extensive forest with magnificent oaks and facilities for visitors including boating, swimming, fishing and camping.

Bourbon-l'Archambault
Remains of a château built by Louis II with a good view from the top.

Musée Augustin-Bernard
Reconstructed home, costumes and local articles.

Souvigny
Church of St Pierre
Priory church with many interesting features including ducal tombs and an old cloister.

Eglise-Musée St Marc
A church converted into a museum with a magnificent carved calendar as well as religious and historical items.

Montluçon
Musée Folklorique
In the fortress-château. Devoted to old industries, ceramics, geology and other aspects of the region.

Musée International de la Vielle
Also in the château. Worth visiting, mainly for its collection of musical instruments.

Néris-les-Bains
Musée Rieckotter
Roman finds and items of local interest.

2
LIMOUSIN

L imousin is a region which, on the map, looks vaguely like a human head turned slightly towards the sunrise. Below a wide forehead there is an ear to the west of Limoges, a heavy jowl along the border with Dordogne, a purposeful chin jutting out towards Aurillac in Cantal and a chubby cheek on a level with the Puy-de-Sancy, the highest peak in the Massif Central. It has been described, somewhat over-enthusiastically, as the land of a thousand lakes; in fact there are only something like a hundred, provided one includes all the lagoons and reservoirs, some natural and others man-made. There are rivers and streams everywhere, each with its full quota of small, picturesque bridges, banks covered with grass and trees that could have been designed especially for fishermen and deep gorges where the normally placid waters tumble over rocks in a brief moment of confusion. The area is essentially a peaceful one, where pastures dotted with sheep and cattle share the land with ploughed fields, healthy-looking crops and extensive woodlands. However, there are parts of Limousin which are as yet untamed; mountains with granite outcrops, natural forests that can include anything from pines to chestnuts and, below the surface, minerals including uranium, much of which is still at the prospecting stage.

Limousin has faced as many trials and tribulations in the past as any other region of comparable size. The earliest inhabitants, who sheltered in convenient caves tens of thousands of years ago, had problems with both survival and the disposal of their dead. There is little evidence that they had either the time or the inclination to paint their living-room walls but in the *département* of Corrèze they have left behind one of the oldest examples of funeral rites so far discovered anywhere in France. The following centuries came and went with very little to mark their passage until the Gauls decided to build a number of fortified strongholds, strictly in the interests of defence. However, this did nothing to deter Julius Caesar once he had set his heart on expanding the Roman Empire. The area was overrun and, in 27BC, became part of the considerably enlarged province of *Aquitainia*.

Christianity was introduced by St Martial around AD250 but it was 400 years before the first abbey was founded at Solignac. After that, building progressed in earnest and by the time Eleanor of Aquitaine married England's Henry Plantagenet in 1152, her dowry included several impressive religious centres. Not surprisingly, the French objected to being part and parcel of each new royal bride's diplomatic luggage and expressed their views vehemently and at frequent intervals. During hostilities in 1199, Richard Coeur-de-Lion was mortally wounded while besieging the castle at Châlus. The Black Prince, whose father gave him Gascony and Aquitaine after he had distinguished himself at the Battles of Crécy and Poitiers, was no more popular and laid waste a large part of the region before his death at Westminster in 1376. By the time Charles VII awarded himself the title of King of France at Mehun-sur-Yèvre less than 50 years later, the French had repossessed at least half of the country. It only needed the inspiration provided by Joan of Arc to drive the English back across the Channel, although they managed to retain a toehold in Calais. The next 500 years were not exactly tranquil, what with the Wars of Religion, sundry revolts, the Revolution and the massacres at Tulle and Oradour-sur-Glane in 1944, but fortunately there were also peaceful landmarks. The discovery of kaolin at St Yrieix-la-Perche in 1771 made it possible for Limoges to create its famous porcelain and the railway arrived on the scene roughly 100 years later. After World War II, the hydro-electric scheme came to fruition and uranium was discovered in Haute-Vienne. The region of Limousin came into being officially in 1964.

It is generally agreed that Limousin, like the rest of the Massif Central, is best seen from its byways though there are major roads linking the three *départements* of Haute-Vienne, Creuse and Corrèze for anyone in a hurry. These have quite a number of secondary routes woven into the overall pattern with a network of lanes and minor roads connecting them at frequent intervals. Very few are unsuitable for cars so, to make life pleasant for non motorists,

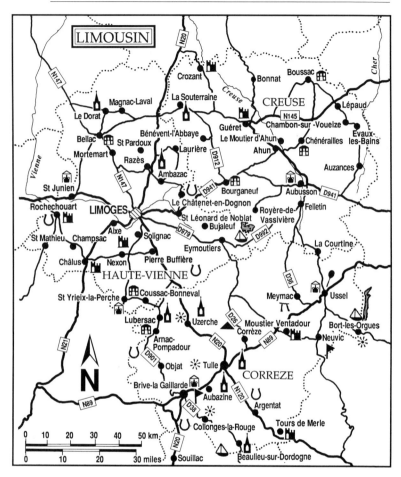

there are bridle paths, about 500 miles of blazed trails for hikers who have no desire to hitch a lift, and river courses where even a novice can paddle his own kayak or canoe without running into serious trouble. It is also quite simple to hire a bicycle. Among the region's many riding centres are a few which will provide a side-saddle or even a gipsy-type caravan.

Sports enthusiasts will find little to complain about. Several of the lakes have beaches which are safe for bathing. Some waterside

Canoeing in Limousin

hamlets will hire out sailing boats and windsurfing equipment, others have motor boats for waterskiing and the majority of those catering for holidaymakers provide at least a couple of tennis courts apiece. Fishing is a popular pastime everywhere and the necessary licences are obtainable from any shop that sells fishing tackle although some places, like the Lac de Vassivière, insist on a special stamp from the Fishing Club as well. All the relevant details such as the best places to go, the length of the season and the size of certain fish that can be taken home for dinner are obtainable from the *Comité Départemental de Tourisme* in either Limoges or Tulle. Golfers have a choice of three courses — at Limoges, Aubazine and Neuvic, the last of which is one of the 9-hole variety and positively welcomes beginners. Kayaks and canoes can also be hired, sometimes with tuition and sometimes without.

Visitors in search of luxurious hotels and super-sophistication will be disappointed in Limousin — with only the odd exception they simply do not exist. However, there are several establishments where one can be very comfortable, cosseted and well fed at prices that compare favourably with popular tourist resorts elsewhere in

France. One step down in the pecking order are plenty of hotels offering comfortable bedrooms with private bathrooms and a range of facilities, although by no means do all of them run to tennis courts and swimming pools. At the tail end come a host of small places which are perfectly acceptable provided one is not looking for up-market amenities at rock bottom prices.

For those who are self-catering the choice is just as wide. Each *département* has literally hundreds of *gîtes* which can be either self contained apartments, houses or country cottages and there are even some, known as *gîtes d'enfants*, where parents can safely leave their children provided they are aged between about six and twelve. In addition, there are holiday villages with well equipped chalets, bed and breakfast establishments and *fermes de séjour* with all the advantages of life on the farm. Special fishermen's rests, known as *hôtels de pêche*, are designed to meet the particular requirements of their guests and some also provide other sports and pastimes for members of the family whose interests do not include a day out with rod and line. Overnight hostels can be found at convenient intervals for the benefit of hikers, cyclists and riders who need accommodation for both themselves and their horses. The camp sites, and there are some 200 of them, range from those in the top category with all the expected facilities, down to a field set aside for the purpose by a local farmer.

When it comes to restaurants much the same description applies — not much in the ultra-expensive bracket but a wide range of places, some delightful and others purely functional, where very few people will find anything to upset them on the grounds of quality, comfort or service. Some of the cafés can be quite atmospheric, serving good if rather basic food with an air that suggests that the staff are enjoying themselves every bit as much as the customers and nothing is too much trouble.

The hotels and larger restaurants provide a variety of menus, priced according to the number of courses and the items included in them, as well as *à la carte* which invariably turns out to be more expensive. On the whole, the dishes are beautifully cooked and attractively served which makes eating even the most modest choice a pleasant experience. Among the specialities to look out for are *foie gras*, potato pâté, duck cooked in a variety of different ways, omelettes with mushrooms or truffles, various fish such as trout or pike, black sausage with chestnuts, madeleine cakes and fruit of all descriptions. It can either be fresh or made into a tart, the best known of which is probably *calfoutis*. This consists of eggs, flour, milk and sugar, flavoured with rum, brandy or something very similar, along with a liberal supply of dark red cherries. However, it is as well to remember that traditionally the cherry stones are not removed, so one's first bite should be a little tentative.

Local events and celebrations can be anything from a religious procession or a folk festival to an art exhibition, a series of concerts, a race meeting or an international canoe rally. For example, Twelfth Night is marked by a fair in Brive, Aubusson makes a feature of its tapestries, Limoges displays its famous enamels and porcelain and Cussac holds a traditional Festival of Healthgiving Fountains. Pageas has a cheese day, St Mathieu prefers ham and beans while Vassivière's contribution is, not unexpectedly, a Freshwater Fish Feast, followed by a Rock and Comic Strip Festival. However, it is left to St Just-le-Martel to organise an international exhibition of comic cartoons. Folk songs and dances are a cause for celebration at Bort-les-Orgues, Chénérailles divides its attention between a medieval pageant and a horse fair whereas the Goateaters Brotherhood invites all and sundry to a feast in Bellegarde-en-Marche. Run of the mill souvenirs can be picked up almost anywhere but the avid collector would do well to concentrate on porcelain, enamels, tapestries and some local crafts.

Haute-Vienne

Limoges, the capital of Limousin, is situated more or less in the middle of Haute-Vienne, the north-westerly *département* surrounded on three sides by Indre, Vienne, Charente and Dordogne with Creuse to the east and Corrèze to the south. It is a pleasant, clean looking city which can trace its history back over some 2,000 years and owes its existence to Agrippa. The Romans ensured that it was well endowed with a forum, an amphitheatre on the site of the present Jardin d'Orsay and a temple, as well as the obligatory aqueducts and thermal baths. However, the town suffered considerably after the fall of Rome and very little remains from its earliest days.

Limoges is only about an hour by air from Paris or Lyon, a 3-hour train journey from Paris or Toulouse and an easy run from most other parts of France along well maintained major roads that radiate out in all directions, rather like the spokes of some gigantic wheel. At one time the city fitted comfortably into a protective bend of the River

Horse riding beside the Taurion River

Vienne but with the growth of commerce and industry it expanded, sending modern suburbs and industrial areas sprawling out into the green countryside all round. While some of this urbanisation is decidedly mundane, it has the advantage of providing a host of outdoor activities for townspeople and visitors alike.

There are two large sports complexes on the outskirts with all the usual facilities including tennis courts and swimming pools. Enthusiastic golfers will find an 18-hole course within easy reach of their hotels while stables in the area cater for experienced riders as well as beginners. Skating is available as is an aero club and there are wide open spaces for walking, jogging or even running. Completing the spectrum are theatre performances, concerts and discos, in addition to which the Association for the Promotion of Baroque Music at 39 Rue des Tanneries encourages musicians who are interested in ancient intstruments and melodies.

As far as accommodation is concerned, there is a sprinkling of comfortable hotels of various sizes including several smaller but quite adequate ones, both in town and beyond. A camp site by the river is a good choice for anyone weighed down with a tent or towing

Fly fishing in one of Limousin's rivers

a caravan. Few of the restaurants are particularly memorable and it would be wise to make a note of the fact that a fair percentage of them close for two or three weeks' holiday in August. One small establishment, 12km (7$^1/_2$ miles) away at St Martin-du-Fault, is short on rooms and tables but is highly rated for its attractive park and exceptionally good traditional cooking. It is fairly expensive by local standards, appreciates anyone who books in advance and not only closes for a week in August but also during January and February.

In its much younger days Limoges was two distinct entities; La Cité, clustered round the cathedral and the site of the Bishop's Palace a short walk from the Pont St Etienne, and La Ville, with its narrow, picturesque streets totally enclosed behind massive stone walls. These have now disappeared, to be replaced more or less accurately by a circle of avenues and boulevards. The best place to start exploring is in La Cité with a visit to the handsome Gothic Cathedral of St Etienne which started life in the thirteenth century but had an extensive facelift 300 years later. The cathedral site is the one thought to have been chosen by the Romans for their temple of Jupiter, long since disappeared, and in fact the crypt and the lower part of the bell tower are all that remain of the original building. The steeple, though still impressive, was partly destroyed by lightning in 1571. The whole effect is rather severe apart from the flamboyant Portail St Jean while inside are the decorative tombs of three medieval churchmen and some colourful if rather sombre stained glass. Incidentally, the art of making stained glass was practised by ancient craftsmen in Limoges to good effect but went into a decline and has only recently been revived.

The city is widely known for its magnificent enamels which have been produced without any serious interruption since the twelfth century. The Bishop's Palace, built about 200 years ago and standing in terraced gardens overlooking the river, is now the Municipal Museum and contains a superb collection of Limoges enamels dating from the earliest times to the present day. In addition, there are rooms devoted to archaeology with bronze statuettes from Egypt and a reconstruction of part of a moderately important tomb at Thebes. Also on show is a fresco recovered from an ancient villa in the Rue Vigne-de-Fer a few blocks away, the usual range of small decorative objects, a mosaic from the tomb of St Martial and an extensive collection of minerals found in Limousin. Two Renoirs — *Colonna Romano* and *Madame le Coeur* — have pride of place in the picture gallery and are surrounded by the works of less well known artists while a collection of contemporary ones have a couple of rooms to themselves. The area immediately around the palace and the cathedral is full of old mansions including the birthplace of Maréchal Jourdan, one of the most outstanding of Napoleon's commanders, who has an attractive square named after him.

A short stroll away, on the other side of the Place Wilson, is La Ville where much of the atmosphere is concentrated in a section known as the Village de la Boucherie. It has been the home of butchers since the tenth century. They formed themselves into a powerful guild during the Middle Ages and still celebrate the good old days with an extremely lively Festival of the Butchers Brotherhood on the third Friday in October. Apart from the attractive, half-timbered houses, it is worth a visit to see the fifteenth-century Guild Chapel of St Aurélien with its statues, *ex voti* and a monolithic crucifix outside the door. The Church of St Michel-des-Lions, close by, is slightly older and can be easily recognised from a distance because of the curious spherical lightning conductor perched on top of the steeple. Inside are the relics of St Martial, the first person to preach the gospel in Limousin, who was originally buried on the Roman road from Lyon to Saintes in the fourth century. The reliquary holding his bones is brought out from behind the altar and carried in procession through the streets once every 7 years, as it has been regularly since the early 1500s.

St Martial's sarcophagus is to be found in a crypt, once part of an important abbey that was finally demolished during the Revolution, and now tucked away snugly under the Place de la République, the city's main administrative, cultural and commercial centre. He and his two companions lay in considerable state below a splendid mosaic ceiling with the tomb of Ste Valérie not far away. The large granite tomb of Tève-le-Duc, dating from the fourth century, has a sanctuary of its own and the other chambers are filled with relics which, under different circumstances, would certainly find their way into a museum. Above, on the Place de la République, there is a ground plan which gives a clear indication of the extent of the original abbey church.

Other places of interest in the vicinity include a group of carefully restored seventeenth-century buildings on the Cour-des-Templiers and the Church of St Pierre-du-Queyroix with a most expressive figure of Christ, carved more than 600 years ago, as well as many other treasures. The former law courts and treasury keep company with a number of elderly private mansions round the Place du Présidial which was the seat of royal government in Limoges during the seventeenth and eighteenth centuries. The present administration operates from an elegant town hall, built in the late 1800s and decorated with two large reclining statues that keep watch over the small but pleasing gardens in front. The Jardin d'Orsay is much larger and, for seekers of antiquity, has just a hint of Roman remains, indicating that the site was not always so green or so peaceful.

Also overlooking the Place Winston Churchill, but a trifle further up on the opposite side, is the Adrien Dubouché National Museum which should definitely not be missed. It houses more than 10,000 items of pottery and porcelain, both home-made and collected from many other parts of the world. There are exquisite oriental examples, typical designs from such famous centres as Meissen, Sèvres and

PLACES OF INTEREST IN HAUTE-VIENNE

Limoges
Adrien Dubouché National Museum
Place Winston Churchill. Outstanding collection of pottery and porcelain, mainly Limoges, augmented with items from many parts of the world. Audio-visual programmes.

Cathedral of St Etienne
Rue de la Cathédrale. Fifteenth/seventeenth-century Gothic construction with older crypt, flamboyant Portail St Jean and fourteenth-century bishops' tombs.

Church of St Michel-des-Lions
Place du Présidial. Relics of St Martial. Fifteenth-century stained glass windows.

Crypt of St Martial
Below the Place de la République. Tombs of St Martial, his companions, Ste Valérie and Tève-le-Duc plus other items of interest.

Jardin d'Orsay
Facing the Place Winston Churchill. Pleasant garden with traces of Roman occupation.

Municipal Museum
In Bishops' Palace close to the cathedral. Magnificent collection of Limoges enamels, antiquities, minerals and pictures.

Village de la Boucherie
Former butchers' quarter with Chapel of St Aurélien and ancient houses.

Workshops
Enamel and porcelain, open to visitors.

Ambazac
Church
Reliquary of St Etienne-du-Muret and eleventh-century mozarab silk dalmatic.

Abbaye de Grandmont
Near Ambazac. Ruins of ancient abbey with small chapel containing some replicas of items connected with the monastery.

La Jonchère-St-Maurice
Arboretum. Rare conifers. Nearby château grounds.

Châteauponsac
René Bauderot Museum
Many archaeological, historical and ethnological exhibits with recorded commentaries.

Church of St Thyrse
Declared an historical monument. Contains many items of interest including relics.

Sous-le-Moustier
Old district with collection of ancient houses.

Le Dorat
Collegiate Church of St Pierre
Impressive exterior and interior with old crypt and sacristy.

Bellac
Maison Jean Giraudoux

Home of the playwright with library containing many souvenirs.

Blond
Frederic Mistral Plaque
Near Blond. Marks the border between the Pays d'Oc and the Pays d'Oil.

Rochechouart
Castle
Renaissance courtyard. Frescoes in hunting gallery. Archaeological exhibits. Gallery of contemporary art.

Ruins of Chassenon
Near Rochechouart. Roman remains including thermal baths.

St Junien
Collegiate Church
Ancient building constantly restored. Tomb of St Junien.

Château de Rochebrune
Near St Junien. Old fortified château with apartments furnished in various styles.

Oradour-sur-Glane
Ruins of village destroyed by the Germans in 1944. Small memorial museum.

Châlus
Châlus-Chabrol Castle
Fortress where Richard Coeur-de-Lion was fatally wounded.

Musée des Feuillardiers
Small museum concerned with the traditions of local craftsmen.

Solignac
Abbey Church
Impressive church on the site of an abbey founded in AD632.

Towers of Chalusset
Near Solignac. Imposing ruins of twelfth-century hill-top fortress reached only on foot.

Coussac-Bonneval
Château de Bonneval
Privately owned château with tapestries, pictures, furniture and manuscripts.

St Yrieix-la-Perche
Porcelain Museum
Collection of china, mainly French.

Le Moustier
Large church on the site of a sixth-century abbey.

St Léonard-de-Noblat
Gay-Lussac Museum
Collection of items including documents from the laboratory of the physicist, who was born locally.

Le Châtenet-en-Dognon
Domaine de St Agnan
Riding centre with horse-drawn caravans for hire.

Delft, contributions from Florence and Madrid, Britain and Sweden and even a few from the little hill village of Moustiers in Provence.

The greatest number and variety of exhibits were made in Limoges itself, exceptionally beautiful articles tracing the history of the industry over a period of some 200 years. It is easy to see how the city came to be ranked amongst the world leaders in this particular art, whether your eye is caught by a tracery of fruit or flowers in pastel shades on a clear white background or groups of figures, delicately and meticulously drawn or painted and positioned like medallions surrounded by iridescent blues or deep ruby-reds. There are also audio-visual presentations showing the whole process from beginning to end.

Compared with enamels, the production of porcelain in Limoges is a comparatively recent innovation. It all started with the discovery of kaolin deposits in St Yrieix-la-Perche, to the south of the region, in 1771. Within a remarkably short time, factories and workshops were turning out beautifully decorated items with a translucent quality that soon made Limoges porcelain famous all over the world. Today it is still a thriving industry and some of the manufacturers are only too happy to welcome visitors and show them round the premises when the artists are at work. The original eighteenth-century moulds are still being used for some articles while others have been developed along more modern lines. When the moulds have been filled with a paste called *barbotine*, consisting of kaolin, feldspar, quartz and water, they are fired at 900°C (1,652°F). The resulting biscuit is given an enamel bath and fired again before being decorated by hand with a whole range of designs and colours which may include 22K gold. Finally, they are fired a further two or three times, after which they are ready to go on sale or display. Anyone on the lookout for a present to send home may find that some producers offer an export refund on more expensive items and even help with packing and posting — a better way of avoiding breakages than slipping them into a suitcase wrapped in tissue paper. At least three enamel workshops are also open to the public. They are just as fascinating despite the fact that the earliest techniques were up-dated during the Renaissance when artists of the calibre of Léonard Limousin perfected the art of painting enamels. An international exhibition is held about every 2 years with exhibits from all over the world, whereas the combined porcelain and enamel exhibition is an annual event at the Pavillon du Verdurier during July and August.

The capital has four historic bridges over the River Vienne. The Pont St Martial owes its foundations to the Romans but much of it had to be rebuilt following the damage inflicted in 1182 by Henry Plantagenet. The workmanship must have left a certain amount to be desired because the whole thing needed redoing after about 100 years. The Pont St Etienne handled most of the road traffic from that time onwards until the Pont Neuf was built in 1840, to be joined by the Pont de la Révolution in 1885. These days, the last two are the main points of departure for motorists on their way to Toulouse, Lyon or Clermont-Ferrand. With all this history so close to hand it is a trifle odd to discover how much of the city is dominated by the Gare des Bénédictins, a great, white railway station at the end of the Avenue Général de Gaulle with a large green dome and a most impressive tower to match. It is a useful landmark, decorated to a certain extent with porcelain and overlooking the Champ de Juillet which is full of grass and trees with fountains playing in a small lake. There is a fair amount of parking space with easy access to all the attractions the older parts of the city have to offer.

Limoges is a good base for anyone who feels like exploring the surrounding country. To the north-east, and no appreciable distance away, is the **Pays d'Ambazac et des Puys et Grands Mont**, an area of round-topped hills set back from the gorges of the Taurion River. It is an ideal locality for ramblers, who can take a leisurely stroll, set out purposefully to climb a mountain, inspect a lake or discover as many out-of-the-way spots as possible. The latter are quite likely to include an ancient stone cross, a megalith or a minute cottage of considerably later vintage.

Ambazac itself is a cheerful little community with a church dating back to the twelfth century where the reliquary of St Etienne-du-Muret, decorated with jewels and enamel, is well worth seeing. A couple of minor roads with pleasant scenery and an occasional view lead northwards to **St Sylvestre** with its own church treasure in the form of a reliquary bust fashioned in gold and silver. Close by are the ruins of the Abbaye de Grandmont, founded in the early twelfth century, which was an important religious centre during the Middle Ages. It suffered in the Wars of Religion, was restored briefly only to be knocked about again when the Order was suppressed a few years after the Battle of Waterloo. There are uranium mines in the vicinity, the Puy-de-Sauvagnac near St Léger-la-Montagne provides a good vantage point and there is a pleasing lake nearby.

The railway station at Limoges

Fishermen tend to gravitate towards **St Laurent-les-Eglises**, due east of Ambazac on the D5, where the pike fishing is highly recommended. Le Pont du Dognon has much to offer, from the site itself and the lake where both motorboats and waterskiing are available, to blazed trails for amblers and gorges for the more adventurous. **Les Billanges**, a short distance away, boasts a fortified church and a collection of thirteenth-century treasures. Beyond it, in the shadow of the Signal de Sauvagnac with its haphazard arrangement of granite blocks rejoicing in the name of Pierre Branlante, is **La Jonchère-St-Maurice**, known mainly for its trees. Places to see include the arboretum, which is full of rare conifers, the grounds of the Château de Valmath and, for the dedicated history lover, a Gallo-Roman stele of the goddess Espona at the almost non-existent Jabreilles-les-Bordes, on the border with Auvergne. Bicycles can be hired at **Laurière** which, like **Bersac-sur-Rivalier** next door, is within easy reach of the forest of Les Echelles and the Rocherolles Viaduct. Local activities include canoeing, riding and tennis and, although hotels are conspicuous by their absence, there are one or two modest *auberges* for anyone in search of a bed for the night.

Hand-painted pottery from the region

The adjoining area of **Le Pays de St Pardoux** prides itself on the variety and quality of its fish which can be found in practically every lake in the vicinity. The biggest of them, called quite naturally the Lac de St Pardoux, is an increasingly popular holiday centre with tennis, riding, sailing, windsurfing, swimming, waterskiing and, of course, fishing. **St Pardoux** village is quite attractive, especially in the centre where a number of old houses jostle together round the church, an elderly market place and a small well. It is a popular venue during the summer and also in October when there is a competition for the Grand Waterskiing Autumn Prize. **Razès**, situated between the lake and the N20, pays equal attention to minerals and a honey farm while pointing visitors in the direction of the rocking stone of Lavaud-Bourgoin and the dolmen of Lavaud-Jalonnaud. **Compreignac**, which is marginally bigger and runs to both *gîtes* and a camp site, still has its ancient church despite the fact that the original suffered at the hands of the English in 1370 and had to be rebuilt and fortified in the fifteenth century. There is not much to do there except hire a bicycle and set out on a much publicised scenic route claiming to take in 120 lakes.

Bessines-sur-Gartempe, sometimes described as the northern gateway to Limousin, is the birthplace of Utrillo's mother, the painter Suzanne Valadon. It is another popular holiday area with a couple of very modest hotels as well as tennis and the Lac de Sagnat quite close by. It makes much of its eleventh-century church containing an altar-piece retrieved from the Abbaye de Grandmont and includes the ruins of the Château de Monishes, the church and gravestones at Folles and the gorges of the Gartempe among its local attractions. They all receive attention during the season although holidaymakers seem less inclined to accept an open invitation to visit the abattoir. Anyone who makes a serious attempt to follow the course of the Gartempe River will come eventually to **Rançon**, a peaceful little place which has preserved a 700-year-old bridge and a graveyard lantern as well as having an attendant forest and an old mill beside the water.

Châteauponsac is rather a different matter with fewer beds but a wider range of offerings. To start with, there is the René Bauderot Museum, housed in an ancient Benedictine priory with a sizeable collection of minerals and fossils. Because space is no problem, as there are fourteen rooms, valiant attempts have been made to trace local history from earliest times to the present day. A bit of everything is on show from funeral urns to pottery, antique jewellery and traditional costumes to statuettes and historical documents covering the past 500 years. An added attraction is that special recorded commentaries are supplied in French, English, German and Dutch on individual cassettes so there is no need to take along a dictionary to appreciate all the various items and their place in the scheme of things.

Close to the museum is the Church of St Thyrse which was originally part of the priory. The choir and transept are pure twelfth century but thereafter a great many details were added such as decorated columns, wooden statues, a stone pulpit and a collection of relics. The town also boasts about its Peyrine gateway, its terraced gardens and Sous-le-Moustier, an ancient district memorable chiefly for its fifteenth-century houses. A miniscule *gîte* township has grown up on the outskirts with all the usual amenities and opportunities for tennis, swimming, fishing, hiking, canoeing and cycling. There is also a choice of souvenirs from a permanent display of local arts and crafts.

To the north of Le Pays de St Pardoux is **La Basse Marche**, an area where the Limoges plateau melts into the plains of Berry and Poitou. It is nowhere near as sports-orientated as its immediate neighbours, being marginally less interested in tourists than it is in sheep and other animals. St Sulpice-les-Feuilles is an important centre for breeding Limousin cattle while St Dorat's horse shows in September attract people from miles around. However, there is plenty to see and do for anyone who wants a quiet and relaxing holiday.

Le Dorat can provide some fairly basic accommodation with good home cooking, a selection of old houses and the remains of its Porte Bergère ramparts as well as a view from the Place de la Libération. But the jewel in its crown is the Collegiate Church of St Pierre on the site of an ancient monastery. Beyond the impressive multifoil west door, refreshingly severe and lacking in superfluous decorations, the inside is vast and cool with plenty of space to admire the large granite font set about with the faces of some friendly-looking lions. Two of the small, tucked away chapels contain the remains of St Israël and St Théobald while those of Ste Anne appear in both the crypt and the sacristy. Every 7 years Le Dorat holds a number of religious ceremonies including pilgrimages and exhibitions of relics whereas the craft fair in July is an annual event.

Magnac-Laval holds its Neuf-Lieues procession in honour of St Maximin every year on Whit Monday followed by an international folk festival on 1 May. During the rest of the year this old town opens its lapidary museum in the hospital grounds to visitors and invites them to inspect a collection of paintings in a small chapel which is also attached to the hospital. **St Sulpice-les-Feuilles** has nothing in the way of great architecture, art or relics but makes up for this omission with two dolmens — La Bras and Bouéry — both within easy reach. Also deserving of mention are the Lac du Mondon at Mailhac-sur-Benaize, the Vallée du Benaize and the Grotte du Martres and Château de Las Croux at Cromac. **Bussière-Poitevine**, the last Limousin village on the road to the west, has its own lake (Lac d'Azat-le-Ris), a twelfth-century church and, for anyone exploring the Vallée de la Brâme, a waterfall known as Le Saut de la Brâme, near Le Thiat.

Turning south again, the ancient town of Bellac on the banks of the Vincou River marks both the beginning of Les Monts de Blond and a staging post on the road from Switzerland to the Bay of Biscay. This area is described as being 'between the *Langue d'Oc* and the *Langue d'Oil*, between the lands of written law and common law.' The names are derived from two old versions of the word 'yes'. *Oc* was spoken in southern Gaul from Roman times onwards and was understood at the medieval courts of England and Italy whereas *Oil*, the forerunner of *Oui*, was largely confined to the lands north of the Loire. In the battle for supremacy, *Oil* won the day to become the official language of France. However, there are still some people who do not go along with what they consider to have been change for the sake of change and stick tenaciously to their ancient dialects, pointing out that what is good enough for the official title of the region of Languedoc is quite good enough for them.

The Monts de Blond region, on the other hand, takes its name from large granite outcrops, worn into strange shapes by time and the elements. There is a slightly untamed air about it, in keeping with the fact that it was invariably in the firing line when its neighbours to the north and south fought one of their frequent battles. In spite of these all-too-regular conflicts, quite a few ancient buildings have managed to survive and it is a happy hunting ground for both history lovers and holidaymakers who have only a minimal interest in the past. There are not a great many hotels around, or even camp sites for that matter, but almost every village can provide *gîtes* of one type or another.

Bellac is by far the largest local town, with a railway station, two major roads that run respectively north-south and east-west, several minor ones and a selection of blazed footpaths up into the hills. The playwright Jean Giraudoux was born there and his old home is now partly a cultural centre and partly a museum. His library, which is full of furniture, photographs and manuscripts, is open from 3-7pm throughout July and August following a special festival held in his honour in late June and early July. At other times of the year the tourist office will arrange special visits provided it is not either a Sunday or a public holiday.

Among other landmarks in the town is the sixteenth-century *hôtel de ville*, overlooking some attractive gardens where a monument to Jean Giraudoux was erected in 1951. It shows him attended by six of his heroines — Ondine, Alemène, Judith, Bella, Isabelle and Suzanne. From the terrace nearby one gets a good view of the Church of Notre-Dame, dating from the tenth century and containing what is reputed to be the oldest shrine in Limousin. The Pont de Pierre may not be the oldest hump-backed bridge in the region but at least it has been doing sterling duty for more than 800 years. As well as tennis and a swimming pool, horses are available at Rançon, slightly to the east and roughly on the demarcation line between Les Monts de Blond and Le Pays de St Pardoux.

Mézières-sur-Issoire, in the opposite direction, is the sheep-breeding capital of the area with markets held regularly twice a month. There is nothing much to see there unless you count a small chapel in the hamlet of Ste Anne which is the focal point of a pilgrimage in July. **Mortemart**, on the road to Limoges, has enough antiquity to make up for both of them. It grew up round the medieval château of the Ducs de Mortemart, still in a reasonable state of repair and the setting for exhibitions of arts and crafts during the summer. One of the most famous members of the family was Madame de Montespan who found fame and fortune in the arms of Louis XIV. There are a couple of old, disused convents, some attractive houses and a covered market which was open for business more than 200 years ago. The church was once a chapel attached to an Augustine monastery and is interesting mainly on account of its oak choir stalls, carved in the fifteenth century. The local tourist office will provide guided tours of the village for anyone who asks to be shown round.

The village of **Cieux**, ideally situated beside a lake, offers its visitors fishing, swimming and long country walks with the added incentives of the rocking stone of Boscartu and the menhir of Cinturat. There is also a small church and a thirteenth-century chapel, some-what oddly christened Le Bois du Rat, where pilgrims congregate twice a year, on the 6 May and 27 December. **Blond** is tucked away in the mountains with an ancient fortified church and a modern railway station. There are plenty of lakes all round for fishing as well as forest paths that can spring a few surprises such as a dolmen, a sacrificial stone or the battered remnants of a Roman construction, deserted and all but forgotten. In the Rochers de Puychaud a memorial plaque to the poet Frederic Mistral, winner of the Nobel Prize for Literature in 1904 and a dedicated supporter of the ancient dialects of the south, marks the frontier between the Pays d'Oil and the Pays d'Oc.

The **Vallée de la Vienne** is somewhat more sophisticated and guards the approaches to Limoges along the course of the river from Aixe-sur-Vienne to St Junien. It is a great place for canoes and kayaks which can be hired by the hour or for a whole trip that includes stop-over camps at convenient intervals. However, it is not calm water all the way. There are the odd rough patches and even obstacles which make it necessary to pick up one's craft and manhandle it across to the other side.

Although the area lives up to its reputation as an ideal venue for country holidays with something to occupy all the family, there is a lot more to it than that. It could be said to wear its history on its sleeve, which includes supporting a handful of traditional industries. **Aixe-sur-Vienne**, for instance, keeps itself busy making porcelain and insists that a Limousin head-dress called the *barbichet* was created in the Rue Rochefroid. The twelfth-century Church of Ste Croix is extremely proud of its stained glass windows although the Chapel of Notre-Dame d'Arliquet has a slight edge as a place of pilgrimage with a procession of original relics at intervals of 7 years. Apart from fishing, tennis and a swimming pool, Aixe-sur-Vienne is the starting point for the GR4, one of the long distance footpaths called *grandes randonnées*, which link up the various regions of France.

Rochechouart, another place that can be reached by train, also parades its sacred relics every 7 years. These events, known as the *ostensions Limousines*, are designed to honour local saints, of which the region has a considerable number. Some are looked on as patrons or protectors while others are venerated for their healing powers. The oldest of these ceremonies originated in the tenth century after a particularly virulent plague. They can be quite simple though picturesque affairs, with masses of flowers and people in national dress, or fully-fledged processions including guards of honour, trumpet fanfares, banners and sumptuous clothes and vestments. Nothing gets under way before the *ostension* is officially declared open with the blessing of a special flag which is then raised to the solemn accompaniment of the church bell. In the case of Rochechouart, it hangs in a curious spiral belfry, added in comparatively recent times to a church that was consecrated a year before the Normans took possession of England.

The town has had a long and somewhat complicated history, including an interesting legend or two, dating from the time when its ruling family got mixed up in the crusades. The ladies of the château were known for their beauty and even the famous medieval troubadour Bertrand de Born was moved to sing the praises of Agnes de Rochechouart. Some years later, the exquisite Vicomtesse Alix had a less enviable experience. A courtier she had turned down started spreading rumours about her, upon which the Vicomte Aymeric shut her up in one of the towers with a hungry lion. When he looked in a couple of days later the lion was sitting at her feet, giving a very creditable impression of an obedient and devoted dog. The lady was vindicated and the courtier was thrown to the lion which immediately recovered its appetite. The château was threatened with demolition during the Revolution but fortunately survived and today includes a granite statue of its famous and most gentlemanly lion. The hunting gallery with its frescoes is worth seeing, along with a museum added in 1894 which is full of archaeological discoveries and other exhibits such as authentic costumes and ancient manuscripts.

In addition to all these attractions, there is the fifteenth-century Maison des Consuls on the Rue Jean Parvy and the Promenade des Allées with some attractive gardens and views across the Graine and Vayres Rivers which meet below the château walls. A lake in the nearby woods of Chenu employs a lifeguard in case bathers get into any trouble. Holidaymakers can also play tennis, go fishing, ride horses or wander off down any of the marked footpaths. A bare 5km (3 miles) away are the remains of a Gallo-Roman settlement including antiquated thermal baths which were once part of the sanctuary of Chassenon. There are hot and cold rooms, sections that were used for treating a variety of complaints and even a special area where the gods were invited to speed a patient's recovery. Guides are on hand every day during the summer and a conducted tour lasts for anything up to 1 hour.

St Junien, about 13km (8 miles) away on the far side of the Vienne River, is a much larger town, second only to the capital. Its local industries include leather, specializing in gloves, paper, weaving and enamel work. Some of the little factories are open to visitors. Sporting activities range from the usual tennis, swimming and fishing to clay-pigeon shooting and a flying club. Bicycles can be hired to explore the Glane Valley, the forest of Brigueuil or for a trip to the Château de Rochebrune, 13km (8 miles) to the north-west. It is an attractive fortress, complete with medieval towers and moats, which was owned in the sixteenth century by the militant Blaise de Montluc who was both a marshal of France and governor of Guyenne. His coat-of-arms is emblazoned over the gateways while the rooms inside are furnished in a variety of styles from the Renaissance onwards. As one might expect, the Empire figures prominently with numerous items that were the height of fashion during Napoleonic times.

The most outstanding building in the town is the Collegiate

Church of St Junien, dating back to the end of the eleventh century but refurbished whenever necessary, such as in 1922 when the tower collapsed and had to be rebuilt. Behind the somewhat severe West Front it has its full quota of decorative stonework, glass and statues. This provides a worthy background for the tomb of the saint, an impressive example of Limousin sculpture, which has survived for 800 years. Running the church a close second is the Chapel of Notre-Dame-du-Pont, overlooking the river and owing much of its elegance to the generosity of Louis XI in the fifteenth century. During the *ostensions* in honour of St Junien, the main street is decorated with foliage to look like part of an ancient forest, an illusion accentuated by cages full of birds suspended from the branches.

A few kilometres to the north-east is **Oradour-sur-Glane** where, on 10 June 1944, the entire population, numbering more than 600 men, women and children, was rounded up by SS troops of the German army and deliberately massacred. Only a handful of people escaped when explosives, hand grenades and machine-gun fire set light to the buildings where they had been herded into groups. A new village has now grown up nearby and a sufficient number of items were recovered from the ruins to fill a small memorial museum, open every morning and afternoon throughout the year.

Le Pays des Feuillardiers, to the extreme south-west of Haute-Vienne, takes its name from the local craftsmen who work exclusively with chestnut wood. They produce fences and hoops for casks, using methods perfected by their predecessors over many generations. It is an area where the wooded hills of Limousin rise up from the green lands of Dordogne and where it is a little difficult to tell which are part of the Massif Central. Generally speaking, the towns and villages are pleasant, quiet and not over-burdened with historical remains although one or two are deserving of mention. **St Mathieu** is definitely sports minded but has also earned a place in several tourist guides on account of its tasty Bean and Ham Fair, held towards the end of August. **Bussière-Galant**, also on the Périgord border, is an undemanding little place with a few minor attractions such as a small lake and an elderly château whereas **Cussac**, which is slightly smaller, is involved in a traditional Bonnes Fontaines pilgrimage on the last Sunday in June In order to hire a bicycle it is necessary to go to **Oradour-sur-Vayres** where the only tourist attraction is the dolmen of La Tamanie.

All in all, the place which arouses the most interest, and rightly so, is **Châlus**. This is largely because Richard Coeur-de-Lion was fatally wounded while besieging the château-fortress during the closing months of the twelfth century. The Château de Châlus-Chabrol is still very much intact from the battlements down to the dungeons. Between the two are rooms where visitors can learn something about the history of the fortress and the life and death of King Richard. A small local museum concerns itself with the traditions of the Feuillardiers.

Gluttons for history and legends will find a fifteenth-century church at **Lageyrat**, springs known as Les Bonnes Fontaines with a reputation for curing ills and granting wishes, as well as the Château de Montbrun, which also proved too much for King Richard. It is a fascinating stronghold, standing on its own surrounded by trees and water and looking very much as it must have done 800 years ago. Sturdy, round towers crowned with battlements stand guard over the central keep, below which is the crypt of an ancient chapel. Visitors are shown round any morning or afternoon whereas one of its neighbours, the Château de Brie, is only open during the afternoon on Sundays and holidays from early April to the end of September.

It is an easy run from Châlus up to Aixe-sur-Vienne and from there, allowing for a short detour, along the Valley of the Briance to **Solignac**. This is a small town dominated by the remains of a large abbey founded in AD632 by St Eligius, also known as St Eloi, who was both a goldsmith and a minister of the crown. Over the years it received the individual and extremely unwelcome attentions of such antagonists as the Normans, the English and the Huguenots, not to mention the French themselves during the Revolution. Under the circumstances, it was lucky to preserve its abbey church, built largely in the twelfth century and well maintained since then without too many obvious additions. The interior is memorable chiefly for its series of domes and its low-key decorations which combine to create a powerful atmosphere so often missing in more ornate surroundings. There is some stained glass of no outstanding merit, the reliquary of St Théau and a likeness of St Christophe which was restored centuries before he was demoted on the grounds that he may not have existed in the first place. The monastery terrace overlooks the river which is crossed by a bridge known as the Pont Rompu, marking an old Roman way that came in useful for pilgrims heading in the direction of Rocamadour or Santiago de Compostela.

Quite close by, along a scenic road that twists and turns enthusi-

Π astically, determined searchers after feudal remains can explore the Tours de Chalusset, provided they have enough energy. This rather fine example of military architecture was built in the twelfth century but largely demolished 400 years later. It stands alone on a rocky spur and the climb up to it takes a good 20 minutes, proving quite hard going for anybody who is not accustomed to clambering up and down mountains. The road also provides a back way in to **Pierre-Buffière** which can, in fact, be reached more quickly along the highway from Limoges or even by train. There is precious little to do there once you have inspected the Roman bridge over the Breuil River and called in at the ancient church but it is a popular spot for concerts and exhibitions and holds an international dog show on the last Sunday in August.

South of Pierre-Buffière is **Le Pays Arédien**, facing the plains of Aquitaine. It has something of interest for everyone, particularly fishermen and other open-air enthusiasts whether they have a mind to explore on foot, horseback or bicycle. The alternatives include the Vallée d'Isle and gorges carved out by the Loue and the Auvézère with wooded slopes on either side. There are forests of oak and chestnut and numerous byways which make it unnecessary to share the main roads with fast cars and heavy vehicles.

Explorers of historic châteaux and tiny medieval churches can have the time of their lives here because most villages of any size have at least one attraction to offer. **Nexon**, for instance, just about half-way between Pierre-Buffière and Châlus, has its own château dating back to the 1400s which had to be extensively restored after the Revolution. There is also a delightful little church, older by some 400 years and noted for its thirteenth-century enamel plaques, wooden statues of Ste Catherine and St Roch as well as its brass reliquary of St Ferréol. Nexon is also a well known centre for the breeding of Anglo-Arabian horses and so, logically, includes riding among its other offerings such as blazed footpaths, a small lake and swimming.

It is hardly surprising that the historic route taken by Richard Coeur-de-Lion should be littered with ancient fortifications. The Château de Lastours is a case in point. It is a splendid ruin steeped in legends with a square dungeon and a son et lumière at the height of the season. A guided tour takes less than half an hour but anyone who wants to look round out of season has only to enquire at the main gate about possible days and opening times, or better still, ring

55.58.38.47 if they do not happen to be in the immediate vicinity. The château is only a short distance from **St Hilaire-les-Places**, a hamlet famous for its flowers which holds an exhibition of crafts during the season as well as providing a lifeguard to keep an eye open for anyone who gets into difficulties on the lake.

Meuzac is a good place to hunt for wild mushrooms, which should only be eaten after they have been approved by someone in the know, or to examine the dolmen of La Ville Dieu. St Germain-les-Belles weighs in with a fortified church and a national horse show in July while **Coussac-Bonneval** is the site of a memorable château, home of the Bonneval family who have owned it since feudal times. It is beautifully panelled, hung with pictures and tapestries and displays several reminders of Bonneval-Pacha who was converted to Islam and helped the sultan of the day to re-organise the Turkish army. There is also a graveyard lantern from the twelfth century which used to light up the entrance to the cemetery and proved a boon to anyone who was travelling at night.

St Yrieix-la-Perche, where kaolin was discovered more than 200 years ago, quite naturally has its own porcelain museum with an interesting collection gathered from all over France and especially from Limoges, although it is a little surprising to find that there is really nothing which was created locally. The Collegiate Church of Le Moustier, built on the site of an abbey founded by Arédius around AD530, is a curious mixture of styles. It is large and much decorated with a treasure that includes a bust reliquary of St Yrieix, although the valuable eleventh-century Bible is lodged in the town hall for safe-keeping. Bicycles can be hired for a trip to one of the local lakes or to the hamlet of Le Chalard, 8km (5 miles) away above the Vallée d'Isle, with its fortified church and medieval cemetery. Additional attractions include tennis, swimming and riding, together with a railway station, good roads leading in all directions and a chance to sample madeleine cakes which are baked locally.

To the north-east of Le Pays Arédien is an area known, not without reason, as **Les Monts et Barrages**. It stretches as far as the Plateau de Millevaches with wooded hills and forests, rivers full of trout, lakes that can be just as full of holidaymakers during the season and several charming little towns and villages. The main centre is **St Léonard-de-Noblat**, 21km (13 miles) from the capital on the road to Clermont-Ferrand and a good place to pause to get one's bearings. It is an atmospheric spot with a couple of modest hotels and a

St Léonard-de-Noblat

collection of houses built between the thirteenth and sixteenth centuries, clustered round their contemporary church. It stands back from a small square on a site which local people will tell you was approved by King Richard and was certainly visited by pilgrims on the way to Santiago de Compostela. Inside there are seven chapels radiating from the choir, chains left behind by prisoners who were no longer forced to wear them and, also made of iron, the last resting place of St Léonard.

The town is so proud of its history and traditions that it holds special festivals — La Bague fair in early July and La Quintaine in November — with medieval equestrian games, a custom so old that nobody seems to know how or when it originated. It also draws the attention of visitors to a museum in the Foyer Rural devoted to the physicist Louis Joseph Gay-Lussac who was born in St Léonard-de-Noblat in 1778. At the same time, ample provision is made for outdoor enthusiasts of all ages and persuasions with a swimming pool, tennis courts, games such as bowls, *boules* and volley-ball. There is also

Horse-drawn caravan from the Domaine de St Agnan

fishing and a camp site about 2km (1¹/₄ miles) away.

For a holiday that is somewhat out of the ordinary there is no need to look further than **Le Châtenet-en-Dognon**, a minute little place due north of St Léonard with a delightful *auberge*. It is the home of the Domaine de St Agnan where it is possible to hire a fully equipped horse-drawn caravan and wander off in search of the gipsy life. Members of the staff keep an eye on their customers to ensure that everything goes smoothly. In addition to this the centre provides bunk beds, a community dining room and large, appetising meals for groups of young people who want to learn all they can about horses. They are taught how to take care of them, what is involved in making horseshoes, cleaning stables and keeping all the equipment in an excellent state of repair. Riding lessons are followed by excursions that can last for hours or even days, with nights spent under canvas. In the unlikely event of an accident, the resident doctor deals with the problem in his own small surgery. By way of a change, there are other attractions such as canoeing and windsurfing.

Anyone exploring the Vallée de la Vienne from St Léonard, and starting from the bridge called the Pont de Noblat, will soon arrive at **Bujaleuf** which has facilities for swimming, windsurfing and water skiing, as well as tennis courts and bicycles for hire. Horse riding is a popular pastime and the main event of the year is an international competition for horse-drawn carriages. A small *hôtel de pêche* caters especially for fishermen, advising them on where to go and even preparing the catch for dinner on their return. Not far away is the Château du Chalard, said to occupy one of the most beautiful sites in the valley. The attendant village is small and pretty with a little fortified church and a medieval cemetery, some eye-catching tombstones and exhibitions which are held in the castle grounds.

Eymoutiers, another riverside resort to the south, has a small church, which is very viewable, picturesque old houses and all the usual sports facilities including long distance footpaths. It also has a delicious way of making mushroom soup. It is mid-way between **Châteauneuf-la-Forêt**, a perfect place for anyone who wants to climb hills covered with many different types of deciduous trees, and **Beaumont-du-Lac** with its own forest and a Ballade fair on the third Sunday in July. Like **Peyrat-le-Château**, which makes a feature of its twelfth-century dungeon and the fact that there are legendary rocks and attractive waterfalls in the vicinity, Beaumont-du-Lac is within striking distance of the Lac de Vassivière. This is a large and beautiful stretch of water which Haute-Vienne shares with Creuse, the *département* adjoining it to the east.

Creuse

The *département* of Creuse accounts for about one-third of Limousin, sharing the 'forehead' section with Haute-Vienne and bordered by Indre to the north, Allier and Puy de Dôme in the east and Corrèze to the south. It is a maze of streams and rivers, the main one being La Creuse, which cuts the area neatly in half from its source in the deep south, to the Barrage d'Eguzon near Crozant. Like all the other waterways, it is fed by a host of tributaries and does rather better than the Gartempe, the Cher or the Petite Creuse when it comes to barrages. In addition there are lakes and forests, hills by the dozen but not much in the way of mountains with spectacular views. Nor does it package itself up into conveniently small sections like Haute-Vienne, preferring to follow what is more like a train of thought than a local boundary. For example, there is the Tapestry Route, the Circuit of Pines and Heathers and, plumb in the middle, an area closely associated with the Romans.

The main town of Creuse is **Guéret**, once the capital of the Comté de La Marche and now the administrative centre. It is fairly large as local towns go with high-rise buildings which are pleasant rather than overpowering, an extremely modern theatre and fountains that have absolutely nothing traditional about them at all. A busy route from Montluçon to Poitiers and, indirectly, to Bordeaux passes slightly to the north with an attractively scenic road running south and a more-or-less direct link with Clermont-Ferrand. Guéret is on the line from Lyon to Bordeaux so it is not the easiest place in the world to get to by rail unless you are prepared to change when travelling from much further afield.

Although quite modern in many ways, Guéret is very much aware of the past and its Municipal Museum is crammed with items of every description. There is a section devoted to the gods of Egypt, India and Ancient Rome while the Salle du Trésor is full of Christian relics from the twelfth century onwards. The various events depicted range from the Adoration of the Magi and the Crucifixion to the martyrdom of St Thomas Becket, the ill-fated Archbishop of Canterbury. Elsewhere in the museum space has been found for weapons and furniture, natural history, pottery and dolls as well as some beautiful old Aubusson tapestries, a large collection of porcelain of every description and, of course, enamels from Limoges. The smaller Creuse Museum in the market place is concerned mainly with local crafts and traditions and is open every day except Tuesday. However, the Hôtel des Moneyroux, ancient home of the Comtes de La Marche, does not welcome casual visitors.

The town is sadly lacking in hotels and restaurants, even if one includes the little villages round about, though it is possible to find a bedroom with a bath. It is certainly worth staying in order to explore places of interest in the vicinity. To the north-west, along the main road out of town, is **St Vaury** which boasts a small church with a couple of thirteenth-century reliquaries and has the popular footpath from the Lac de Vassivière to the Lac de Chambon passing by the door. A minor road, skirting an equally minor lake, leads to **Roche** where there is a good view of the Vallée de la Creuse and the hills of Ambazac. It is useful to know that the small, well equipped camp site on the edge of the lake is open throughout the year. A clutch of small churches can be found to the north and east of Guéret. The first, at **Glénic** on the River Creuse, is a fortified example from the fourteenth century with a somewhat older entrance and a fresco of Adam and Eve. **Jouillat**, an even smaller hamlet just off the D940, has both a church and a château, as well as a choice of small roads leading down to **Ajain** where the 800 year old church is also fortified.

Another attractive byway circles round to **Ste Feyre** which is dominated by an elegant château with a small fortified church thrown in for good measure. However, if one is in the vicinity between July and September, the place to call in at is the Château du Théret where the guided tours last about half an hour. It is an interesting place which takes pride in its old furniture, splendid fireplaces and a room in the west wing where the Grand Condé is said to have spent the night. The large Forêt de Chabrières is almost on the doorstep, full of birch and beech, oak and pine with paths for anyone who feels like wandering about under the trees.

Still further west, Bénévent-l'Abbaye, the site of a monastery founded in the eleventh century though now all but disappeared, is worth visiting for its ancient church and the nearby Puy-de-Goth. Sightseers who attempt an undemanding half-hour climb to the top are rewarded by a view over the surrounding hills towards the Puy-de-Dôme and the Puy-de-Sancy in Auvergne, both of them visible but only on a clear day.

A well maintained secondary road cuts across country, through Le Grand-Bourg, to **La Souterraine** which had Roman connections but lost sight of them during the Middle Ages. It is a town well worth viewing and has, among other little establishments, a small hotel facing the church which is known for its traditional cooking. A couple of restaurants offer more modern food such as pizzas and there are facilities for tennis and swimming as well as a convenient lake for picnics. The Church of the Assumption dates mainly from the thirteenth century although the crypt was originally part of the Abbaye St Martial de Limoges and is older by some 200 years. There are traces of the earlier building inside the church, along with a twelfth-century altar, but nothing much in the way of treasures. The Tour de Bridiers, a keep that proved its worth in feudal times, the remains of the ramparts punctured by fortified gateways, a graveyard lantern and a number of ancient houses all add to the general atmosphere.

A short distance away at **Bétête**, the ruins of a Cistercian abbey are used for exhibitions during the summer. Among the neighbourhood attractions are a thirteenth-century château at **St Germain-Beaupré**, the Chabannes Woods near **St Sulpice-le-Dunois** and the gorges of the Creuse, best seen from the hamlet of **Anzême**.

The Circuit de la Petite Creuse could be said to start at **Crozant** which contributes a ruined fortress that withstood an attack by the Black Prince. Unhappily, the Wars of Religion, ably assisted by an earthquake in 1606, succeeded where he had failed. There is a fair amount to see provided you are there between Easter and the end of September when the ruins are open all day. Excursions are arranged to the Barrage d'Eguzon at the height of the summer, some of them only when twenty or more people are anxious to make the short trip. There are some good views, facilities for tennis and a small *auberge* beside the lake.

This is an area where almost anything goes — from ancient legends to moto-cross, long distance walks to a day out in a canoe, horseriding to fishing. To the east is **Fresselines**, a village known principally for artists who hold exhibitions of their work at quite regular intervals. **Bonnat**, further to the east, has two very small camp sites that are open throughout the year, a market every four weeks or so and a fortified church which is all lit up on summer evenings, while **Châtelus-Malvaleix** boasts a 700-year-old church of its own.

By far the most impressive place in the Vallée de la Petite Creuse is **Boussac**, standing at a point where it joins the Tapestry Route. The village is dominated by a splendid château that really should be seen for the first time from a stretch of road running alongside the river towards some elderly cottages and a picturesque bridge. This rather severe stone fortress rises above a wooded hillside on a site first chosen by the Romans. The original medieval stronghold was virtually destroyed by the English, only to be rebuilt almost immediately by Maréchal Jean de Brosse, who fought alongside Joan of Arc. The antiquated dungeons underneath are closed to visitors whose tour, lasting nearly 1 hour, begins in the old guardroom and neighbouring kitchen both of which have stone floors, enormous fireplaces and a sprinkling of appropriate furniture and other articles against a background of superb tapestries.

It is hardly surprising that tapestries are to be found everywhere in the Château de Boussac because it was here that the famous series of six known as the *Lady with the Unicorn* was discovered and later transferred to the Musée de Cluny in Paris. Monsieur Blondeau, who lives on the premises, is not only an expert who is able to repair even the oldest examples but also arranges exhibitions during the season. A wide, circular stone staircase leads up to the first floor which is sheer eighteenth century, beautifully decorated and furnished and looks as though the family of the day might appear at any moment. Apart from the main salons, there is a small secluded bedroom with a canopied bed and a tea tray close to hand. This is where George Sand wrote part of *Jeanne*, no doubt pausing at intervals to look out at the magnificent view across the valley.

Boussac itself has inherited the coat-of-arms of Jean de Brosse and is a delightful place with a number of ancient houses, a small church and a modest *auberge*. The local inhabitants, who are mostly farmers, are both friendly and helpful. Quite nearby, on the D917, is the Commanderie de Lavaufranche which once belonged to the Knights of St John of Jerusalem. They managed to hang on to this valuable piece of real estate until the Revolution when they were forced to move out, leaving much of interest behind them including the sculptured tomb of the commander Jehan Grimau, dated 1480. Unlike the Château de Boussac, the Commanderie de Lavaufranche is only open during July and August when visitors are shown round the chapel with its thirteenth-century frescoes, the commanders' apartments and the rooms set aside for the knights. It also has a large collection of popular works of art and items connected with folklore and traditions which it augments with tapestry exhibitions during the season.

An alternative road from Boussac winds its way through pleasant country to a spot near **Les Pierres Jaumâtres**, a heap of strange granite rocks about 15 minutes' walk up the hill from a small parking area. The most eye-catching of them, shaped from one viewpoint rather like an escaped bread roll from some enormous shopping basket, is balanced precariously on a central point with all the rest suspended in mid-air. There must be some logical reason why it does not topple over but the explanation would not be half as much fun as the legends that have grown up over the centuries. It is only a few kilometres from **Toulx-Ste Croix** which is an historical site with a splendid view from the church tower.

Lépaud, on the other hand, has no ancient attractions but it does possess a small airfield and is quite close to the Complexe du Golf de la Jochère. In addition to a club house, a restaurant and plenty of opportunities to improve one's game under the watchful eye of a professional, there are stables, a day nursery and some small, individual cottages to rent. A brief detour to the east, along a comparatively quiet road, festooned on either side with delicately coloured wild roses and purple-red foxgloves in the late spring and early summer, is **Chambon-sur-Voueize**. Like both Lépaud and Boussac it is on a dual long distance footpath — namely the GR41 and the GR46 — is conveniently close to the gorges of the Voueize, opens its quite large and moderately well equipped camp site from June to September and has two small holiday *auberges*. Apart from yet another château belonging to the Comtes de La Marche, who seem to have collected them rather like other, less well-heeled people collect postage stamps, there is an attractive bridge over the river.

The outstanding place of historic interest in Chambon-sur-Voueize is the Abbey Church of Ste Valérie. It is said to be one of the most important and most interesting of its kind in Limousin. A priory was originally built on the site to guard the remains of the saint but the church was only completed around the end of the eleventh century. It is a fairly large granite building, with a bell tower and porch that were added about 200 years later, and a well decorated interior. The centrepiece of its treasure is a partly-gilt bust reliquary of Ste Valérie enhanced by the presence of several paintings like *The Death of the Virgin*, Ribera's *David and Goliath* and the *Décollation de Sainte Valérie* by the Maître de Moulins.

About 5km (3 miles) away is **Evaux-les-Bains**, discovered in the first instance by the Romans and still the only spa in Creuse. It is open from March to October and offers its clients a choice between an *auberge* attached to the baths, half a dozen other small establishments, several furnished apartments and a camp site which operates all through the year. Its tourist attractions consist of a few fragmentary remains of the Roman baths, one or two archaeological bits and pieces in the care of the *syndicat d'initiative* and the fifteenth-century Church of St Peter and St Paul. There is good fishing to be had in the vicinity, a couple of tennis courts for people whose rheumatism and other ailments are responding to treatment and long distance footpaths heading both north and south as well as into Auvergne. A good secondary road of no particular merit leads south from Evaux-les-Bains to Auzances but there is a pleasant shortcut which saves a few kilometres for anyone who wants to explore more places in the north-west corner of the *département* and, at the same time, rejoin the Tapestry Route.

Gouzon has nothing much to offer apart from a small church whereas **Chénérailles** has an elderly one which is not a great deal more viewable but includes the added advantage of a fine three-tiered relief dedicated to its founder, St Bartolomé de la Place. The Crucifixion occupies the top section with a hive of activity surrounding the Virgin and Child in the centre and mourners gathered round the

Château de Boussac

tomb of the saint at the bottom. It can be seen at any time except on Sunday afternoons. A kilometre or two beyond the town is another of the family de la Marche's fortified country residences. Its title is the Château Villemonteix, it dates from the fifteenth century and it is open for inspection from early June until All Saints' Day. The highlights of a guided tour, lasting about 1 hour, are some interesting tapestries woven in Aubusson during the seventeenth century.

Chénérailles is a great believer in annual celebrations. Horse fairs are held on the second Sunday in May and the second Sunday in October with a wool fair in June, a medieval festival on the first Sunday in July and national equestrian events during the last fortnight in August. Sporting activities include fishing in the small Etang de la Forêt and tennis with the option of one covered court or two in the open air. Anybody who is interested can take a mini-course in the art of making cheese by telephoning Monsieur Briat on 55.62.37.11.

Salon Vert, Château de Boussac

Ahun is also in the cheese-making business, can provide a few beds in two quite basic holiday inns and places for tents and caravans on its local site. Otherwise, its claims to fame lie in the Church of St Sylvian. The crypt was not only there when the Romans arrived but also contains an extremely ancient tomb, much venerated in the dim and distant past though nobody appears to have discovered the reason. Strangely, none of this is at odds with the statues of St Gilles and St Sylvian, the fifteenth-century Pietà or an even older granite font in the church itself.

Ahun's closest companion is **Moutier-d'Ahun** which has certainly had its historical ups and downs. The village started off quite well about 1,000 years ago when the newly founded Benedictine monastery looked all set for an important role in church affairs. However, the English put an end to its aspirations during the Hundred Years War and, although it staged a brief revival, this literally went up in flames at the time of the Wars of Religion. The Revolution also took its toll but somehow the abbey church managed to survive, preserving its beautifully carved choir stalls and some seventeenth-century panelling that are well worth seeing. A few relics from the old monastery can be inspected in the sacristy between May and October but visitors who turn up at other times of the year have to content themselves with the exterior decorations, some of which are fascinating, and just a trace of the fourteenth-century fortifications. Ahun stages an international moto-cross event on the second Sunday in August and a folk dance festival on the 15th of the month. Moutier-d'Ahun, not to be outdone, turns out for its annual Procession of St Roch on 16 August.

The most famous town in Creuse is **Aubusson** which has been producing superb tapestries for close on 700 years. Legend has it that the Saracens, after their defeat at Poitiers in the eighth century, retreated into the area, settled down and started weaving. However, historians are inclined to believe that the art was introduced from Flanders in the fourteenth century by Marie de Hainaut who, as one might expect, became the Comtesse de La Marche. It took 200 years for the local workshops to reach their peak and gain long overdue recognition as the official suppliers of tapestries to the French court. When the Edict of Nantes, giving freedom of worship to the Huguenots, was revoked in 1685, they left in droves to avoid persecution and, as a large percentage of them were industrial workers, Aubusson suffered as a result. Several attempts were made to revive the art of tapestry weaving with the assistance of painters like Watteau and Boucher but the Revolution did not help matters and, for the most part, the industry was left to get along as best it could.

The artist Jean Lurçat was largely responsible for breathing new life into this ancient art shortly before the outbreak of World War II and today the weavers are hard at work again, to everybody's complete satisfaction. Aubusson tapestries are woven on a horizontal loom with the warp running lengthways and the wool or silk, with perhaps a touch of gold or silver thread, following the design which is slotted in underneath. It is a fairly complicated procedure, requiring infinite skill and patience to achieve high-quality results.

Without in any way ignoring the traditional subjects, which covered the whole spectrum from religion to history and leisure to colourful flights of fancy, the modern works have enlarged their horizons to incorporate strictly twentieth-century designs and even an occasional cartoon or two. Artists such as Vasarely, Dom Robert and Picart Le Doux are deeply involved and their ideas appear regularly at exhibitions held every year at selected places along the Tapestry Route such as Boussac, Felletin and in Aubusson itself.

Each workshop is run by a master weaver, who may have a highly trained staff to help, and about half a dozen of these little enterprises are open to the public during working hours.

The Tapestry Museum, situated in the Jean Lurçat Cultural Centre, was opened in 1981, partly to display some very fine early examples and partly to draw attention to the modern versions which are just as fascinating in their own way. Exhibitions are also held in the museum during which visitors can learn something about the history of the craft and find out exactly what is involved. The town hall has its own selection of wall hangings and carpets open to view from mid-June to the end of September.

The Maison du Vieux Tapissier keeps to the same opening hours but has one or two additional attractions. It is housed in a fifteenth-century mansion that was once the home of the Corneille family who were leading tapestry-makers in their day. A traditional workshop has been reconstructed on the first floor with a good deal of early equipment along with designs and embroidery of comparable age. Elsewhere in the house are examples of local furniture, books and manuscripts dealing with the history of the town and everything one needs to know in order to set up a loom of one's own — and far more complicated venture than would appear to be the case at first glance.

The old part of Aubusson is full of atmosphere, created by houses which have been close companions for several hundred years. There are also all the predictable little shops selling everything from antiques to souvenirs, an elderly fountain in the Place de la Libération and two trees, said to be 400 years old, alongside a picturesque bridge over the River Creuse.

The thirteenth-century Church of Ste Croix, restored almost beyond recognition about 100 years ago, contains four tapestries, one of which recalls the vision of Constantine the Great. The Emperor, on his way from southern France to Italy, is reputed to have seen a giant cross in the sky conveying a message to the effect that he would win his forthcoming battles provided he did so in the name of Christianity. Win them he certainly did but there are people who maintain that his future tolerance towards the Christians was motivated more by politics than conviction.

The ruins of an ancient castle, which in this instance belonged to the Viscomtes d'Aubusson along with a round clock tower and a few ramparts, stand guard over the town. For anyone who has had a surfeit of tapestries and old buildings, there are tennis courts and a

PLACES OF INTEREST IN CREUSE

Guéret
Municipal Museum
Near the Avenue de Laure. Wide selection of exhibits of all descriptions including Limoges enamels and Aubusson tapestries.

Creuse Museum
In the market place. Local crafts and traditions.

St Germain-Beaupré
Near Guéret. Moated castle.

Glénic
Church
Fortified in the fourteenth century with twelfth-century doorway and fresco.

Ste Feyre
Château du Théret
Near Ste Feyre. Interesting château with guided tours.

Puy-de-Goth
Views from the top.
Reached on foot.

La Souterraine
Decorative church with crypt.

Open in July and August.

Bétête
Remains of Cistercian abbey with exhibitions during the summer.

Crozant
Ruins
Remains of ancient fortress.

Boussac
Château
Interesting fortified château famous for tapestries. Old guardroom and beautifully furnished eighteenth-century apartments.

Commanderie de Lavaufranche
Near Boussac. Fortified old headquarters of the Knights of St John of Jerusalem. Exhibits and exhibitions.

Les Pierres Jaumâtres
Granite rocks near Boussac.
Reached on foot.

Chambon-sur-Voueize
Church of Ste Valérie
Interesting church with several

swimming pool with fishing and canoeing in the vicinity.

Hotels and restaurants are not quite so easy to come by. However, it is possible to find a bed and a bath, plus a garage, close to the river and one or two little places just outside the town. A case in point is **Felletin**, 12km (7$^1/_2$ miles) distant along the Tapestry Route, which has a restaurant with rooms attached. This specialises in traditional dishes but its menu also includes *Fondant Amer au Chocolat Sauce Anglaise*, which by no stretch of the imagination could have been left behind by the Black Prince!

treasures including reliquary and pictures.

Chénérailles
Château de Villemonteix
Near Chénérailles. A mixture of old fortress and country mansion. Some interesting tapestries.

Moutier-d'Ahun
Abbey church
Once part of an ancient abbey. Some very fine wood carving.

Church of St Sylvian
Ahun. Carved sixteenth-century woodwork and very ancient crypt.

Aubusson
Tapestry Museum
In Jean Lurçat Cultural Centre. Both old and contemporary tapestries. Exhibitions. Audio-visual presentations.

Maison du Vieux Tapissier
In Maison Corneille, Rue Vieille. Fifteenth-century mansion with reconstructed workshop, furniture, manuscripts and books.

Tapestry workshops

Some open to visitors.

Church of Ste Croix
Much restored church with interesting tapestries.

Castle ruins
Round clock tower, some ramparts and ruins with view over the town.

Felletin
Eglise du Moûtier
Old church reconstituted in fifteenth century.

Notre-Dame-du-Château
Former church now used for exhibitions.

Bourganeuf
Tour Zizim
Three towers and remains of château.

Hôtel de ville
A fine eighteenth-century Aubusson tapestry in the Salle du Conseil.

Lac de Vassivière
Large lake with many sporting facilities. Island with open-air museum. Small marina.

The monastery church, dedicated to Ste Valérie, was founded in the twelfth century but up-dated 300 years later, making it a contemporary of the former Church of Notre-Dame-du-Château where tapestry exhibitions are held during the season.

The village offers a reasonably sized camp site beside the river as well as tennis and riding and makes much of its folk dance festival at the beginning of August. In addition, it draws its visitors' attention to a few remnants from the distant past discovered at St Georges-Nigremont, a vantage point to the south-east and a short drive away.

The Circuit des Chevaliers is rather more concerned with knights than it is with tapestries although **Bourganeuf,** capital of the region at the time of the Templars, has a particular regard for Prince Zizim, son of Mahomet II. After a spot of family intrigue in Constantinople he was told by Pierre Aubusson, the Grand Master of the Order of St John of Jerusalem, that a visit to the Massif Central would be both wise and beneficial. He arrived in Bourganeuf in 1483 and was installed in the Tour Zizim where he is said to have created an atmosphere better suited to the Arabian Nights than the Hospitallers. Inevitably, stories and legends grew up round him, especially after he died in Naples in 1495, reputedly poisoned by the Borgias.

Along with two other towers and the remains of the twelfth-century Château de Grand Prieuré d'Auvergne, the Tour Zizim vies for attention with a particularly fine tapestry hanging in the *hôtel de ville.* It is an enchanting town with streets so narrow and winding that cars towing caravans have to go round the outside. There are some enticing little shops, a clutch of modest *auberges,* a selection of tennis courts — two in the open and three under cover — a riding centre and immediate access to the *randonnée* GR4 for long distance walkers who are heading either east or west.

The circuit also includes the **Forêt de Mérignat,** once the happy hunting ground of the Grand Prieuré d'Auvergne, the 14m (46ft) **Cascade des Jarreaux** near St Martin-Château and yet another group of granite rocks not far from Le Monteil-au-Vicomte which, according to legend, are associated with the devil. The countryside is pleasant without being at all remarkable and is criss-crossed with little roads in a good state of repair that take in a gorge or two, an occasional view such as the one from the Signal du Pic, but not a great deal in the way of picturesque villages.

The main attraction in this part of Creuse is the large and lovely **Lac de Vassivière.** It spreads itself out in all directions, surrounded by woods and open moorland, with sandy beaches where it is not impossible to imagine that one is within reach of the sea. It is essentially a holiday area, providing all manner of water sports, tennis courts, fishing, a riding centre, blazed footpaths that wander about for miles and a camp site close to the water. There are boat trips round the lake from May to September along with regattas, equestrian events, a *café-théâtre* festival and a popular song contest for young holidaymakers. Towards one end of the lake is the Ile de Vassivière, a wooded island where there are paths designed for botanists and an open-air museum of modern sculpture. Artists of several different nationalities are represented, having qualified for inclusion on the grounds that they work in granite. A road follows the contours of the lake, calling in at the little marina, crossing the barrage and, at one point, changing direction briefly to pay its respects to **Royère-de-Vassivière** where there is an elderly church. Stonemasons usually find time to visit **Gentioux-Pigerolles**, their own special village with a statue of Our Lady of the Building Trade. There are opportunities to study forestry, learn to fish, sail, windsurf or water ski, inspect archaeological sites at **Chadièras** or relax in the Forêt de la Feuillade. Further afield, **Gentioux** marks the source of the Taurion River while **La Courtine** offers a handful of small *auberges*, a traditional restaurant and views across the Plateau de Millevaches and the mountains of Auvergne.

Corrèze

The third and most southerly of the *départements* of Limousin is Corrèze which covers the entire width of the region and has Dordogne, Lot, Cantal and just a fraction of Puy-de-Dôme for its other neighbours. Although it lacks the famous tapestry weavers of Creuse and the equally widely acclaimed porcelain manufacturers of Haute-Vienne, there are just as many historical associations and up-to-the-minute holiday attractions to satisfy all but the most critical visitor.

The area has its fair share of lakes and rivers, densely wooded hillsides and verdant pastures. Cattle are raised on the Plateau de Millevaches, which is shared with Creuse, and there is a spot of prospecting for uranium at Chaumeil. The roads are generally good and there are some impressive views up in the mountains as well as a gorge or two along rivers like the Cère and the Dordogne as they wander through the area. It is, in fact, a place of contrasts where the only consistent features are the warmth of its welcome and the almost total lack of sophistication.

Although Brive is considerably larger and more business-like, **Tulle** is the chief town of Corrèze. It sits comfortably astride the river which shares its name with the *département*, following it along the valley in either direction in a rather aimless way. This impression is no doubt due to the fact that, although it has a plentiful supply of streets, hardly a single one of them is straight. There is a railway station, a number of modest hotels with all the necessary amenities

Windsurfing on the Lac de Vassivière

but nothing in the luxury class, a couple of quite acceptable restaurants and a recreation centre for people who feel in need of a little exercise. The choice is varied with a swimming pool and tennis courts as well as canoeing and fishing in the river. A camp site within walking distance is open right through the year.

Rising high above the rooftops is the 73m (240ft) bell tower of the Cathedral of Notre-Dame, standing on the site of an abbey which was founded at the beginning of the twelfth century. It is only a stone's throw from the water and there is generally somewhere to park the car nearby. The interior is unusually sombre in spite of some interesting stained glass, added in 1979. The accent is on melan-

choly, recalling both the martyred bishop Dumoulin-Borie and the townspeople who were massacred by the retreating German army in June 1944.

One of the cathedral's most treasured possessions is a statue of St John the Baptist, carved from wood in the sixteenth century. Each 23 June, a procession takes place through the streets of the town in honour of St John, just as it has done for several hundred years. The cloister, built in the early thirteenth century but much restored at intervals thereafter, is certainly worth seeing. Apart from a doorway, added to commemorate an apparently friendly visit by Charles VII in 1442, there is a theatre where concerts are held throughout the year and the comprehensive André Mazeyrie Cloister Museum. Part of this is, quite naturally, given over to sacred art but there is also a section tracing the history of Tulle and an attractive collection of porcelain and pottery.

A decidedly warlike atmosphere is introduced on the upper floor. The town started manufacturing arms and armaments towards the end of the seventeenth century, receiving the seal of royal approval in 1777, and the display of pistols and other weapons produced around this time, and during the next 200 years or so, tells the whole story.

A much sadder and more recent story unfolds in the Musée Départemental de la Résistance et de la Déportation. It recalls how the town was liberated by the Maquis, only to have the Germans recapture it and take their revenge by hanging ninety-nine people in the streets and deporting as many more to end their lives elsewhere.

The old district of Tulle, known as the Quartier de l'Enclos because it was once protected by ramparts, starts just across the Place Gambetta to the north of the cathedral. It is partly a pedestrian precinct, with a number of streets that are more like staircases, some delightful medieval houses and the general air of a backwater that has been trying hard, but not always successfully, to ignore the passage of time.

The much decorated Maison de Loyac, with the Rue de la Tour-de-Maïsse climbing up one side, is the most noteworthy of all the ancient buildings and still displays the emblem of Louis XII, which was emblazoned outside when it was built at the beginning of the sixteenth century. It only takes about half an hour to inspect the entire district, even if one pauses to admire the sculptured façades that appear without warning in the Rue des Portes-Chanac and the Rue Riche, both of which are open to traffic.

Tulle lays on several exhibitions, including a display of special crafts during the summer, is host to an international meeting of accordionists in the first half of July and celebrates Liberation Day on 17 August.

To the east of Tulle, 12km (7^1/$_2$miles) distant along an attractive winding road, is **Gimel-les-Cascades**. Anyone who is prepared to take a short and undemanding walk will be rewarded with the sight of three impressive waterfalls, the highest of which, the Queue de Cheval, would reach very nearly to the top of the cathedral spire in Tulle. They make a splendid sight as they plunge down the gorge into the aptly-named Gouffre de l'Inferno. Just as memorable in its own way is the Châsse de St Etienne, a beautiful reliquary, richly decorated with enamel and dating from the twelfth century, which is the centrepiece of the treasure house in the little local church.

Further along the same route — the D978 — is **Clergoux**. It has little to offer apart from a small *auberge* but it is conveniently close to the isolated Château de Sédières. Standing close to a waterfall and flanked by two small lakes, it was built in the fourteenth century for the local bishop whose family made several improvements during the next 200 years. It is used for music festivals and various exhibitions during the summer and offers guided tours each morning and afternoon from the beginning of July to the end of August.

Naves, an even smaller village just off the main road from Tulle to the north (the N120) is the proud possessor of a fifteenth-century church with a fortified turret added 200 years later. It is nicely placed for anyone who is interested in exploring the area and calling in at the little town of Corrèze. This has a large church and just a trace of the ancient fortifications, an hotel which can also supply studios on request and a number of modern attractions such as a swimming pool, tennis courts and a sauna as well as boating on the lake. Alternatively, one can press on by way of various narrow, twisting roads, to the Suc-au-May where there is an excellent view over the mountains of Corrèze, Cantal and the Mont-Dore.

The determined searcher after exceptional ruins would be well advised to head straight for **Moustier-Ventadour** where the remains of a massive twelfth-century fortress are perched precariously on the top of a rocky spur. It takes about half an hour to climb up the narrow pathway and appreciate that the resident duke was not boasting when he told Louis XIV that all the straw in his kingdom would not be enough to fill the moat. In spite of being completely satisfied with their almost impregnable eyrie, the Ventadour family gradually came to realise that an isolated country residence had certain disadvantages when it came to everyday living. As a result they moved down to a much more convenient home in **Ussel**, leaving their feudal château to the none-too-tender mercies of time and the weather.

The Hôtel de Ventadour, built in the late 1500s, stands on the corner of the Rue du Marché and the Rue de Ventadour. It is obviously small by comparison and has an odd turret, a modest entrance and very little outward decoration. No doubt the inside was both palatial and comfortable but unfortunately it is not open to the public. However, there are plenty of other reasons for visiting Ussel.

In the first place, it is a viewable town with some well restored

PLACES OF INTEREST IN CORREZE

Tulle
Cathedral of Notre-Dame
Between the Place Gambetta and
the Place Emile Zola. Statue of St
John the Baptist. Original stained
glass.

André Mazeyrie Cloister Museum
Adjoining the cathedral. Items of
sacred art. History of Tulle. Pottery
and porcelain. Display of weapons
manufactured locally between
1696 and 1900.

Musée Départemental de la
Résistance et de la Déportation
2 Quai Edmond-Perrier. Activities
of the Maquis in World War II. The
massacre and the German
deportation camps.

Quartier de l'Enclos
Old district with several attractive
houses but none open to the
public.

Gimel-les-Cascades
Church with several treasures
including an exceptional reliquary.

Cascades
Near Gimel-les-Cascades.
Impressive waterfalls, reached
only on foot.

Clergoux
Château de Sédières
Attractive fortified château.
Concerts and exhibitions during
the summer.

Suc-au-May
High vantage point in the Massif
des Monédières with a splendid
panoramic view.

Ventadour
Near Moustier-Ventadour.
Magnificent ruins of an ancient
fortress.
Can only be reached on foot.

Ussel
Hôtel du Juge Choriol
Museum of traditional crafts with
reconstructed workshops of
especial interest.

Bort-les-Orgues
Orgues-de-Bort
Large natural rock formation
overlooking the village.
Can only be reached on foot.

Lac de Bort
Large, man-made lake. Hydro-
electric power house with audio-
visual presentation explaining the
system.

Château de Val
On the Lac de Bort. Atmospheric
fortress of interest. Also used for
summer exhibitions.

Neuvic
Musée de la Résistance
Henri-Queville
Contents divided between the life
of the politician who was Minister
for Agriculture on several occasions and the role of the Resistance Movement in World War II.

Meymac
Marius-Vazeilles Foundation
Archaeological museum in the
former Abbey of St Andrew, Place
du Bûcher. Special attention paid
to the Plateau de Millevaches.

Abbey Church
Contains a twelfth-century Black
Madonna and relics of St Léger.

Bac les Cars
Near Meymac. Gallo-Roman
remains.

Treignac
Maison Marc Sangnier
Devoted to the arts and traditions
of the Upper Vézère.

Uzerche
A very atmospheric village on the
River Vézère. Well worth seeing
for itself. Old houses and a fortified
gateway.

Church of St Peter
Twelfth-century building, subse-
quently fortified and restored.
Attractive interior.

Lubersac
Village with interesting church.

Arnac-Pompadour
Château-Pompadour
Impressive fortified castle given to
Madame de Pompadour by Louis
XV. Only the grounds are open to
the public.

Haras
Stud farms founded by Louis XV
and now part of the national stud.
Many different breeds of horses.
Racecourse with meetings and
other events in July, August and
September.

Brive-la-Gaillarde
Home of Edmond Michelet
Museum mainly concerned with
the Resistance Movement and the
German deportation camps.

Church of St Martin
Place Charles-de-Gaulle. Much
up-dated twelfth-century church
with a decorative interior and quite
an extensive treasure.

Noailles
Le Gouffre de la Fage
Swallowhole and palaeontological
museum.

Turenne
Castle Ruins
Remains of a fourteenth-century
fortress with a memorable view.

Collonges-la-Rouge
Medieval village built of red
sandstone and well-worth seeing
in itself.

Beaulieu-sur-Dordogne
Abbey Church of St Peter
Outstanding doorway carved in the
twelfth century. Wood carving and
large collection of relics.

La Chapelle-aux-Saints
Near Beaulieu-sur-Dordogne.
Underground cave and collection
of archaeological finds.

Reygade
The Mystery of Reygade
An outstanding fifteenth-century
tomb, the work of an unknown
artist. Audio-visual presentation in
the chapel.

Tours de Merle
Near Argentat. Ruins of a superb
medieval fortress town, reached
only on foot. Son et lumière during
the summer.

Le Coiroux
Sports complex with an 18-hole
golf course, archery butts and a
wide variety of other activities.

Aubazine
Abbey Church
The tomb of St Etienne.
Stained glass.

Monastery
Religious centre built on the site of
a twelfth-century Cistercian
monastery founded by St Etienne.

houses lining the Rue de la Liberté, at one end of which is the old Church of St Martin, updated at intervals and given a new bell tower about 100 years ago. It is not particularly memorable and anyone whose time is limited would be well advised to call in at the Hôtel du Juge Choriol instead. This lies a few blocks away and is a three-storey mansion devoted entirely to traditional crafts. A blacksmith's forge has been reconstructed with all the equipment necessary for his trade. Visitors can study the art of weaving, see how wooden shoes and leather clogs were made, discover how many different articles could be constructed out of straw and examine the manu-scripts left behind by local scribes, long gone but not entirely forgotten.

The Chapelle des Pénitents has also been converted into a museum but in this case the theme is a religious one. Roughly half-way between the two museums, in the Place Voltaire, is a Roman eagle made of granite, which is 2m (6ft) tall, weighs just short of 1 ton and was found in the vicinity of the town.

Ussel has one or two quite adequate *auberges* and a couple of camp sites, one of which is particularly well equipped and has bungalows to rent, besides staying open throughout the year. It is possible to hire a bicycle or a pedalo, ride, play tennis, call in at the aero club, spend the day fishing or go for walks along any of the footpaths which have been marked out in the surrounding country-side. There is also bathing in the lake not far away. In addition to all this, the town holds an exhibition of paintings and sculptures which lasts for most of July.

Motorists who feel like doing a bit of exploring in the area can choose the main road to La Courtine, across the *département* border in Creuse, opt for another in the same category which heads eastwards into Auvergne or follow a secondary route that skirts a couple of lakes on its way to **Bort-les-Orgues**. This is an agreeable village in the Dordogne Valley, strung out along the water's edge with one small hotel that caters for handicapped guests and two or three others which are somewhat more basic. The only tourist attraction in town is the old church with its twelfth-century choir, a statue of Ste Anne and a brass reliquary decorated with enamel.

It is interesting to see how much enamel is used in churches when one considers the old legend associated with it. The story goes that Lucifer, Satan and Mephistopheles met to discuss earth, fire and water and, as a result of their deliberations, mankind produced enamel and porcelain. Incidentally, it is a mistake to think that all three were the same devil. Lucifer was the son of Aurora and was translated in the Old Testament from the Hebrew word *Hélèl*, which meant 'shining one'. Mephistopheles, on the other hand, is part of German legend, appears in the old *History of Dr Faustus* and was a much less powerful demon than Satan.

The main reason why people visit Bort-les-Orgues is to see the Orgues de Bort, a series of gigantic pieces of phonolite rock, worn down over hundreds of years until they look rather like enormous pillars standing guard over the town from a dizzy height. To get a closer view of these so-called 'Organ Pipes' it is only necessary to drive a short distance, park under the trees, and set off on foot. There is a well worn track leading up from a small souvenir shop with very run-of-the-mill merchandise on display, an extensive view and an orientation table that could be quite an attraction if someone would only recondition it. At the moment the surface looks more like the top of a picnic table in need of a good scrub than a contour map of the surrounding country.

Fractionally to the north is the **Lac de Bort**, a splendid, artificial lake stretching for more than 17km (11 miles) along the river course with a barrage which plays a principal part in the overall hydro-electric system. The power house is open to visitors every day with an audio-visual programme explaining how the whole system works. There are trips round the lake by motor launch, starting either from the barrage or from the nearby Château de Val.

The fortress has a Grimms' Fairytale look about it with sturdy round towers topped by pointed roofs that put one in mind of witches' hats, broomsticks and magic spells. It was, however, built for strictly military purposes during the Hundred Years War. These days it stands on an island attached to the bank by a strip of ground which, under present circumstances, could hardly be described as a cause-way. There is a fair amount of space for parking, woods where visitors can picnic, a small marina tucked in behind the château and a great many tourists in the high season. A stone lion guards the main courtyard which was presented at some stage with the basin of a Roman fountain.

The other attractions include a couple of beautiful Renaissance fireplaces, a small chapel and an impressive line in staircases. Apart from guided tours that last for anything up to 1 hour, the château is used for art exhibitions at fairly regular intervals and is floodlit on

Tapestry-making in Aubusson

summer evenings. The lake provides ample opportunities for bathing, sailing, windsurfing, waterskiing and fishing. Bicycles can be hired in Bort-les-Orgues where there are also tennis courts available, while walkers will find enough blazed trails to keep them happy for hours. The town is also well known for its international folk dance festival which attracts even larger crowds at the beginning of August.

Half a dozen minor roads, twisting their way between wooded hillsides, head in the direction of St Nazaire, a beauty spot with views of the gorges created by the Dordogne and the Diège Rivers as they join forces down below. However, a bit of back-tracking is necessary in order to inspect the Barrage de Marèges before driving on to **Neuvic**. It is an old town with little to say for itself except for the Musée de la Résistance Henri-Queville. He was a politician with a particular interest in agriculture who did a great deal for the farmers of France. Part of the house where he lived is devoted to his life and work and part of it to the Resistance Movement, with special emphasis on the local Maquis. There are a great many documents, photographs and souvenirs of the men and women who fought the long, underground war against the Germans. One section is almost entirely concerned with the parachute forces, large numbers of whom were dropped in the area just ahead of the advancing Allied armies in 1944.

On a more peaceful note, the town caters for sports enthusiasts, having a 9-hole golf course, tennis courts, riding stables and bicycles for hire. The Lac de la Triouzoune provides opportunities for bathing, sailing, windsurfing, waterskiing and fishing, as well as having plenty of footpaths. The town is definitely short of accommodation when it comes to hotels but tries to redress the balance to a certain extent with four camp sites, one of which has both static caravans and mobile homes to rent.

Meymac, about 30km (18$^1/_2$ miles) to the north beyond the Château de Ventadour, fares no better when it comes to *auberges*, nor does it have a golf course, but it does offer a number of alternative attractions that are worth considering. To start with, it has a picturesque old quarter, with decorative medieval houses in the immediate vicinity of the church whose main claims to fame are the twelfth-century Black Madonna and relics of St Léger. About 1,000 years ago the village was the site of a Benedictine abbey and what little remains of it today serves a useful purpose, partly as a contemporary art centre and partly as the home of the Marius-Vazeilles Museum. This concentrates mainly on archaeology and, in particular, on the history of the Plateau de Millevaches, which is practically on the doorstep.

The whole area is a good place to explore, whether one is interested in tracing a river such as the Vienne, the Vézère or the Creuse back to its source, rubbing shoulders with the ghosts of ancient Celts at Le Rat, where there are some strange rocks, a small chapel and an exceptional view, or coming to terms with the Romans at Bac les Cars. Admittedly these ruins are fairly modest, little more than foundations surrounded by undulating grasslands, but it is possible to make out part of the settlement, the site of the temple and the mausoleum. Alternatively, there are high-rise points from which to admire the beautifully wooded countryside, among them Mont Besson and the Signal d'Audouze, small villages clustered round elderly churches, and even an occasional fortress like the Château de Rochefort. Meymac is also a good centre for canoeing, fishing, riding, bathing and windsurfing. One can play tennis or hire a pedalo for a leisurely trip round the lake. There is a camp site within easy walking distance, complete with a bar and a restaurant, which is open all year. The whole summer is taken up with events of one kind or another, many of them with a distinctly rural flavour.

Treignac, somewhat further to the west, has all the same sporting facilities including a good view from the Rocher des Fées, half an hour's walk away. The town is old, has its obligatory church, a Gothic bridge over the Vézère and a museum of arts and traditions in the Maison Marc Sangnier. It is also on the way to **Uzerche**, frequently described as the Pearl of Limousin, and not without good cause. It is an exceptionally fascinating little town, all stone walls, slate roofs and turrets climbing up a fairly steep hillside and neatly contained in a hairpin bend of the Vézère River. Its more 'modern' section is connected by two bridges more or less in the centre of the loop.

The whole scene is dominated by the twelfth-century Church of St Pierre with its original bell tower which has survived intact despite a number of unpleasant experiences such as the Hundred Years War. It is well worth visiting, mainly on account of the interior decorations, its beautiful little chapels and the ancient crypt containing a highly-prized fourteenth-century tomb, although nobody seems to know who is buried in it.

Uzerche was well fortified when it attracted the attention of the Saracens after the Battle of Poitiers and withstood more than one siege during the Middle Ages. Sadly, the Porte Bécharie, with its modern statue of the Virgin, is the only original gateway still in existence. The Esplanade de la Lunade, looking out over the valley on the opposite side of the church, has taken the place of the ancient ramparts which once enclosed a sizeable collection of fifteenth-century houses, most of them still in private hands. The best places to see these are in the Rue Pierre Chalaud, the Rue Gaby-Furnestin and the Rue Jean-Gentet which run together in a more or less straight line from the Place Marie-Colein on the main through road from Brive to Limoges. Just beyond the Porte Bécharie a few steps, known as the Escalier Notre-Dame, lead down into the Place des Vignerons, an ancient fruit market with an even older Chapel of Notre-Dame tucked away in one corner.

Uzerche is undoubtedly a town to be savoured unhurriedly, especially as there are at least two small hotels providing rooms with private bathrooms and restaurants on the premises as well as a camp site with little put-you-ups called *huttes de France*. The best place to go for an overall view of the old town is the district of Ste Eulalie, on the road to Eymoutiers in Haute-Vienne.

If one is heading in a north-westerly direction from Uzerche there are three different places worthy of note. The first is **Lubersac** where the curious little eleventh-century church is open to view every day with the exception of Saturday afternoons and Sunday mornings. The considerably younger Maison des Archiprêtres stands in the main square and was all but reconstructed about 100 years ago.

Among Lubersac's nearest neighbours is **Ségur-le-Château**, full of old houses and thought to occupy the site of an early Gallo-Roman settlement. It was an important centre during the Middle Ages and had royal connections. This was firstly on account of the local Vicomtes de Limoges, then through Jean d'Albret who was born in 1470 and went on to become the first king of Navarre and eventually by way of his grand-daughter Jeanne d'Albret, known principally as the mother of Henry IV. The Maison Henri IV was so-called in honour of the d'Albret family, a compliment echoed today by a little *auberge* of the same name which is more of a restaurant than anything else.

Royal patronage is far more apparent at **Arnac-Pompadour**, a short distance away. The splendid fifteenth-century castle, complete with towers, ramparts and a moat, was a present from Louis XV to his famous mistress, Jeanne Antoinette Poisson, in 1745. At the same time he made her a marquise. Madame de Pompadour showed her appreciation by carrying out many of the king's state duties and encouraging the writers and artists of her day. She became a duchess 7 years later and died at Versailles in 1764. The rooms, which were rebuilt after being destroyed during the Revolution, are unfortunately closed to the public but sightseers are shown round the terraces each day except for Sunday afternoons.

Three years before the death of his favourite, Louis XV founded two stud farms at Arnac-Pompadour which provided it with the additional titles of Cradle of the Anglo-Arab Breed and The Horse Lover's City. Both the racecourse and the *haras*, now part of the national stud, are close to the château which is used as a home for its officials. They, in turn, open up the terraces on race days to give punters an uninterrupted view of all the events. Both stud farms are open to visitors at various times, although La Jumenterie de la Rivière, where the mares are kept, restricts its hours to weekday afternoons between July and November with special arrangements on Sundays, public holidays and race days.

The only other building of note is the Eglise d'Arnac, a severe-

Marina on the Lac de Bort

looking, granite church built in the twelfth century just outside the town. Arnac-Pompadour has a couple of small hotels, opens its swimming pool during July and August, provides tennis courts and, as one would expect, ample opportunities for riding.

There are a number of different routes leading southwards, one or two of which are quite straightforward while others twist and turn through hilly country, providing some attractive scenery and an occasional view along the way. The route through Chabrignac and Objat has so many ups and downs that it begins to feel vaguely like a switchback after a while but the surface is good. Some stretches are delightfully scenic, especially along two short deviations, one to the left and the other to the right, just short of Juillac. There are few villages in the area bordering on Dordogne and even the hamlets seldom consist of more than one or two houses facing each other across the road. Anyone in search of solitude would unquestionably find it in this part of Corrèze but, for the majority of people, a better plan might be to follow the D7 in an easterly direction as far as **Vigeois**, on the banks of the River Vézère.

This is another village that carries the hallmarks of history, having

Château de Val

been the site of a monastery founded in the sixth century which was destroyed by the Normans 300 years later. The church is something like 800 years old but it was overhauled thoroughly in 1866 and again in 1908. Vigeois is only some 10km (6 miles) from Uzerche and 16km (10 miles) from **Chamboulive** which was inhabited in the Neolithic period and later had a visit from the Romans. It has both an ancient church and a medium sized *auberge* offering about two dozen rooms, half of them with private bathrooms, a garage, a garden and good traditional cooking.

A major road, partly dual carriageway, heads south from Uzerche to **Brive-la-Gaillarde**, by far the largest town in the area and much concerned with trade and industry. There is a comfortable hotel just inside the tree-lined boulevards which surround the old part of the city. Another of similar stature can be found on the outskirts to the west while, slightly further on, is the first class Château de Castel Novel, standing alone in its large park with every facility including tennis and swimming, a handful of private apartments and an excellent restaurant. Other hotels and restaurants of various sizes are scattered around quite liberally, some of them are fairly well equipped, others unexpectedly basic. There is also a camp site beside the river with attractions such as tennis, riding, sailing and swimming nearby.

The town itself has bicycles for hire as well as swimming pools, tennis and squash courts, a practice golf course, riding stables and a skating rink which is open from mid-September to mid-May. Visitors can either explore on their own or call in at the tourist office where English-speaking guides are on hand to show them round.

Brive has surprisingly little of interest for the average sightseer and all its attractions are grouped together in the old centre with the Church of St Martin right in the middle. This first saw the light of day in the twelfth century but it was extensively restored and re-modelled about 100 years ago. The main things to look for are the choir stalls and the examples of mythological wildlife such as winged serpents and griffins which, for some reason, were chosen as appropriate decorations. Its quite extensive treasure, housed in the sacristy, includes a reliquary bust known rather extravagantly as *The Seven Thousand Virgins*.

The streets all round are small, a bit winding in places and contain a number of old houses, the most eye-catching of which is the sixteenth-century Hôtel Labenche on the Rue Blaise Raynal. The only museum is restricted almost entirely to the Resistance Movement during World War II, recalling the activities of the local Maquis and the infamous German deportation camps, and is found alongside a study centre in the Maison Edmond Michelet.

As one would expect, Brive celebrates at regular intervals throughout the year, with *foie gras* and truffles playing an important part in the Twelfth Night Fair in January. The Limousin Bourrée Festival takes place in July with a melon fair on the last Sunday in August followed a month later by a fresh walnuts festival and a book fair early in November.

Anyone who is interested in the early history of the area has only to drive to **Noailles**, some 12km (7$\frac{1}{2}$ miles) to the south, where there is a palaeontological museum, open every day from April to September, along with a swallowhole known as Le Gouffre de la Fage. Leaving the major road at Noailles in favour of a scenic byway that leads due east, opens up a whole new range of possibilities. The first might well be **Turenne**, once the home of the Tour d'Auvergne family who ruled it without interference from anybody else from the Middle Ages until the Revolution.

It is a picturesque little village of ancient houses, with a Capuchin friar's chapel, a 400-year-old church and some impressive castle ruins. They are open every day from Easter until October and a tour includes the fourteenth-century keep with its guardroom and quarters set aside for horsemen as well as the so-called 'Caesar Tower' commanding a magnificent view.

The most noticeable thing about this area is that everything, apart from the trees and the grass, is red. The roads corkscrew their way up and down between banks of dark red soil with rocks and boulders of the same colour popping up everywhere, and even the cattle have a russet hue about them. As a result, it is hardly surprising to find that **Collonges-la-Rouge** is built almost entirely of red sandstone. It is a totally enchanting medieval village with, unfortunately, quite a lot of twentieth-century tourist overtones.

In bygone days, Collonges belonged to the Viscounty of Turenne and was the site of holiday homes for important officials who wanted to get away from the seat of government every now and then. The most outstanding of these palatial country residences is the Castel de Vassinhac whose owners protected themselves from surprise attacks by adding small overhanging turrets to the already extremely secure outside walls. The Castel de Maussac put its faith in a tall, square tower while its neighbours contented themselves with round constructions, topped occasionally by a witch's-hat type of roof. As far as visitors are concerned, the little narrow streets are for pedestrians only and to this end a fairly large parking area has been constructed for cars and coaches on the main road just outside.

Beyond the Porte Plate, which was once a doorway in the original fortifications, there is a small, rather bare fifteenth-century Chapel of the Penitents and a very much older church. Built in the eleventh century, it was fortified during the Wars of Religion 500 years later and still retains its watch tower. The village has a great deal of atmosphere, which is somewhat spoiled by chairs and tables set out under the trees, stands full of postcards and most unoriginal souvenirs.

Collonges has both a small *auberge* which serves good food at reasonable prices and a fairly large camp site nearby. There are opportunities for many sporting activities, from tennis and swimming to sailing, riding and fishing in the immediate vicinity. Exhibitions of various kinds are held during the summer in the House of the Mermaid and also in the Chapel of the Penitents, added to which the whole village is floodlit from 10-12pm throughout July and August.

Collonges-la-Rouge

Meyssac, built in the same red mould as Collonges-la-Rouge, is larger but somewhat less atmospheric. It boasts an old fortified church and a collection of fifteenth-century houses grouped round an elderly corn exchange but has no tavern or camp site. Slightly further up the road, just before St Julien-Maumont, there is a comprehensive view over the countryside with its patchwork fields and woods, small functional houses, switchback roads and signposts indicating the way to **Beaulieu-sur-Dordogne**.

Beaulieu is another very attractive town with a clutch of small, quite acceptable hotels and a whole range of attractions available for its guests. At one time it was an inland port where flat-bottomed sailing barges put in to unload their wares and there are still some really lovely old houses lining the waterfront. The Maison de Clarisse is especially memorable with its wooden balcony and two square towers, now inhabited by pigeons. It was once home to boatmen and fishermen who earned their living on the Dordogne. Also overlooking the river is an ancient sanctuary, with a gable on the belfry wall that is high above five empty archways and mirrored on the usually placid surface of the water.

A small backstreet in Collonges-la-Rouge

Beaulieu-sur-Dordogne came into existence in AD855 with the building of a Benedictine monastery of considerable importance which, like so many other centres of power and learning, fell on hard times, during the Wars of Religion. Nevertheless, the Abbey Church of St Pierre managed to survive. It was built in the twelfth century by the monks from Cluny and has a particularly impressive south doorway, profusely carved with biblical scenes including depictions of Daniel in the Lions' Den and the Last Judgement. Inside are some excellent wood carvings, a few additional lions and a large collection of relics. The most noteworthy of these is a statue of the Virgin, though a thirteenth-century enamelled reliquary runs it a close second. Cheek by jowl with the church are some ancient houses including one known as the Maison d'Adam et Eve, much decorated with statues and medallions, which stands in the Place de la Bridolle.

Turning to its more up-to-date attractions, the town has bicycles for hire, a miniature golf course, tennis courts and a swimming pool. There is organised canoeing on the river with trips lasting for anything up to 4 days, as well as bathing, boating and fishing on the Lac d'Aubarèdes and blazed trails for walking. Beaulieu organises an annual exhibition of paintings and regional art which opens in mid-July and closes at the end of August, just in time for the Feast of the Holy Relics, held traditionally during the first weekend in September.

There are plenty of things to see in the surrounding area, starting with the underground cave of La Chapelle-aux-Saints. It is mainly of interest to archaeologists who went through it with a fine tooth-comb after a remarkably well preserved prehistoric skeleton was found there in 1908. A small display of things like fossils and flints, plus documents relating to the Neanderthal community who are thought to have lived there, is open on Sunday and Monday mornings.

Slightly further afield, **Reygade** is known simply and solely on account of a fifteenth-century tomb in the churchyard. It shows the body of Christ about to be wrapped in a shroud by two men, one of them Joseph of Arimathea, while five women including the Virgin Mary stand watching. All the figures are intricately carved and the clothes worn by the mourners are full of detail and painted meticulously in a range of different colours. It is described as the 'Mystery of Reygade' because no-one has any idea who the artist was or who commissioned him. The tomb is so highly thought of that son et lumière performances are held in the little chapel from 9am to 6pm every day throughout the year with plenty of free parking for cars.

Another son et lumière which attracts large crowds is staged at the **Tours de Merle**, just short of the border with Auvergne. This is a most imposing medieval ruin, rising out of a craggy mountaintop in the middle of nowhere, which can only be reached on foot. In its heyday Merle was a fortress town capable of holding up to 2,000 people, in spite of the fact that the eleventh-century lords of Merle had planned it simply as a defensive outpost. The fortress naturally attracted the attention of the English during the Hundred Years War but was saved, partly because of the intervention of Pope Gregory XI.

The Huguenots also tried to capture it in 1547 but were forced to give up the idea. It was after this that the inhabitants began to drift away, to be replaced briefly during the seventeenth century by a garrison of falconers in the employ of the Duc de Noailles.

For anyone who can face the long climb to the top it is a fairytale place with the remains of towers and terraces, an ancient keep, a few battlements and remnants of the Chapel of St Léger and the Château d'Hughes et Fulcon de Merle at the highest point. Medieval displays are held there from mid-July to mid-August, followed by the son et lumière. However, the latter entertainment actually starts much earlier with Saturday night performances in June, which are stepped up to one a night for the next two months, and revert to Saturdays only in September. St Geniez-ô-Merle, nearby, is the site of a little holiday village composed of *gîtes* which can be rented during the season.

Although the Tours de Merle give every impression of being half way to the end of the world, they are, in fact, only 20km (12$^1/_2$ miles) from **Argentat**, another extremely atmospheric little town on the banks of the Dordogne. At one time it was a lightermen's port and many of their excessively elderly houses still look out from under stone-tiled roofs in the shadow of a small but in no way remarkable church. There are a handful of small hotels and a well equipped camp site as well as the usual facilities for bathing, sailing, fishing and canoeing. The town runs to tennis courts, riding stables and a miniature golf course. It also hires out bicycles and maintains a series of blazed footpaths in the vicinity. It holds an international canoe rally on the first Sunday in July and a boating festival on 15 August.

Amongst the various places worth seeing are the Barrage d'Argentat, linked to the general hydro-electric system, and the Xaintrie plateau which covers the area between the gorges of the Dordogne and those of the Cère.

One scenic route follows the Dordogne up past the Château du Gibanel to **Glény**, where there is a little chapel left over from a larger church, and on to the Barrage du Chastang, returning by way of Servières-le-Château. Another makes for **St Chamant** where the only attraction, apart from the church, is its proximity to the Cascades de Murel and the **Roche de Vic**. The latter is wreathed in large blocks of granite and a short walk to the top is rewarded by a panoramic view stretching as far as the Massif des Monédières in the north and southwards to the Causse du Quercy.

A touch further on lies Quatre Routes which lives up to its name

Travelling with donkeys in Beaulieu

by offering a choice of four main routes heading due east, south, north and west. You can take your choice between Aurillac in Cantal, Figeac across the border in Lot, Tulle to the north and Brive slightly further off in a westerly direction. In addition, many of the minor roads offer their own alternatives, among which is the large holiday complex of **Le Coiroux**. Its many attractions include an 18-hole golf course beside the water, which is open all the year round and has a club house where one can take a shower, have a drink in the bar and reserve a table in the restaurant.

Le Coiroux also has archery butts, tennis courts and blazed footpaths as well as a lake for bathing, fishing, windsurfing or messing about in pedalos. All this is within striking distance of **Aubazine**, the site of a monastery which welcomes visitors every afternoon except Mondays during the summer but only at weekends for the rest of the year. The abbey church, dating from the twelfth

Tours de Merle

century, is worth seeing for its original stained glass, the tomb of St Etienne and an unusual oak cupboard of comparable age.

Apart from the Hôtel du Coiroux, where visitors can book in for a comprehensive golfing holiday, there are two small establishments with nearly as many facilities and a modest *auberge* with a nice line in home cooking. Aubazine is only about 14km ($8^{1}/_{2}$ miles) from Brive which, as the gateway to the south, is a good starting point from which to explore other parts of the Massif Central as they finger their way down in the direction of the Mediterranean, beyond the borders of Limousin.

3

MIDI-PYRENEES

M idi-Pyrénées is one of the larger provinces of France, leaning comfortably against a backrest of the Massif Central with its feet on the Spanish frontier. It is divided up into eight *départements*, only three of which have any relevance here, namely Aveyron and, to a certain extent, Lot and Tarn. La Montagne Noire marks the southernmost point of the Massif, a rather bleak area relieved by forests of oak or pine and the occasional lake. The stark limestone plâteaux, known as the Causses, lie to the north and east. Rivers such as the Agout, the Tarn, the Aveyron and the Lot have carved out gorges for themselves which have canyons and grottoes. Sheep are more numerous than cattle or pigs on the windswept highlands but once the land becomes attractively fertile they are joined by everything from horses, mules and donkeys to poultry and bees.

History has left its mark all over the region in the form of prehistoric dolmens, caves resplendent with rock paintings, solidly built châteaux, mouldering fortresses and more than a few small towns and picturesque villages. Many of these have become so accustomed to their ancient Roman churches that they seldom think of mentioning them at all. Souvenir hunters may be a trifle disappointed because items of this kind are rather thin on the ground but there is plenty of folklore adding colour to the various fêtes and festivals and, generally speaking, the cooking is both tasty and traditional.

Lot

The *département* of Lot came into existence in 1790. It was created out of part of the old province of Guyenne and corresponds roughly to the area known as Quercy. Its neighbours include Corrèze and Cantal to the north and Aveyron in the east while a fringe of hills separates it from the plains of Aquitaine. North of the Dordogne River is the Causse de Martel, crossed by a scenic highway that heads south from Limoges on its way to Toulouse. Just beyond the border the road forks, heading due south for Souillac and Cahors or slightly south-east past Martel and Rocamadour towards Figeac. It is down in this area that rivers like the Célé, the Lot and later the Aveyron appear, fed by higher than average rainfall that soaks into the limestone plâteaux and reappears later as springs which soon eat away narrow, very viewable courses for themselves. It is predominantly sheep country although crops of wheat, maize and rye are grown quite extensively. There are also some vineyards and the woods produce quantities of chestnuts and walnuts with truffles as an added luxury.

Holidaymakers who enjoy exploring historic towns, visiting a variety of châteaux, churches and museums and wandering through small, medieval villages will find plenty to interest them but there is just as much to occupy the sporting fraternity. Canoes can be hired at several places along the Célé, the Lot and the Dordogne where novices as well as experts can find the conditions best suited to their capabilities. Fishermen also have a choice of different types of water, backed up by any help or advice they may need from more than twenty different centres maintained by the Association de Pêche.

There are just as many riding stables with horses available for day trips or longer excursions. These follow a network of bridle paths which call in at most of the towns and larger villages but also have special stopping places of their own, some with *gîtes* and camp sites run by the authorities. Cyclists are just as well catered for with suggested circuits covering anything from 50 to 100km (30 to 60 miles) or a round tour of the *département* that involves travelling at least five times as far.

Les Sentiers de Grande Randonnée are every bit as enterprising, linking all the main tourist centres and providing conveniently located *gîtes* and camp sites, particularly on the GR6 from Souillac to Figeac and along the GR651 in the direction of Cahors. Hotels, on the whole, are fairly modest, there is no shortage of furnished accommodation,

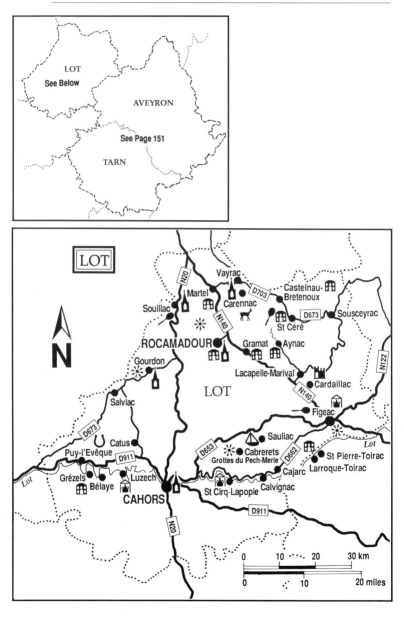

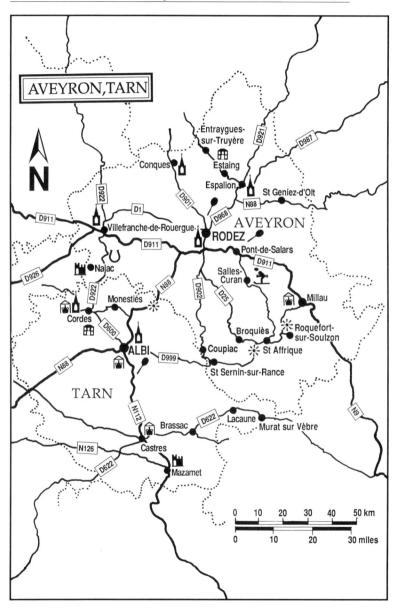

augmented by holiday villages and camp sites, and it is possible to find farmers who are willing to accept paying guests.

The history of Lot is similar to that of its neighbours, with traces of human habitation going back many thousands of years. There are caves and grottoes north of Rocamadour, at Cougnac, and along the Célé Valley as well as one of the largest collections of dolmens to be found anywhere in France. However, there is not a great deal of evidence of Roman occupation, despite the fact that Caesar's legions were no strangers to the area. They were followed by other invaders, among them Richard Coeur-de-Lion and his brother Henri Court-Mantel, at the time when the greater part of south-western France was in English hands after the marriage of Henry Plantagenet and Eleanor of Aquitaine. Obviously the local people did not take kindly to their sudden change of fortune and many a feudal castle was badly battered during the Hundred Years War.

The Wars of Religion that followed were just as damaging to both life and property and even as recently as 1944 death and deportation were commonplace for the members of the Resistance Movement who had waged a constant underground battle against the Germans for nearly two years. Few of the industries that sprang up throughout the country after the war extended as far as Lot. However, craftsmen of all kinds took a liking to the region and set up small workshops where they keep alive traditional arts and also run courses for beginners who are interested in learning to weave, make pottery or even work with iron.

To the west of Lot the mountains and the provincial boundary fail to coincide in many places which means that an occasional sortie is necessary in order to visit an attractive town or a site of particular interest. The latter almost invariably fall into the prehistoric category because the western edge of the Massif Central is said to have been inhabited for something like 200,000 years. There are several hundred caves and grottoes strung out along the Vézère Valley at places like **Le Moustier**, where the excavations are under cover in the village itself, and **Les Eyzies**, the self-styled prehistoric centre of the world.

Apart from Les Combarelles, which has about 300 different paintings, there are several other areas of exploration as well as the extremely informative National Museum of Prehistory, housed in an ancient fortress. Although the famous Lascaux caves have been closed to the public in order to preserve them, 90 per cent of the art work has been faithfully reproduced at **Lascaux II** nearby. Forty people are allowed in at a time for an inspection which lasts about three-quarters of an hour.

For anyone who wants to make a detailed tour of this part of Périgord, beyond the border with Lot, a good base would be **Sarlat-la-Canéda**, founded by the Benedictine monks 1,200 or more years ago, a few kilometres north of the Dordogne River. It is a delightful place grouped round, but not overawed by, its Cathedral of St Sacerdos. The old quarter is a maze of tiny streets and alleyways bordered on either side by medieval houses, several of which are worth more than just a passing glance.

The Maison de la Boétie, dating from the early sixteenth century, is a perfect example along with the Hôtel de Maleville and the somewhat older Hôtel Plamon which looks out on the Rue des Consuls through windows that would do justice to a church. However, the most curious building is the Lanterne des Morts, a twelfth-century tower constructed in honour of St Bernard, who paid Sarlat a visit in 1147. Other attractions include the Museum of the Chapel of the White Penitents, and the Aquarium museum, as well as sports facilities, some attractive gardens and a handful of small hotels.

Back in Lot, the first town of any size is **Gourdon**, a good deal smaller than Sarlat but equally well worth visiting. The old section is restrained by a circlet of avenues and boulevards and still has its original fortified gateway protecting the Rue du Majou, once the most important road into the town but now a pedestrian walkway. It runs between lines of elderly houses from the Chapelle de Notre-Dame du Majou to the Place de la Mairie and the Eglise St Pierre which started life in the early fourteenth century. It was once attached to the Abbaye du Vigan, 5km (3 miles) away to the east, and has some rather nice panelling added during the seventeenth century. Just as viewable is the starkly impressive Eglise des Cordeliers, on the far side of the Allées de la République which marks the line of the old ramparts. However, all this takes second place to the Grottes de Cougnac, a few minutes' drive away.

The first three caves are quite small and full of stalactites all bunched together like icicles on a cold winter's morning, whereas the larger Salle des Colonnes is relatively spacious. It is a fine sight although, for many people, it is overshadowed by the Salle des Peintures Préhistoriques with its cave paintings harking back to the days when mammoths lived in Europe. The drawings are extremely

The Grotte de Font de Gaume, near Les Eyzies

Sarlat

vivid and are almost on a par with those of Lascaux, claimed to be the most outstanding discovered anywhere in the world. The town of Gourdon, while not overblessed with hotels, has a few small *auberges* and provides its guests with facilities for tennis, swimming, riding, fishing and potholing. As far as long distance walkers are concerned, it is a good place to join the GR64 heading north towards the Dordogne.

The main centre in this area is **Souillac**, a small town in the heart of a fertile region with a long history, a large abbey church and enough other advantages to make it a popular holiday resort. There are several *auberges*, most of which have restaurants, private baths or showers and parking space for cars. Some also run to private pools while the town itself provides tennis and swimming, fishing, riding, potholing, canoes for exploring the Dordogne and a series of marked footpaths. There is also a well shaded camp site on the river bank which is open from mid-June to mid-September and furnished accommodation in local farmhouses, one of which offers its guests a whole range of sporting facilities including mini-golf.

The ancient monastery in Souillac, having survived the Hundred Years War without too much trouble, had a bad spell during the Wars of Religion before disappearing altogether at the time of the Revolution. The twelfth-century Church of St Martin fared rather better and succeeded in preserving a magnificent doorway and most of its decorations as well as the ancient tombs in the crypt. There are statues of saints, episodes from the Old Testament and a noteworthy bas-relief of the prophet Isaiah obviously drawing the attention of Israel to the long list of troubles ahead.

Martel, which gave its name to the Causse north of the Dordogne, was the centre of a family row involving England's Henry II, who owned most of western France at the time, his wife Eleanor of Aquitaine and two of their sons, Richard Coeur-de-Lion and Henri Court-Mantel. Court-Mantel found himself disinherited in favour of his brother and desperately short of funds so he attacked the monastery at Rocamadour and made off with its treasure. By the time he reached Martel he was overcome with fever and remorse, confessed his crimes, was forgiven and died in the Maison Fabri in 1183. Other places of interest in the town include streets full of atmospheric and ancient houses, the Church of St Maur, the Cloître de Mirepoises and the eighteenth-century market place. The Hôtel de la Raymondie has, behind its fourteenth-century arcaded façade, a small museum with bits and pieces unearthed near Vayrac, a short drive to the east.

The Puy d'Issolud, on the outskirts of Vayrac, is one of the spots considered by experts to be a possible site of *Uxcellodunum*. Whether it was the ancient battle ground or not, there is little doubt that the Gauls dug themselves in there in a last, vain attempt to halt the Roman advance in 51BC. Their obstinacy in the face of over-whelming odds annoyed Julius Caesar so much that he retaliated by cutting off the right hands of all his prisoners. Anyone who wants to take a longer look at Martel and its Causse will find a couple of small hotels in the town, a camp site and opportunities for playing tennis, swimming, fishing, walking and potholing.

On the opposite side of the Dordogne and due south-east of Vayrac, **Carennac** has not a great deal to offer in the way of hotels but it is extremely well placed for canoe trips along the river as well as being on the GR652 to Aurillac, in Cantal. The main bridle path which tours the north of the *département* passes close by, with a camp site where riders can pause for a while. The original entrance to the old town is well fortified, though not in any way spectacular, but beyond it are some attractive old houses and the Eglise St Pierre with a doorway that was beautifully sculptured in the twelfth century. A relatively small road leads back across the southbound route from Martel, follows the Dordogne past some small hamlets and pauses briefly at the **Grottes de Lacave**, within sight of the river.

These caves were discovered in 1902 and provided a rich harvest in the form of prehistoric tools and weapons, bones and animal horns as they were gradually excavated before being prepared to accept visitors. The site is open for much of the year when a small electric train and a lift transport customers into the bowels of the earth to be greeted by stalactites and stalagmites, an illuminated Sal du Lac and the much-decorated Sal de Merveilles. An additional attraction is the nearby Château de la Treyne, now a comfortable hotel.

After rejoining the main route to Cahors, more or less on a level with Gourdon, there are not a great many places to see on the western side before dropping down into the Lot Valley. However, for the dedicated searcher after small villages, one or two are worthy of mention in passing. **Salviac**, for instance, contributes a small church which has managed to preserve some fragments of fourteenth-century stained glass recalling the murdered St Eutrope while **Catus** takes equal care of the remnants left over from an ancient priory.

For some reason, the Lot Valley is frequently ignored by tourists

PLACES OF INTEREST IN LOT

Le Moustier
Prehistoric excavations. A site in the village, Le Ruth and a troglodyte settlement in the cliff.

Les Eyzies
Many prehistoric discoveries including the Grotte de Combarelles, the Gorge d'Enfer and Laugerie Basse. Small safari park.

National Museum of Prehistory. In the fortified castle in Les Eyzies. A collection of relics and explanations of the ancient crafts as well as the techniques used to discover them.

Lascaux II
North of Sarlat. Reproductions of the cave drawings of Lascaux.

Sarlat-la-Canéda
Museum of the Chapel of the White Penitents
Rue Jean-Jacques Rousseau. The Museum of the Société des Amis de Sarlat.

Cathedral
Twelfth-century Chapel of the Blue Penitents and traces of the old abbey and the ancient cemetery.

Lanterne des Morts
Opposite the cathedral. A twelfth-century tower.

Aquarium Museum.

Gourdon
Eglise St Pierre
Twelfth-century church with decorations added in the seventeenth century.

Grottes de Cougnac
Caves with stalactites, stalagmites and wall paintings.

Souillac
Abbey church. A twelfth-century church. Bas-relief of Isaiah and magnificent doorway.

Martel
Hôtel de la Raymondie
An attractive, medieval mansion with a small local museum concerned mainly with items discovered on the site of an old Gallic defensive position near Vayrac.

Cloître de Mirepoises
An attractive, old cloister open to visitors during the summer.

Carennac
Eglise St Pierre. A well decorated church with a fine doorway, a *mise au tombeau* and a flamboyant cloister.

Grottes de Lacave
On the Dordogne north of Rocamadour. Fascinating underground caves reached by a small train and a lift.

Château de Bonaguil
An impressive fortress near Fumel of particular interest to students of military architecture.

Grézels
Château de la Coste.
A sturdy fortified chateau with towers and a small chapel.

Luzech
Armand Viré Museum

Cahors
Cathédrale St Etienne
Ancient doorway, decorative interior and impressive cloister. Chapel housing a collection of treasures.

Pont Valentré
A much fortified bridge, said to be the only one of its kind. The central tower is open to summer visitors.

Maison de Roaldes
An ancient house associated with Henri de Navarre, restored in1912.

Eglise St Barthélémy
The original Church of St Etienne-de-Soubiroux which changed its name in the thirteenth century. Contains a bust of the local pope, John XXII.

Municipal Museum
In the Parc A. Tassart, exhibits associated with Pope John XXII and the statesman Léon Gambetta.

Mont St Cyr
View of Cahors.

St Cirq-Lapopie
Musée Rignault
Small museum with widespread interests including items from China and some African masks.

Château de Cénevières
Near Calvignac. Fortified château with tapestries, very viewable rooms and terraces with views over the Lot Valley.

Château de Larroque-Toirac
Typical fortified medieval château

Grotte du Pech-Merle
Near Cabrerets. Interesting underground caves with many prehistoric decorations.

Figeac
Hôtel de la Monnaie
Museum in the Place Vival, related to the town's history.

Musée Champollion
4 Impasse Champollion. A museum concerned with the life and work of the Egyptologist Jean-François Champollion.

Château d'Aynac
Near Lacapelle-Marival. Particularly suited to horse-lovers.

Rocamadour
Hôtel de ville
A fifteenth-century mansion with a tapestry exhibition in the summer.

Grottoes of the Nativity, the Sepulchre and the Cross of Jerusalem. All places of pilgrimage which can only be reached on foot.

Basilique St Sauveur
Eleventh-century church in a religious complex which includes some impressive chapels and a museum of treasures.

Chapelle Notre-Dame
Ancient chapel, much restored. Famous Black Madonna and votive offerings.

Château
Also part of the complex with ramparts and an exceptional view.

Musées de Cire Roland-le-Preux et de l'Historial.
Small displays of local interest and associated with the history of the town.

Gouffre de Padirac
Near Carennac. Magnificent caves with an underground river and lifts for easy access. Also a small zoo.

Château de Castelnau-Bretenoux
Large medieval fortress. Interesting interior, a small chapel and decorative furnishings.

St Céré
Vintage Car Museum
Not the most comprehensive collection but interesting.

Casino
Exhibition of tapestries during the summer: the work of Jean Lurçat and his weavers in Aubusson.

Château de Montal
Near St Céré. Medieval château with some attractive stonework and pleasing interiors.

though it is a favourite haunt of travellers and like-minded people who prefer to do their sightseeing in peace and comparative solitude. This is all the more strange when you realise that a well maintained road accompanies the river from Villeneuve-sur-Lot all the way along the valley, passing atmospheric little villages, elderly châteaux and an occasional ruin, not forgetting the ancient city of Cahors.

The Château de Bonaguil, on the western boundary with Lot-et-Garonne, is a splendid fortress and a perfect example of military architecture in the early sixteenth century. It has a double line of defences, the outer walls protecting a group of towers overlooking the central courtyards, with an unusually shaped keep in the middle and living quarters all round. The ramparts were designed to withstand any siege but, as was so often the case, they were not proof against either famine or treachery.

The first town of any consequence along the river is **Puy-l'Evêque** which is not nearly so militant, despite its early fortifications. The keep is all that remains of the thirteenth-century castle with an attractive church marking the north-eastern end of the original defences. Between them is a jumble of old houses lining the narrow streets and clustered round a fourteenth-century church. The village boasts a small inn and a camp site with tennis, swimming, canoeing and fishing. There are also riding stables in the area, well marked footpaths and a small road up to Martignac where some frescoes in an excellent state of preservation were discovered in the local church in 1938.

On the far side of the river, round the next bend, is the seemingly self-important Château de la Coste at **Grézels**, perched on a hilltop with twin towers flanking the battlements and a history going back more than 700 years. Further on, past Bélaye with its view along the valley, **Luzech** is even older and just as fascinating. It is protected on all sides by the river, suspended like a giant drop pearl on a short necklace, with a thirteenth-century keep dominating the village at the entrance and a patchwork of fields and trees beyond.

Because of its obvious strategic advantages, it has been a popular stronghold since prehistoric times. The Gauls made good use of it before they were moved on by the Romans and Richard Coeur-de-Lion captured it in 1188. The stronghold also featured in the crusade against the heretics of Albi and was a bargaining counter between the French and English during the Hundred Years War. However, time and a good deal of reconstruction have healed many wounds and today it is a charming, rather sleepy medieval village with some understated chapels, typical houses and a collection of relics from the past in its mini-museum. For travellers in search of up-market accommodation it is useful to know that the Château de Mercuès, which also dates from the Middle Ages, has been turned into a comfortable hotel surrounded by terraces and gardens and commanding a splendid view.

Cahors comes next, full of atmosphere, history and hotels. The town, virtually enclosed in a tight, horseshoe-bend of the river, was well known to both the Gauls and the Romans. The latter liked it so well that they settled down and built themselves a forum, theatres, temples, villas and the obligatory baths, all protected by ramparts. However, not a great deal has survived from those early days and one tends to think of it as a dignified, medieval city with a wealth of tiny, narrow streets, shady squares and beautiful old houses like the Maison de Roaldes where Henri de Navarre stayed briefly at the end of the sixteenth century.

The most memorable building is arguably the magnificent Cathédrale St Etienne, built on the site of a sixth-century church which has been improved and refurbished at intervals ever since. The ornate north door is a fair indication of things to come, which include paintings and statues, decorated chapels, an exceptionally viewable cloister and a collection of treasures spanning about 1,600 years.

Fine as it is, the cathedral has a rival in the form of the Pont Valentré which was built, according to legend, with the help of the devil. It is an extremely martial construction with three tall, square towers, a once-fortified gateway and additional vantage points over-looking the river for extra protection. From the bridge it is a tidy walk to the Municipal Museum, housed in the ancient episcopal palace and half surrounded by gardens on the other side of the station.

Its exhibits are many and varied, from Roman remains and medieval sculptures to religious relics, china and souvenirs of people like Pope John XXII and Léon Gambetta. The pope was baptised in the Eglise St Barthélémy, a stone's throw from the waterfront, and founded the city university in 1332. Gambetta, the son of a local grocer, was a staunch Republican who became Minister for War in 1870, served briefly as premier and was accidentally shot at his villa near Sèvres soon afterwards.

Like the Pont Valentré, several other places of interest are

Cahors Cathedral

The Pont Valentré, Cahors

marked by towers. One is all that remains of a palace owned by the pope's brother, Pierre Dueze, another belongs to the ancient college of Jesuits, a third was part of a hall of residence for impoverished students attending the university while a fourth was attached to a former prison, now known as the Château du Roi. It is definitely a town which needs to be explored at leisure and anyone who has difficulty in getting their bearings has only to climb to the top of Mont St Cyr for an informative, bird's eye view. However, wandering round is just as straightforward if you remember that the Boulevard Gambetta, slicing a path along the line of the ancient ramparts, neatly separates the old quarter from the rest of the city.

Beyond Cahors the road and the river keep each other company, past the little Chapel of Notre-Dame de Veles to **Bouziès**. It is near here, just beyond a small tunnel cut through the rock, that visitors should keep an eye open for the so-called Maison Anglais. It is an amazing little place, built into a crevice between the rocks high above the road with mini-battlements and the air of a small fortress that is ready and willing to pit its strength against all comers.

Its nearest neighbour is **St Cirq-Lapopie**, elegantly draped over a steep hillside on a sharpish bend in the river. It is justly proud of its reputation as the First Village of France although it has changed a bit since the English yeomanry gave it a good deal of attention towards the end of the twelfth century. To start with, its castle was demolished on the orders of Louis XI in 1471 and the Huguenots did not help when they made good use of the ruins during the Wars of Religion. Nevertheless, it has a Rip van Winkle quality about it with a number of enchanting little alleys, some of which look as though they have not received much attention since the Romans were fighting the Gauls, and antiquated houses that do nothing to break the spell. There is also a small church and the Musée Rignault containing, amongst other things, some unlikely exhibits from as far away as China and Africa.

Further up stream there are not many more places to see along the Lot before it is crossed by the *département* border south of Figeac. However, the Château de Cénevières is one of them, built in the thirteenth century and still retaining its original keep, attractive Renaissance courtyard and rooms hung with tapestries. **Calvignac** has less to offer because it lost nearly all its fortress many years ago while **Montbrun**'s only claim to fame is a ruined château that belonged in its heyday to a member of Pope John XXII's family. Finally, Larroque-Toirac and St Pierre-Toirac weigh in with a small fortified church and a château, decorated in the style of Louis XIII, which welcomes visitors.

The River Célé, which joins the Lot in the vicinity of St Cirq-Lapopie, has just as many attractions, ranging from secluded hamlets and long-established châteaux to the prehistoric **Grotte du Pech-Merle**. Only a few of the caves and galleries are open to visitors, with guided tours both before and after lunch during the summer months, but even so it is an opportunity not to be missed. The walls are covered with strange signs and symbols, designs apparently traced by ancient fingers in soft clay and beautifully executed drawings of animals. There are also ghostly, disembodied hands, looking more like rubber gloves, and footprints left behind by an early inhabitant which became petrified at some time during the past 20,000 years.

The adjacent village of **Cabrerets** has a ruined Devil's Castle, a château that turns its back on visitors and the Musée du Cazals within easy reach. A small, comfortable hotel on the outskirts is set in more or less formal gardens sloping down to the river where guests can swim, fish or drift up and down in a modest boat. However, it is often fully booked in which case an acceptable option is the local *auberge* with nearly twice as many rooms, some with baths attached, that charges less than half the price. Its residents can also swim, fish, go potholing or take long walks in the forest.

From Cabrerets the road follows the course of the Célé through a series of small villages, each of which has something to offer the traveller who has plenty of time to spare. **Marcilhac-sur-Célé** still retains the tall, square tower which was part of its ancient abbey and points its guests in the direction of the Grotte de Bellevue, discovered in 1964, while **Sauliac-sur-Célé** shares the open-air museum with Cuzals which specialises in popular art and traditions, rural architecture, farming equipment and flowers. **Ste Eulalie** has a prehistoric grotto which is of no interest to visitors because they are not allowed inside whereas **Espagnac** possesses the remains of an ancient monastery and a bell tower that must be one of the strangest in the area. It looks more like a large dovecote with an eight-sided pointed hat on top.

Figeac, almost at the end of the line, is a good deal bigger than its neighbours with an attractive old quarter full of picturesque houses, two elderly churches that were updated in the seventeenth century and a museum devoted largely to Jean-François Champollion. He was the first person to compile an alphabet from hieroglyphs and is generally regarded as the founder of Egyptology, having had a special professorship created for him in Paris before his early death in 1832. The Eglise St Sauveur is quite ornate inside, with several small chapels, notably the Chapelle Notre-Dame de Pitié, and a memorial to Champollion dating from 1870. The town also boasts a comfortable hotel with facilities for both tennis and swimming, a couple of the smaller, less well equipped variety, a sports stadium and a leisure park with 150 sites for caravans plus a restaurant and organised entertainments during the season.

Capdenac, south of Figeac and only a short drive away, is believed by some historians to be the site of *Uxcellodunum* where the Gauls made their final stand against the advancing Roman legions. Whether or not Caesar was there, it continued to be a warlike entity, getting caught up in the fracas between the Church of Rome and the Albigeois, the religious sect who refused to believe in the birth of Christ and described the world and everything in it as the work of the devil. Much affronted, the Catholics mounted a crusade which lasted

Figeac

for 20 years and only ended when the sect was exterminated by Simon de Montfort when he captured their Mont Ségur stronghold in 1245. Nothing daunted, Capdenac threw itself with equal enthusiasm into both the Hundred Years War and the Wars of Religion so it is mildly surprising to find so much of it still standing.

Meanwhile, **Cardaillac**, reached by way of a very minor road off the main route to the north, provides its own interest in the form of a twelfth-century fort. The countryside beyond is pleasant without being particularly exciting, with byways keeping for the most part to the valleys, not a great many hamlets and few if any tourist attractions along the unmarked border with Aveyron.

In complete contrast, a fork in the main road slightly further on reintroduces that all-too-frequent feeling of indecision. To the left are Gramat and Rocamadour, to the right Lacapelle-Marival and Aynac, which no-one in search of an unusual holiday can afford to ignore. Lacapelle-Marival is a delightful little place dominated by a large

Château d'Aynac

thirteenth-century keep left over from the days when it was extremely well fortified.

On the other hand, the Château d'Aynac with its domed towers and shuttered windows, is anything but forbidding. It is the home of the Tourisme Attelé which caters solely for people who are interested in horses. It is possible to study the whole subject from start to finish, both in theory and in practice, and once a visitor is at home in the saddle, excursions are organised into the surrounding country. They range from a day out in the woods, with horse-drawn carriages for anyone who is only going for the drive, to longer trips designed to include places of outstanding beauty, popular locations and historic sites. Day to day living is comfortable and easy but it is not the place for tourists in search of organised entertainments or city lights.

Gramat is rather more interested in dogs which it trains for the French police force at the Centre de Formation, established there at the end of World War II. Visitors are allowed in on Thursday afternoons during the summer to watch the lessons and displays while at other times they can play tennis, fish, swim, ride, walk, investigate potholes or go to the races. One or two small hotels are augmented by the more up-market Château de Roumégouse, about half way to Rocamadour, generally agreed to be one of the most eye-catching towns in the region.

Rocamadour is best seen for the first time from L'Hospitalet, so named because it was once an important stopping place for pilgrims who wanted to wash and brush up before reaching the end of their journey. The hospital, like the ramparts, is now in ruins but the view is unchanged. Rocamadour itself is steeped in legends, most of them contradictory but all attributing its origins to one saint or another. Even St Amadour is thought to have been an assumed name although who assumed it and why remains a mystery. The fact is that the town has been a place of pilgrimage since the Middle Ages, playing host to kings and cardinals, saints and sinners while establishing outposts as far afield as Spain, Portugal and Sicily.

Now, as then, Rocamadour clambers up the side of the Canyon de l'Alzou, finding its feet on rocky ledges between the trees until it reaches the Basilique St Sauveur and its neighbouring castle at the top. Beyond are the Grottoes of the Nativity and the Sepulchre and, a short walk away, the venerable Cross of Jerusalem. Many places can only be reached on foot although there is a road, the ancient Rue de la Mercerie, winding its way up from the bypass which carries on singlemindedly near the bottom of the canyon.

Ardent pilgrims, who tend to arrive these days on wheels rather than on foot, are sometimes inclined to negotiate the Grand Escalier, or Via Sancta, on their knees but ordinary tourists can discover less painful approaches to the Basilica with its attendant chapels and the Crypt of St Amadour. The Chapelle Miraculeuse is the home of the famous Black Madonna, referred to locally as the Saint of Saints, full of votive offerings and decorated with frescoes including yet another version of the *Danse Macabre*. The Chapel of St Michel, partly built into the rock, is distinguished by two ancient frescoes in an excellent state of preservation while the *hôtel de ville*, housed in the fifteenth-century Maison des Frères, is equally proud of its modern tapestries depicting the flora and fauna of the Causse.

A fifteenth-century gilded silver chalice, along with sculptures, reliquaries, pictures and vestments, can be seen in the Musée Trésor which also has a good view of the canyon though the panorama from the castle ramparts is much more spectacular. Rocamadour is certainly a place to linger a while, especially as there is one comfortable and fairly spacious hotel, a number of smaller ones, a restaurant with rooms attached, two small museums and son et lumière during the season. If the past becomes a trifle overbearing there are long, invigorating walks — the GR46 is close at hand — and opportunities for a quiet day's fishing in the River Alzou.

To the north-east of Rocamadour, on the far side of the main highway and beyond the rather forgettable hamlet of Alvignac, is the magnificent **Gouffre de Padirac**. It was officially discovered in 1889 but is generally believed to have provided a refuge for local people in the Middle Ages while one war after another raged above their heads. Legend has it that Satan created the enormous caverns and the spectacular underground river for his own benefit before he met his match in St Martin who stumbled across them by accident. Apparently, the saint's mule refused to enter the devil's territory, there was a confrontation, good triumphed over evil and St Martin and his mule continued on their way.

A tour of the Gouffre de Padirac begins in comfort with lifts whisking visitors down to the lowest level. This is followed by a stroll along the Galerie de la Source in the company of a guide who points to the various items of interest and trots out relevant statistics which include the fact that it is 2,000m (6,500ft) below ground level and the temperature never drops to less than 13°C (55°F).

At the far end of the Galerie a flotilla of small boats continues the journey over limpid water, past the Grande Pendelogue, a giant stalactite in the Lac de la Pluie, as far as the uncomfortably named Pas du Crocodile. This is where the boats turn round to collect the next group of sightseers while their passengers continue on foot past Lac Supérieur and through the Sal des Grands Gours, with its pools and natural waterfall, before starting the journey back. The whole visit takes roughly 1½ hours although it would last a good deal longer if one decided to use the stairs in preference to the lifts. Back at ground level there is the added attraction of a small zoo with animals like bears, llamas and monkeys as well as cages of exotic birds.

The surrounding area is well supplied with byways, some of which lead to far less memorable caves and grottoes while others discover a small, health-giving spa, look in at Autoire with its old houses and even venture as far as **Castelnau**. The main reason for making this short detour would be to visit the Château de Castelnau-Bretenoux, an extremely elderly fortress which insists that it withstood every attack except one — and then only surrendered to Henry II of England in 1159 because its defenders were literally starving to death. It has

Rocamadour

Château de Castelnau-Bretenoux

its fair share of tapestries, furniture and objets d'art as well as a small chapel, added in 1429, and a fourteenth-century tower which is not open to visitors.

From Bretenoux a road of no particular merit wanders off southwards towards **St Céré** which is pleasant and unassuming with an ancient quarter tucked away beside the river and sprawling suburbs. It boasts several old houses which have changed very little since the Middle Ages and an ornate water pump in the Place du Mercadial. There is no sign of a basin to catch the water but it is topped by a delightful little figure, peering back over her shoulder as if to discover where her bathwater had gone. There are a couple of small hotels, along with a camp site, everything one could wish for in the way of sporting activities, a vintage car museum and a casino which holds exhibitions of modern tapestries at the height of the season. During its annual music festival, St Céré makes a point of including masterpieces by composers of the calibre of Mozart and Verdi while at the same time introducing its audiences to a whole range of lesser known works.

The Château de Montal, beyond the outskirts of St Céré, was built on the orders of Jeanne de Balzac in 1523. It had a rather checkered career and was in a sorry state when a certain Maurice Fenaille came to its rescue in 1908. The whole building has been particularly well restored from its solid stone foundations to the 'witches' hats' which sit easily on top of its various towers. It is worth noting the astonishingly lifelike busts of its original owners keeping watch from sculptured niches in the west wall before going inside to inspect the interior decorations.

From St Céré a secondary road wanders across the countryside to the comparatively remote village of **Sousceyrac**. Here the highlight is a typical little hotel offering a warm welcome and dishes like trout soufflé, fresh salmon or sweetbreads in an onion sauce for the benefit of anyone looking for somewhere to spend the night en route to Aveyron.

Aveyron

For all practical purposes, Aveyron marks the south-western boundary of the Massif Central, sandwiched between Lot and Lozère, with Hérault separating it from the Mediterranean. There are volcanic highlands round Aubrac which can be snowbound in winter but burst into flower in the spring, turn pleasantly warm during the summer months and then become enveloped in autumn mists as a prelude to renewing the cycle. The tree-covered slopes of the north give way to bleak, rather rocky terrain which can be either fascinatingly remote or depressingly isolated, depending on one's frame of mind.

Rivers, the most important of which are the Lot, the Aveyron and the Tarn, have carved out beds for themselves with sides that can reach a height of 1,500ft or more. Where the ground is softer they have created warm, sheltered valleys full of meadows, orchards and vineyards. Chestnuts, the main source of starch before the Spaniards introduced potatoes from Peru in the early sixteenth century, are still very much in demand, providing everything from *marrons glacés* to food for the animals.

The farmlands are a patchwork of small fields devoted mainly to potatoes, fodder and pastures for the cattle while the sheep graze at slightly higher altitudes. At one time they were highly prized for their wool but nowadays play an even more important role in the manufacture of cheese. Neither mining nor light industry contribute very much to the local economy although there is a modicum of coal and small deposits of iron and zinc.

The area is peppered with dolmens and there are traces of Roman occupation as well as small towns and villages that suffered repeatedly in the days when religious differences were settled with guns and swords. Replacement populations, brought in to fill the gaps left by constant battles between the established church and the heretics of Albi, took no chances and protected their settlements with high defensive walls.

It is generally agreed that one of the most beautiful towns in the *département* is **Conques**, a showpiece of golden-beige houses clustered round the imposing Cathedral of Ste Foy and spilling down the terraced hillsides towards the Dourdou River and the Ouche Valley. It was an important place of pilgrimage in the Middle Ages, especially for travellers taking the long road to Santiago de Compostela which lies on the far side of the Pyrénées.

The town is in an exceptionally good state of repair due mostly to the determined efforts which were made to restore and refurbish it in 1974. It is almost impossible to find a bed, let alone a bath, during the season because of the lack of hotels but there is one delightful *auberge* across the road from the cathedral where it is worth enquiring in case there has been a cancellation. Nor does Conques put itself out to entertain visitors. Crowds arrive in cars and coaches, walk round the little streets that are delightfully free of obtrusive souvenirs, pay their respects to Ste Foy and leave again by nightfall.

Apart from the Chapelle St Roch, which can only be reached on foot, the Porte de la Vinzelle and some picturesque old houses, the sole place of interest is the cathedral. Behind the splendid twelfth-century doorway, the church is unusually austere with an arcaded cloister that was much restored in 1975. However, the treasures are anything but muted. The tenth-century statue reliquary of Ste Foy, seated in a decorative chair, is encrusted with gems and, somewhat unusually, holds a tiny vase in either hand, just large enough to take a flower or two. There are a number of other impressive reliquaries, silver statues and a processional cross as well as a reference to Charlemagne who, it is said, listed all the main abbeys of Gaul according to their importance, starting with Ste Foy. The life of the saint is told in a series of tapestries woven in Felletin, the small but much respected centre of weaving just south of Aubusson.

From Conques a well surfaced road runs along the banks of the Lot past the Pont Coursavy, passing several nice little villages, each with its characteristic country inn. There are a few camp sites by the

Conques

water and an occasional notice to the effect that canoes can be hired. The houses are mostly built of stone, with slate-tiled roofs, small vegetable gardens and garages. The overall impression is one of contentment and wellbeing.

The River Truyère joins the Lot at **Entraygues-sur-Truyère** where it is crossed by an extremely picturesque thirteenth-century bridge which is still very much in operation. Modern houses with shuttered windows nudge each other up the hillside, and the village also boasts a minute old quarter where the Rue Basse is reserved for pedestrians only. There is an ancient château, a church of no particular merit and two *auberges* offering most aids to comfort, including lifts. It is a good centre for anyone with a little gentle

Thirteenth-century bridge at Entraygues-sur-Truyère

exploration in mind, especially as visitors can hire bicycles and park a caravan. One acceptable excursion would be along the River Truyère which earns its living by providing hydro-electric power but also has some attractive gorges and a sizeable reservoir.

Meanwhile, the Lot continues peacefully on its way through wooded and increasingly rocky country, past the Barrage de Golinhac, to **Estaing**. This is a typical waterside hamlet dominated by a fifteenth-century château, one of whose previous owners became involved in the intrigues surrounding Marie Antoinette and consequently lost his head. The village has its own Gothic bridge with a statue of François d'Estaing, a small church, several elderly houses and two rather basic inns. There is a local camp site, swimming and canoes for hire in addition to blazed trails through the gorges.

Espalion, further up stream, is a small village in very much the same mould as its neighbours with an old château, a less arresting thirteenth-century bridge and the ancient Eglise St Jean which has been converted into a folklore museum. On the outskirts, a gentle stroll away, is the Eglise de Perse, dating from the eleventh century, which pays equal attention to St Hilarian and the Last Judgement.

At this point, one can leave the Lot Valley for a short detour northwards across the stark, rocky highlands to Aubrac. The town was built in 1120 for the benefit of pilgrims on their way from Le Puy-en-Velay to Santiago de Compostela. It has probably seen little change since then though the Tour des Anglais was added a bit later to make life difficult for the English during the Hundred Years War.

There are one or two small hotels and the old Pilgrim Church of Notre-Dame-des-Pauvres but nothing in the sporting line apart from the usual marked footpaths. Included among them is the GR65 down to **St Chély-d'Aubrac** where one can play tennis in summer, ski in winter, put up at a basic tavern, cross into Lozère or head back to **St Geniez-d'Olt**. From here a fairly ordinary road provides an easy run through to Laissac and on past the Forêt des Palanges to **Rodez**.

There is no doubt that the town's most prominent attraction is the Cathedral of Notre-Dame, which is extremely decorative but rather severe. The west face was at one time part of the citizens' first line of defence and has all the hallmarks of a fort with businesslike towers and hardly any windows worth mentioning, whereas the upper part of the bell tower is splendidly ornate. The interior is equally full of contradictions with some beautiful wood carving but at least one chapel where the statues have seen far better days. The cathedral looks out over the Place d'Armes and down the arrow-straight Avenue Victor Hugo while the old quarter hides behind its skirts. Among the many aged and attractive houses are the decorative Maison d'Armagnac, the Maison Molinier and the Musée Fenaille, full of archaeological discoveries, old furniture, manuscripts and pottery from La Graufesenque, which was produced in Roman times.

Beyond the encircling boulevards, the Musée des Beaux Arts displays paintings and sculptures, both ancient and modern, with particular attention to local works. It is a good idea to walk round the line of the ancient ramparts in order to see the different views — northwards from the Square Monteil to the mountains of Aubrac and Cantal, east from the Square des Embergues where there is an orientation table and south from the Square François Fabie, watched over by a statue of the poet. The town has its own local airport, a sports centre and several small hotels with two comfortable establishments on the outskirts. The best equipped of these provides tennis, two swimming pools and a few apartments and can be found at Onet-le-Château, slightly off the road to Marcillac-Vallon.

From Rodez a major road leads westwards to **Villefranche-de-**

Rouergue with, perhaps, a minor detour to Belcastel on the Aveyron and the nearby statue of Notre-Dame-de-Buenne where pilgrims gather on the last Sunday in May and again on the last Sunday in August to receive a special blessing. Villefranche-de-Rouergue itself, also on the Aveyron, is a busy market town with fewer hotels than Rodez but it contains probably the biggest bastide of all. This was started in 1099 by the Comte de Toulouse and completed around 1256 under the direction of Alphonse de Poitiers, the brother of St Louis. It consists of parallel streets with any number of intersections, most of which are blind alleys.

The focal point of the bastide is a beautiful arcaded square in the middle, overlooked by the Church of Notre-Dame. It is tall and faintly warlike with an enormous door, a touch of fifteenth-century stained glass and carved wooden stalls that were badly damaged during the Wars of Religion. The Chapelle des Pénitents Noirs, not far off, did not escape lightly either so most of its main features were added in the eighteenth century. The Ancienne Chartreuse St Sauveur, well away from the bastide, managed to save its structure during the Revolution because the town needed a hospital and it was perfectly willing to oblige. The small chapel with its own tiny cloister and the refectory on the other side would fit quite easily into half of the Grand Cloister, reported to be the largest in France.

Lovers of old ruins need look no further than **Najac**, 24km (15 miles) to the south-west. It is an atmospheric little place overshadowed by the remains of a hilltop fortress, part of which was built in the thirteenth century. The original defences suffered at the hands of Simon de Montfort during his crusade against the Albigeois. When Alphonse de Poitiers decided to do some restoration work he made the inhabitants pay for their past misdeeds by building a new church. Today, Najac is much more interested in peaceful pursuits, offering its visitors a choice of small hotels, a camp site, bicycles for hire, tennis, riding and country walks. South of Najac the Aveyron is joined by the River Viaur which is not an important waterway but has a few attractions for anyone who is determined to see the rest of Aveyron before crossing the *département* border into Tarn, further south.

A series of little roads make their way by one means or another to connect with the main route from Rodez to Albi near the ruined Château de Thuriès. This was a valuable military outpost during the thirteenth century but has nothing better to do these days than keep an eye on the barrage. Further east, the isolated **Eglise de Las**

Château l'Ouradou, Estaing

A bridge over the Aveyron at Villefranche-de-Rouergue

Viaduc du Viaur

Planques is out of reach to anyone who is not prepared for a long but not particularly demanding walk up to its mountain eyrie. The building is extremely matter of fact with its eleventh-century foundations, some art work that was added 300 years later and a commanding view of the country all round. As there is unlikely to be anyone about when you get there, it is essential to collect the key from either the town hall or the Hôtel du Nord in Tanus before setting off.

A short detour from here will take you to the **Viaduc du Viaur**. This 100 year old structure jumps the narrow valley with a single leap and has the same openwork appearance as the Eiffel Tower. Yet another detour is necessary in order to visit the Château de Bosc where Toulouse-Lautrec spent much of his childhood. It still belongs to members of his family and contains, among other things, some beautiful Aubusson tapestries, a quantity of drawings and a small museum crammed with memorabilia.

It is possible to find any number of back ways across to the Lac de Pareloup, one of the biggest lakes in Aveyron and a popular holiday resort. The main village is Salles-Curan with nothing of historical or architectural interest but plenty of sporting activities. There is a sailing school, and visitors can hire a boat or a pedalo, practise water skiing and windsurfing, play tennis or ride. There are roads and footpaths beside the water, some of which are pleasantly scenic, and opportunities for cross-country skiing during the winter.

The camp site is often crowded during the season, as are the *auberges*, one of which is in a fourteenth-century château with an ivy-encrusted tower and produces some delectable menus. **Pont-de-Salars**, a short drive to the north, has its own lake with all the same sports facilities apart from skiing which it makes up for by providing supervised bathing and bicycles for hire. It also lies on the main road from Rodez to Millau, the starting point for a trip across the border into Lozère and along the impressive Gorges du Tarn.

Millau was founded by the Romans around 121BC when they started up potteries which kept the town busy and prosperous for centuries after they had left for home. The products from La Graufesenque were so highly regarded that choice pieces were exported in large quantities and have turned up in places as far afield as Scotland and Germany as well as beneath the ashes that buried Pompeii. It is still possible to visit the site of all this feverish activity on the outskirts of the town but all finished products were transferred out of harm's way a long time ago with an interesting collection housed in the local museum for safekeeping. Millau is still busy and prosperous, having turned its attention first to the manufacture of woollen goods and then to leather, specialising in gloves.

Places of interest in the old quarter include the Church of Notre-Dame, built on the site of a Roman temple but owing considerably more to the nineteenth and twentieth centuries. There is also an ancient fortified gateway and the remains of a twelfth-century tower belonging to the original *hôtel de ville* which ended its medieval life as a prison. The most attractive square is the Place du Maréchal-Foch with arcades, some of them more than 800 years old, and a Roman column bearing the inscription '*Gara que faras*' which could be taken to mean 'Watch how you go'. There are two comfortable hotels, one large and one small, both taking great pride in their cooking and closing resolutely in mid-winter. They are augmented by a number of smaller, perfectly adequate establishments, some supplying lifts and private baths.

Two major roads lead south from Millau, offering a choice between crossing the semi-deserted Causse du Larzac into Hérault or staying within the provincial border and taking a trip to **Roquefort-sur-Soulzon**, which is famous the world over for its cheese. There is little else of particular interest in the town though the local museum does provide an alternative in archaeological exhibits from the surrounding area, mostly dating from the Bronze and Iron Ages.

The accommodation is fairly ordinary but the limestone caves where the cheeses are left to mature are certainly worth seeing. Hundreds upon hundreds of round cheeses are stacked up neatly in racks. Here they wait for the humidity, helped by carefully regulated currents of air and constant attention, to develop their familiar blue-veined appearance. Something like 16,000 tons are sent out every year from these vast underground caverns which have been modernised quite considerably since the days when their most important clients were Roman emperors, war lords like Charlemagne and rich merchants who supplied the courts of France.

St Affrique, happily settled in a small depression further south, on the banks of the Sorgues, has no such claims to fame. However, it did provide a refuge for the saint when he was on the run from the Visigoths and subsequently took his name. Many centuries later it was the birthplace of General de Castelnou who defended Nancy against the Germans in World War I. His statue in the public gardens, across the river from a very ordinary little church, is the only village

PLACES OF INTEREST IN AVEYRON

Conques
Cathedral of Ste Foy
A large, austere building with a beautiful west door, twelfth-century grilles and attractive cloister. The church treasures are definitely worth seeing.

Lot Valley and Gorges
A most attractive stretch of river with several delightful and picturesque small villages.

Estaing
Château
Fifteenth-century building housing a religious order which is willing to accept visitors.

Espalion
Eglise St Jean
A former church which now houses a small museum.

Eglise de Perse
Near Espalion. A small church and cemetery dating from the eleventh century.

St Geniez-d'Olt
Small village in farming country known for its strawberry fair and Procession of White Penitents.

Rodez
Cathedral of Notre-Dame
An impressive, fortified church with an outstanding bell tower and much to see inside.

Musée Fenaille
Rue St Just
A mainly archaeological museum with some medieval sculptures and furniture, religious exhibits, old manuscripts and Roman pottery.

Musée des Beaux Arts
Off the Boulevard Denys-Puech. A collection of paintings and sculptures with the emphasis on local artists.

Notre-Dame-de-Buenne
Near Belcastel. A pilgrim chapel with special gatherings in late May and late August.

Villefranche-de-Rouergue
The town includes a massive bastide surrounding an attractive square.

Eglise Notre-Dame
An impressive, thirteenth-century church overlooking the main square in the bastide with sculptures and an aged iron grille.

landmark but the residents compensate by making much of two other attractions in the vicinity. One is the Dolmen de Tiergues which is an excellent example of the type of megalithic monument to be found in the region while the other, the Rocher de Caylus, is all that remains

Chapelle des Pénitents Noirs
Boulevard Haute Guyenne. A
chapel in the form of a Greek cross
with some viewable contents.

Ancienne Chartreuse St Sauveur
On the road to Albi. An enormous
cloister with a small chapel and a
refectory.

Najac
Ruined château
A good example of thirteenth-
century military architecture with a
view across the Valley of the
Aveyron.

Church
A small, attractive church closed
during the winter.

Château de Thuriès
On the road from Rodez to Albi.
Another thirteenth-century fortress
with a reasonable view.

Eglise de Las Planques
An isolated, hilltop church which
can only be reached on foot.

Viaduc du Viaur
A metal construction 460m
(1,500ft) long and 116m (380ft)
high built by Paul Bodin between
1897 and 1902.

Château de Bosc
Off the Rodez to Albi road. Pleasant
château filled with reminders of
Toulouse-Lautrec who lived there as
a child.

Millau
Museum
Place du Maréchal-Foch. It is mainly
concerned with pottery produced
locally in Roman times.

Beffroi
The original *hôtel de ville* with a
twelfth-century tower.

Roquefort-sur-Soulzon
Caves de Roquefort
Vast, underground limestone caves
where the famous cheese is
matured.

Archaeological museum with
exhibits mainly from the Bronze Age
and the Iron Age.

St Affrique
Dolmen de Tiergues
7km (4 miles) from St Affrique. An
accessible dolmen of the type found
throughout the region.

Rocher de Caylus
Sparse remains of a château
destroyed in 1238 and a reasonable
view.

of a château which stood out against the Comte de Toulouse with
disastrous results. From here the main road presses on westwards
to **St Sernin-sur-Rance** which has a small inn, some fifteenth-
century houses and a river rich in crayfish and trout, before winding

its way out of the valley and across the border in the direction of Albi.

Tarn

Tarn, like Aveyron, is a long way from being the cosiest *département* in France but that does not mean it has nothing to offer the tourist. On the contrary, there are splendid towns like Cordes and Albi, granite plateaux typified by Le Sidobre, and rock formations eroded into weird and wonderful shapes by the elements. The rivers, eating ever more deeply into their allotted courses, are a treasure house of caves and grottoes, some well known and frequently visited while others give the impression that nobody has set foot inside them for many thousands of years. There are artificial lakes, particularly in the Monts de Lacaune, and La Montagne Noire has brooding forests of oak, spruce and pine as well as gold mines that were exploited by the Romans before the birth of Christ. There are also a variety of light industries, introduced much more recently. History has left its mark too, in the form of ruined châteaux, small fortified villages and other all too familiar relics from the conflict between Catholics and Protestants.

There is little doubt that **Cordes**, across the River Aveyron from Najac, stands out as one of the most memorable centres in Tarn. It rests on a hilltop, rather in the manner of the Ark, and is designed on the lines of a ship with a main street down the middle and slightly curved roads resembling catwalks and enclosing the old city from stem to stern. It was built by the Comte de Toulouse 700 years ago and has lost very little of its original character and certainly none of its charm. The huddle of ancient houses, cobbled streets, medieval mansions and the defiant Church of St Michel were all enclosed in three lines of ramparts pierced by strategically placed gates, five of which are still standing.

Although it is possible to drive up and down, it is better to be on foot, starting at the prow by climbing the Pater Noster stairway to the Clock Gate, along a winding road through the Barbacane Entrance in the next line of defences to the sturdy Victory Gate beyond. Even here, invaders would still have had the Painted Gate to contend with, although the only reason for stopping there these days would be to visit the Charles Portal Museum next door. Its main interest is archaeology, with a hoard of coins, jewellery and other items discovered on the site of a Gallo-Roman temple along with prehistoric relics unearthed by the Spelaeological Club of Cordes. In addition there is a faithful reproduction of a typical farmhouse with all manner of articles that were in general use at the time.

The main street follows an uninterrupted line past a series of noteworthy mansions to the fourteenth-century market place. Here the roof, supported by more than twenty stone pillars, protects an ancient well which goes down nearly 122m (400ft) and never runs dry. It is said that three members of the Inquisition who were rash enough to speak their minds during a fact-finding tour were promptly pushed over the edge by an enraged crowd and left to drown. Among many other places of interest is the House of the Great Staghunter, decorated with lively little faces and appropriate scenes including one of a sculptured horseman on a mettlesome charger about to do battle with an abnormally large wild boar.

The Church of St Michel, distinguished by its octagonal belfry and adjacent square fort, is less absorbing than one might expect but it is worth taking a turn down alleyways like Cold Street, Hot Street and even Obscure Street, the latter doing its best to live up to its name. The town hall shares the Maison du Grand Fauconnier with an exhibition of works by Yves Brayer, the artist who breathed fresh life into Cordes when he opened a school of painting there in 1940. As a result, the town has become a 'Mecca' for traditional craftsmen and this has produced a great many small shops aimed at the tourist trade which, for some visitors, strike a slightly discordant note.

There are some atmospheric hotels headed by a palatial establishment full of antique furniture which has taken over the House of the Great Equerry, once a hunting lodge belonging to the Comte de Toulouse. The town has tennis courts, a modest night club, a well equipped camp site with a swimming pool, and a lake stocked with fish. Anyone in search of local excursions should call in at the Château du Cayla with its decidedly literary flavour, followed by a visit to Monestiés where the Chapelle St Jacques has an exceptionally fine *mise au tombeau*.

Further south, Castelnau-de-Lévis, on the banks of the Tarn, is a ruined thirteenth-century fortress commanding a splendid view of **Albi**, totally dominated by the enormous Cathedral of Ste Cécile, claimed to be one of the biggest in France. The modern suburbs have spread themselves out on either side of the river to accommodate a host of light industries which have turned Albi into a busy centre with a thriving economy. There is not a great deal left from the Middle Ages when the city was torn apart in the interests of religion and its name

Broquiès near St Affrique

became synonymous with heresy and bloodshed.

 The eleventh-century Pont Vieux leads straight across the river to the old city where its first call is at the Palais de la Berbie, once the archbishop's palace but now home to the most extensive collection of the works of Toulouse-Lautrec in the world. The nucleus was a present from his mother in 1922 and this has been enlarged at intervals by various relatives and a few close friends. The old mansion where he was born in 1864 is close by and, although it is still owned by members of the family, they are perfectly happy to show visitors round between mid-June and mid-September.

The cathedral, a few steps from the Palais de la Berbie, dates back to the thirteenth century and is a magnificent sight, especially

Coupiac near St Sernin-sur-Rance

The River Tarn near Coupiac

when it is illuminated on summer evenings. The exterior is rather severe, as befits a church that was expected to defend itself in the face of an attack, but, once inside, it is little short of breathtaking. There are statues everywhere, ranging from prophets like Isaiah to personalities of the calibre of Charlemagne and Constantine, ornate tombs, aged stained glass, gold and silver plaques and beautiful wood carvings. A staircase leads up to the top of the bell tower where anyone with enough stamina to complete the climb is rewarded with an unsurpassed view across the town and along the valley.

The Eglise St Salvy is somewhat older, not nearly so overpowering but equally viewable in its own way. A twelfth-century statue of the saint and a medieval Piétà are on view in the sacristy which keeps rather unusual hours but is always open on Sunday mornings. Two elderly mansions and a decorative thirteenth-century fountain in the Parc Rochegude, a tidy walk away, complete the list of tourist attractions. However, there is a month-long music festival starting in mid-July with a short international event featuring the efforts of amateur film-makers sandwiched in the middle. Naturally, Albi has some comfortable hotels, one standing in its own grounds beside the river which adds tennis and swimming to its other facilities.

Due south of Albi and 42km (26$^1/_2$ miles) away on the extremities of the Massif Central, the town of **Castres** has grown up on the site of a Roman settlement. Its history is beset with very much the same religious problems as its neighbours and it emerged from them with little to show for its trouble. Nevertheless, although it is a bit dour and industrial, there is one particularly good reason for including it in any tourist itinerary and that is the Musée Goya.

The *hôtel de ville* shares the old bishops' palace with the museum, surrounded by superb formal gardens that were the brainchild of Le Nôtre. The rooms inside are viewable in their own right with sixteenth-century tapestries and a marble fireplace but this is overshadowed by the collection of Goyas, ranging from a large painting of an audience in the presence of Ferdinand VII to sorcerers, devils and some outlandish monsters. In addition, there are photographs, letters and documents illustrating the life and times of Jean Jaurès, the politician and newspaper owner who was assassinated in Paris in 1914. The Cathedral of St Benoît, opposite the museum, is quite small by comparison but has a few marble statues and Gabriel Briard's *Resurrection of Christ*. Castres is also a good base for touring the Monts de Lacaune and La Montagne Noire and to this end the town has one or two hotels, though the most comfortable of them does not include a restaurant.

Mazamet, less than half an hour's drive to the south, also has a comfortable hotel on the outskirts with both a park and a dining-room but there is nothing of interest as far as sightseers are concerned. The town makes its living by importing skins from Australia, South Africa and the Argentine, going to work on them and then exporting the treated leather to customers all over Europe and the United States. However, it is well placed for anyone who is determined to explore La Montagne Noire without looking for anything particularly unique or spectacular. There is the small Lac des Montagnés, with an attendant long distance footpath and an occasional ruined church or château, the best of which are probably the **Châteaux de Lastours**, though these can only be reached after a long, brisk walk from the nearest parking spot.

The villages are rather nondescript, like Salsigne which produces arsenic, bismuth and gold. Vines can be found in the Gorges de la Clamoux and the **Grottes de Limousis** are worth a visit. The caves were discovered at the beginning of the last century and are a pleasing mixture of limpid pools and crystalline rock formations. The roads hereabouts are small and very winding, especially round the Pic de Nore, and it takes quite a while to climb up and down between one main route and another.

Instead of driving down to Mazamet from Castres, a secondary road and a handful of rather tortuous byways wander eastwards through **Le Sidobre**, which is full of natural attractions that entail leaving the car at frequent intervals and taking to the footpaths. An almost inexhaustible supply of large granite rocks balanced at incredible angles, but apparently quite stable, have given rise to stories of strange animals which can converse with you if you run across them on a dark winter's night or invade their privacy in the caves where they hide by day.

On a less fanciful note, **Ferrières**, overlooking the River Agout, has a sixteenth-century château housing the Musée du Protestantisme en Haut-Languedoc and a Centre d'Art Ferrières which arranges everything from musical events and various exhibitions to long, informative walks. Further upstream, the little industrial village of Brassac has both a small scenic route along the river to the Lac de la Raviège and a slightly bigger road linking it with Lacaune, which is quite a holiday centre. Apart from an elderly fountain, two quite ac-

PLACES OF INTEREST IN TARN

Cordes
Charles Portal Museum
An interesting museum in an old mansion concerned mainly with archaeology and the history of the town.

Musée Yves Brayer
Maison du Grand Fauconnier. A collection of works by the artist.

Eglise St Michel
An ancient church with decorations and an organ added in the nineteenth century. A good view from the top of the tower.

Château du Cayla
Near Cordes. A collection of items which belonged to Maurice de Guérin and his sister Eugénie who were literary figures and contemporaries of George Sand.

Chapelle St Jacques
Monestiés. A small chapel with some good statues.

Castelnau-de-Lévis
A ruined thirteenth-century fortress with a good view of Albi and the Tarn Valley.

Albi
Cathedral of Ste Cécile
A magnificent church, liberally decorated and with a great deal to see inside.

Musée Toulouse-Lautrec
Palais de la Berbie. Very large collection of the works of Toulouse-Lautrec with some other artists also represented.

Toulouse-Lautrec birthplace
Boulevard Roger Salengro.

Medieval mansion with family possessions, many of them associated with the artist.

Eglise St Salvy
Rue Mariès. Elderly church originating in the eleventh century with statues, sculpture and woodwork as well as the remains of the old monastery.

Eglise St Michel de Lescure
An old priory church which includes the Musée de la Carte Postale, concerned with local art.

Castres
Musée Goya
A collection of the works of Goya in the ancient bishops' palace with formal gardens laid out by Le Nôtre.

Musée Jean Jaurès
In the same building as the Musée Goya and the *hôtel de ville*. Papers and photographs covering the career of Jean Jaurès, the French Socialist politician and owner of the paper *L'Humanité*.

Châteaux de Lastours
A collection of ruined châteaux which formed part of the isolated Fortress de Cabaret. Reached only on foot.

Grotte de Limousis
A collection of caves with pools and rock formations.

Ferrières
Musée du Protestantisme en Haut-Languedoc
A small museum in a sixteenth-century château and including the Maison du Luthier.

The Elm Gate in Cordes

ceptable hotels and a camp site, it boasts a casino, a heated swimming pool, riding stables, tennis courts, blazed footpaths and cross-country skiing in the winter. It is also well endowed with minor roads that make off in all directions including a very manageable one through Murat-sur-Vèbre and into Languedoc.

4

LANGUEDOC-ROUSSILLON

Languedoc-Roussillon is a long, rather narrow province bordering on the Mediterranean and stretching from Provence round to the Spanish frontier. It is made up of the *départements* of Pyrénées-Orientales, Aude, Hérault and Gard which take up the whole length of the seaboard, leaving Lozère tucked away inland between Midi-Pyrénées, Auvergne and the Vallée du Rhône. Although the province is saturated with history, typified by ancient cities like Nîmes, Montpellier, Narbonne, Carcassone and Perpignan, only a very small section can actually be described as being part of the Massif Central. This consists of Lozère, the Parc de Haut-Languedoc, which Hérault shares with Tarn, and two small sections of Gard clambering up towards the crystalline plateau edged by the Cévennes.

Along the way are abandoned terraces, once covered with mulberries that were essential for the production of silk 400 years ago, as well as a scattering of almonds, olives, vines and chestnut trees. Beyond these lie limestone tracts where very little grows apart from Mediterranean scrub. As these intrusions are rather limited, none of them merits a section to itself, so they all appear under the heading of Lozère.

Lozère

Lozère is essentially a land of contrasts, known as the Department of the Springs because of the number of brooks, streams and tiny waterfalls that feed rivers like the Lot and the Tarn, helping to swell three of the country's main waterways — the Rhône, the Loire and the Garonne. Conversely, there are desolate and arid limestone plateaux in the south-west, punctured by sinkholes and sliced with deep gorges, as well as the granite mountains of La Margeride where the forests are filled with bilberries and mushrooms. Even more bleak, the volcanic area of the Aubrac has lakes and rough pastures which are strewn with rocks but carpeted in wild flowers once the snows of winter have melted.

Wheat is grown along the fertile Lot Valley, where there are orchards and forests of chestnut trees, herds of cattle grazing contentedly on fresh, green grass and sheep which provide wool for spinning and milk for cheese. Other local occupations include beekeeping, furniture-making, the manufacture of wooden shoes and small-scale copper, lead and silver mining.

Lozère has few towns of any size, the main one being Mende, but this is offset by any number of ancient churches with small villages in attendance, as well as quite a few castles, towers and ramparts. There are literally hundreds of dolmens, standing stones, and antique bridges, together with bread ovens and the once-essential blizzard bells. Although the *département* is determined to extend its tourist attractions well beyond the confines of the famous Gorges du Tarn, it still has a fair way to go when it comes to providing accommodation for people who like their creature comforts.

Mende, Le Rozier and Meyrueis all have comfortable hotels, though they close with one accord during the off season, while places like Florac, Aumont-Aubrac, Bagnols-les-Bains, La Canourgue and Langogne can provide the necessary facilities but not many frills. Elsewhere, the inns are usually modest but adequate, augmented by guest houses, furnished apartments, *gîtes* and camp sites, many of which are located along the river banks.

Historically, the region can hold its own with any of its neighbours. It boasts Neolithic caves and was home to the Gabales, who had their original capital at Javols in the north-west corner. This was eventually moved to Mende where the local bishops were granted sovereign rights over the territory by the kings of France in the early fourteenth century. The area suffered as much as anywhere else during the Hundred Years War and the Wars of Religion, was terrorized by the legendary Beast of Gévaudan between 1764 and 1767 and ended its official existence at the time of the Revolution when Gévaudan was eliminated and Lozère took its place.

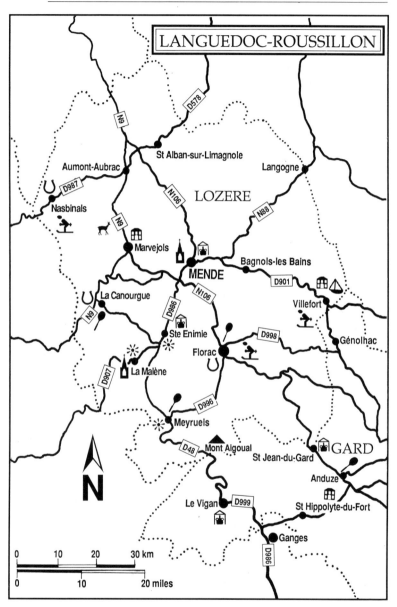

The Gorges du Tarn

The newly-created *département* had a hard time during the last century when more than half the population took to their heels but things started to improve when Edouard-Alfred Martel decided to exploit the Gorges du Tarn in 1890. Since then, life has become a little easier for the local inhabitants, many of whom concentrate on tourism and are keen to make sure that their guests have everything they need for an enjoyable holiday.

Lozère is an especially good area for the outdoor enthusiast. There are literally hundreds of kilometres of marked footpaths, with detailed maps to go with them, and just as many bridle paths and stables which organise anything from a training course to a pony trek. Canoes are available on all the main rivers and tuition is provided when necessary, while instructors are on hand to help would-be climbers, potholers or anyone who wants to explore a sinkhole or an underground river. Sailing and windsurfing are popular on three different lakes and fishermen have a choice of trout, char, dace, gudgeon or barbel. There are courses in hang gliding at Chanet, with facilities for experienced flyers at Mende, and at least thirty villages are equipped with tennis courts.

Cyclists can take their choice from a number of forest roads or join an organised round trip of 890km (552 miles). Facilities for archery and golf are also promised for the near future. In addition to this there are folk festivals and other events inspired by anything from the harvest in Langogne, cabbage soup in Le Malzieu-Ville and ovenbread in La Canourgue to music in Florac, comic strips in Marvejols or historical activities during the Mende Festival.

Mende, the main city of Lozère, is situated right in the middle of the *département* and makes a good starting point for trips in any direction. It is a pleasant, small town which has expanded to accommodate such additions as the railway station, administrative buildings, schools, sports facilities and small factories engaged chiefly in the manufacture of various fabrics. The city owes its existence to St Privat, the Bishop of Javols, who retreated to a hermitage built into the side of Mont-Mimat after his own capital had been destroyed. He was killed there by the Vandals in AD265 but the village which had grown up at his feet continued to expand until it emerged as the capital of the Gévaudan district in the fourteenth century. Inevitably, it became involved in the conflict between the Catholics and the Protestants and was partly destroyed by the Huguenots in the battles of 1579 and 1580. Rebuilding started in the seventeenth century when, among other restoration work, a tower belonging to the ancient citadel was used as a belfry for the Church of the Penitents.

Mende's main attraction is the Cathedral of St Pierre, founded in the fourteenth century by Pope Urbain V, who was born in the area. It also had to be restored after the Huguenots tore it apart when they occupied the town, though they did leave the ancient crypt intact. It still contains the remnants of an early Roman structure as well as the tomb of St Privat and is said to be one of the oldest in France. Among the cathedral's other possessions are a number of Aubusson tapestries depicting the life of the Virgin Mary, fine sixteenth-century candlesticks and some beautifully carved wooden stalls.

The Musée Ignon Fabre is full of interesting exhibits going back to prehistoric times. The displays include Bronze Age jewellery, vases and other ornaments, bones and even plaits of hair as well as weapons, relics discovered in Javols and ancient pottery from Banassac. Special exhibitions are organised to draw attention to local folklore and the history of the capital from its earliest days.

The streets of the old town take in the sparse remains of the ramparts, a number of medieval houses, a thirteenth-century synagogue and the elderly Couvent des Carmes which, these days, acts as a shop window for local arts and crafts. Anyone who wants to get out and about will find several *grandes randonnées* to choose from, offering tours of the Aubrac or the Cévennes, jaunts to mountains such as Mont-Aigoual and excursions across the provincial boundaries to St Flour or Conques. Much closer to hand there is a 10km (6 miles) circuit up to Mont-Mimat with its hermitage of St Privat, an orientation table and a view across the Valley of the Lot. On the way back it calls at the deserted villages of Le Gerbal and La Chaumette. The town has one comfortable hotel and several smaller ones, two or three restaurants and a couple of camp sites in the vicintiy which are reasonably well equipped.

Marvejols, 29km (18 miles) to the north-west of Mende, is another atmospheric small town with an equally bloodstained history and an impressive seal to prove that it was granted the status of a royal city in 1696. Its most eyecatching gate is the Porte du Soubeyran, an antiquated fortified archway set between two sturdy, round towers with an odd-looking communal roof which gives the impression of having been balanced on top as an afterthought. Outside in the square is a modern statue of Henri de Navarre who was responsible for rebuilding the town after it was bombarded and captured by the Duc de Joyeuse. Far from being magnanimous in victory, he put three-quarters of the inhabitants to death despite having promised them safety if they surrendered.

There are other fortified towers marking the line of the old ramparts and an ill-assorted collection of sculptures, including a bust of the African explorer Savorgnan de Brazza, who married a local girl, a medallion of the banker René Luche and a wolf-like impression of the Beast of Gévaudan. The hotels provide bedrooms with baths en suite, restaurants, lifts and car parks.

There are a number of good reasons for exploring the surrounding countryside. These include the Plateau du Poujoulet with its dolmen-like, Gallo-Roman cave, the ruins of the feudal Château de Baldasse and the Wolf Park at Ste Lucie. More than fifty wolves have been re-introduced into the area from Canada and various parts of Europe and appear to have settled down extremely well in their new home. In addition to the animals, there is a Wolf Museum which divides its attention between facts and fairy tales. It includes Little Red Riding Hood and the Big Bad Wolf gazing at each other across a miniscule cottage which neither of them could possibly get inside.

A view from one of the roads to Mende

The village is fairly new, but built on traditional lines, and includes a hotel-restaurant and self-catering *gîtes* of assorted sizes.

There are quite a few little villages dotted about the Aubrac to the north. One such is **Nasbinals** where the taverns are modest, the eleventh-century church has been declared an historic monument and the plateau stretches away into the distance on every side. It is a good place for walking, cycling, riding, canoeing and fishing as well as being ideal for cross-country skiing, but it is certainly no place for the sophisticated visitor. The Festival de l'Accordéon in mid-July is fun with a rural flavour, as are the local fairs in August and September and the stories of ancient battles and chance encounters with wolves, which improve when told round blazing log fires in the depths of winter.

At **St Alban-sur-Limagnole** the tales are more likely to be concerned with the pilgrims who passed by on their way to Santiago de Compostela or the Beast of Gévaudan which apparently accounted for more victims in the immediate area than anywhere else in the district. Nobody knows if it was a giant wolf, some other vicious animal or even a human being, but two centuries of speculation have

PLACES OF INTEREST IN LOZERE AND GARD

Mende
Cathedral of St Pierre
Restored fourteenth-century
church with tapestries and some
fine wood carving.

Musée Ignon Fabre
Mainly archaeological exhibits
with special items from the
Bronze Age and pottery from
Banassac.

Château de Baldasse
Ruins
Near Marvejols.

Ste Lucie
Wolf Park and Museum
Large wolf pack. Museum deals
with both fact and fiction.

Château de Montferrand
Ruins
Near La Canourgue.

Gorges du Tarn
Magnificent gorges with impres-
sive view from the Point Sublime.
Also scenic road along the river.

La Malène
Small town in the Gorges du
Tarn with river trips through the
most impressive section, the
Cirque des Baumes.

Aven Armand
Spectacular caves with stalagmites. Reached by a small
underground train.

Ste Enimie
Le Vieux Logis
Small rural museum near the old
monastery and the Fontaine de
Burle. Also an up-dated twelfth-
century church.

Mont Aigoual
Highest peak in the area with a
meteorological station and
splendid views. An arboretum,
the 'Garden of God', near the
summit.

Grotte de Dargilan
Near Meyrueis. Large, subterranean cavern well equipped for
visitors.

Le Vigan
Musée Cévenol
Small local museum concentrat-
ing on all aspects of life in the
Cévennes.

Parc de Prafrance
Large bamboo plantation with
some attractive gardens.

Musée du Désert
Near Mialet. Museum concerned
with the Protestant fight for
survival with particular reference
to the Cévennes area.

Grottes de Trabuc
Near the Musée du Désert. Said
to be the largest underground
complex in the area with pools
and strange rock formations.

St Jean-du-Gard
Musée des Vallées Cévenoles
Small museum dealing with local
matters.

Château de Castanet
Medieval fort with exhibitions
during the summer.

La Garde-Guérin
One of the most impressive local
ruins with a large keep.

added a supernatural dimension which no-one seems anxious to disprove. The village has a typical small church built on the site of an ancient monastery and an equally characteristic small *auberge*. It also holds a dog show in mid-July and follows that with a cheese fair in August.

The Margeride region in the north-east of Lozère is just as rural, with a fair number of tiny hamlets but very few larger villages or places of historic interest. A certain amount of work is being done on the roads which means that there are good surfaces interspersed with some pretty rough patches, but even these present no real problems. **Langogne**, on the road to Le Puy-en-Velay, is one of the bigger villages, with quite an attractive old church, whereas **Bagnols-les-Bains**, further south and only 20km (12^1/$_2$ miles) from Mende, has updated its thermal baths and provides a handful of quite basic hotels as well as furnished accommodation and a camp site nearby.

The tourist outlook to the south of the capital is rosier in every respect. **La Canourgue**, for example, is an attractive little place hidden away in a hollow with a reasonable hotel, tennis courts, a heated swimming pool and opportunities for canoeing, cycling, riding, fishing and walking. The narrow streets are lined with old houses and the main attractions include a twelfth-century church and a tower which was once part of the fortifications. **Banassac**, quite close by, was an important pottery centre in Roman times and keeps a selection of relics dating from AD1 to AD300 on permanent display in the Mairie. Also within easy reach is a rock known as the Sabot de Malepeyre and the ruined Château de Montferrand. However, all this is merely a prelude to the famous **Gorges du Tarn**.

One of the best places to join the Tarn is just inside the border with Aveyron, slightly east of Millau. The scenery begins quite gently as the road follows the river bank between wooded hills, past attractive little hamlets. Most of these have a small *auberge*, private houses, tiny garages and shaded camp sites close to the water's edge. All along the way there are cherry trees, loaded in the early summer with dark red fruit that flavours a whole range of dishes, especially a memorable rabbit stew. At **Le Rozier**, a comfortable hotel looks down on the river, crossed by a modern bridge and dotted with inflatable rafts, canoes and other small craft. Within a short distance, the sides of the gorge become steeper until, beyond the ruined Château du Blanquefort, the road divides at the village of Les Vignes.

The main route continues, following the contours of the river round the massive natural amphitheatre known as the Cirque des Baumes. To the right a less well used road crosses to the other side for a trip across country before rejoining the Tarn at La Malène while the left-hand fork climbs resolutely up to the Point Sublime where there is a superb, pilot's eye view of the river as it snakes its way through the gorges. The Tarn is quite shallow in places with deep pools much frequented by fishermen and a boat trip through the colourful Cirque des Baumes under towering limestone cliffs is an experience not to be missed.

At the moment, anyone towing a caravan would be well advised to park it at Les Vignes before starting the climb up to the Point Sublime. The road is narrow and very steep in places with a series of tight, hairpin bends calling for low speeds and unfailing concentration. There are very few places to stop in the early stages, and not all that many further up, but road widening is in progress which will eventually make life much easier for everyone. In addition to a restaurant and a ruin perched on top of an adjoining hill, the main distraction, apart from the view, is the variety of wild flowers growing along the roadside. These include white and mauve daisies, heather, gorse and clover, as well as honeysuckle, delicate pink roses and bright red poppies, with what looks like small delphiniums adding a brilliant shade of blue.

Point Sublime itself is wide open to the elements with a modest restaurant and a shop filled with all the usual souvenirs as well as articles made from animal skins in a complete range of natural colours. Having admired the panoramic views from a vantage spot high above the gorges, drivers are faced with two alternatives. They can either negotiate a small, scenic route across the Causse and rejoin the river at La Malène or return the way they came to inspect the Cirque des Baumes at close quarters. The latter is interrupted here and there by a tunnel through the overhanging cliffs.

La Malène is a pleasant little village with an eleventh-century church, some elderly houses and a small hotel. This makes a good base for river trips or an excursion to the Roc des Hourtous with its grotto and view of the canyon. From here one can also take long walks, or a less exhausting drive, over the Causse Méjean to the Caves of Aven Armand. This splendid subterranean complex was discovered by Louis Armand, working with Martel, just over 100 years ago but it was some 30 years before it was opened to the public.

Today's visitors travel part of the way in a small underground train

Boating in the Gorges du Tarn

to inspect the gigantic cavern filled with hundreds of stalagmites that fully justify its title of the Virgin Forest. Martel, incidentally, referred to it as the 'Dream of a Thousand and One Nights', though it might just as easily prove to be a nightmare for anyone suffering from claustrophobia. In this case there is an easy alternative in the form of a leisurely lunch or a long, cool drink near the car park at ground level. If the hotel at La Malène is full, or your bank balance is looking reasonably healthy, the fifteenth-century Château de la Caze, a little further up the river, has been converted into a comfortable hotel with extra apartments in a farmhouse in the grounds.

Above the Cirque de St Chély, which has its own grottoes as well as a hamlet with elderly houses and a small chapel, the river runs through **Ste Enimie**, the largest village in the Gorges du Tarn. Legend has it that the lady in question, a beautiful princess no less, refused all offers of marriage because she wanted to devote her life to God. When the king chose a husband for her she promptly caught leprosy which put an end to all her father's plans. One day she was informed by an angel that she would find a cure in Gévaudan and set out immediately for Bagnols-les-Bains. Once again the angel ap-

Ruined bridge in the
Gorges du Tarn

peared and told her that she had chosen the wrong place so she travelled on as far as the Fontaine de Burle where she plunged into the water and emerged without a trace of leprosy. However, as soon as she set off for home again the marks returned and she had to dash back to the fountain for a second miraculous cure. After that she very wisely decided to stay where she was and spent the rest of her life in the convent where she died in AD628.

The fountain is still there, along with a twelfth-century church, the remains of the old monastery and a small museum concerned exclusively with local affairs. There is also a grotto a longish walk away which is believed to have sheltered Ste Enimie. Visitors are not allowed into the chapel but there is nothing to stop them admiring the view which is unforgettable, especially at sunrise. Ste Enimie is also a good place for classical concerts which are held in the open air beside the river but it is short of both hotels and camp sites.

From Ste Enimie the road continues to keep company with the gorges, past the ruins of Castelbouc which are floodlit during the summer, to the ancient bridge. This was built on the orders of Pope Urbain V so that pilgrims could visit the sanctuary at Quezac without getting their feet wet. It serves the same purpose nowadays, especially on the first Sunday in September when there is a special pilgrimage in honour of the Virgin, whose statue was discovered nearby in 1050.

Ispagnac, which marks the eastern end of the Gorges du Tarn, is a thoroughly go-ahead little place whose residents keep themselves busy growing fruit, especially strawberries, tending the vineyards and catering for tourists. Hotels are definitely not its strong point but there are places for tents and caravans, facilities for tennis, riding and cycling, potholes to explore, marked footpaths for hikers and a direct link with **Florac** less than 10km (6miles) away.

This slightly larger centre boasts a couple of modest hotels and all the same sports facilities, plus canoes for hire and opportunities for cross-country skiing in winter. It is a charming little town overlooking the Tarn Valley and set against a backcloth of high cliffs which characterise the Rocher de Rochefort. At one time it was the capital of its own region, a fact born out by the Couvent de la Présentation, built by the Templiers in the Middle Ages. Florac is conveniently placed on the main road from Mende to Alès with the sparsely populated Causse Méjean to the west and the Cévennes National Park curving southwards beyond **Meyrueis** on the border between Lozère and Gard.

There is nothing particularly memorable about this small town apart from its having all the necessary sports facilities, including a heated swimming pool, as well as possessing some lovely old houses and two comfortable hotels. One was originally a Benedictine monastery, converted into a very desirable country residence in the sixteenth century. Its famous guests have included Blanche de Castille and, much more recently, General de Gaulle and Chancellor Adenauer. The other is a 400 year old manor house, full of antique furniture, engravings and objets d'art, which takes great pride in its traditional menus and careful choice of wines.

Meyrueis is within easy reach of Aven Armand and the **Grotte de Dargilan**, another impressive underground cavern discovered by Martel in 1888 and subsequently fitted with steps, ramps and passageways under the direction of Louis Armand. **Hures-la-Pa-**

rade, nearby, is a tiny hamlet which was attacked by the Germans in May 1944 during their search for the famous Maquis group known as Bir-Hakeim. Thirty-two members of the Resistance Movement were killed in the fighting and after the war a memorial was erected to them beside the road that links Meyrueis with Ste Enimie. To the south an extremely winding route into the Cévennes National Park skirts round the Château de Roquedols, which can supply a wealth of information about the area, and continues through the mountains in search of other worthwhile places to visit.

Mont Aigoual, the highest point in the southern Cévennes, definitely falls into this category. The slopes have narrow passes at frequent intervals, forests full of beech and pines, great chunks of rock and occasional waterfalls. Near the top is an arboretum called 'L'Hort de Dieu', or 'The Garden of God', laid out by the botanist Charles Flahault with the blessing of Georges Fabre, the chief forester who was responsible for the area. Fabre was also instrumental in building the meteorological station at the summit in 1887 to monitor the weather and give advance warning of high winds and torrential rainfall which can cause havoc throughout the region. The views all round are spectacular and it is claimed that, on a clear winter's day, it is possible to see the Alps, the Monts du Cantal, the Mediterranean and the Pyrénées from the top of the tower.

South from Mont Aigoual the road drops steeply past the ski village of L'Espérou towards **Le Vigan**, an atmospheric little place, with huge chestnut trees. It has nothing much to offer in the way of sporting activities but makes up for this with a clutch of modest hotels, an ancient bridge and a most informative local museum housed in an old silk factory. Any number of extremely minor roads potter about the Cévennes, some of them more suitable for jeeps than cars. This makes it an ideal place to explore, especially for people who enjoy walking.

It is easy to see why the local Protestants, known as Camisards, retreated into the area after Louis XIV revoked the Edict of Nantes in 1685. They staged a revolt at the turn of the century and held out for 2 years against the thousands of troops who were sent in to subdue them. The villages, some deserted and falling into ruins, are often rather dark and brooding. However, with the growth of tourism, efforts are being made to restore not only the old houses, some of which are being snapped up as second homes by townspeople, but also communal bread ovens and water troughs that pass for fountains.

Canoeing in the Gorges du Tarn

Having got as far as Le Vigan, the easiest round trip is south to Ganges, a forgettable little town in Hérault, next to St Hippolyte-du-Fort and then across country to **Anduze** where there is one comfortable hotel nearby, a couple of smaller ones and facilities for tents and caravans. This is an attractive little place with an elderly château, a fourteenth-century clock tower and a maze of narrow streets and alleys to tempt the visitor. It also provides tennis, riding, potholing and a selection of long country walks.

Other attractions in the vicinity include an enormous bamboo forest in the Parc de Prafrance, created by Eugène Mazel in 1855, complete with a replica of an Asian village, magnolia trees and lotus ponds. Alternatively, there is the Musée du Désert, near Mialet, which tells the story of the Camisard revolt and occupies the house where its leader, Roland, was born. A little further afield are the **Grottes de Trabuc**, a collection of vast underground caverns, pools and rock formations with a strange group of stalagmites called the 'Hundred-thousand Soldiers', because of its resemblance to an advancing army.

St Jean-du-Gard, remembered chiefly as the place where

Robert Louis Stevenson and his donkey parted company, is only a short distance away. It has its share of modest *auberges*, a little steam train that puffs its way through the mountains and the Musée des Vallées Cévenoles where visitors can learn all they need to know about the past life of the region — everything from growing chestnuts to keeping silk worms. A secondary road running through the town follows the Corniche des Cévennes back to Florac. There are other ways of cutting across country to join up with the main road to the south but they require more time and effort.

Lozère's north-eastern section of the Cévennes, beyond the Florac to Alès road, is every bit as time consuming for anyone who intends to explore its out-of-the-way places. These include the Ecology Museum at **Le Pont-de-Montvert**, where the Protestant revolt started, the red-roofed village of **Génolhac**, with its old houses and shaded river frontage and **Villefort**, nestling in the heart of the mountains near the provincial border.

This little centre is working extremely hard to become a popular tourist resort and has already achieved some success. It provides sailing, waterskiing and windsurfing on the picturesque lake nearby, and camp sites in among trees at the water's edge. Fishing is available along the rivers and in the Etang de la Bastide, bridle paths and *randonnées* take off in all directions with ski slopes at the Mas de la Barque, 14km (9miles) away. Anyone interested in old castles can visit the sixteenth-century Château de Castanet, partly surrounded by water and built of granite with towers that have flat, sloping roofs which make them look vaguely like giant refuse bins.

Another local attraction is La Garde-Guérin, a village which was fortified in the twelfth century to protect the Chemin de Regordane and is now the proud possessor of some very viewable ancient ruins and a small *auberge*. Villefort is surrounded by some splendid, rugged country. It also keeps contact with Mende, Nîmes and Montpellier by way of Alès, and is linked with Les Vans, across the border in Ardèche, which is useful for anyone planning a trip northwards along the Vallée du Rhône.

5

VALLEE DU RHONE

It would be quite wrong to suppose that Vallée du Rhône as a whole is part of the Massif Central but it does flirt with the mountains now and again and for this reason deserves at least an honourable mention.

The province had its own prehistoric communities, thrived under the Romans, built churches and castles and defended them vigorously whenever the occasion demanded, though most of the activity took place along what was known as the Rhône Corridor. Anyone in search of museums — Lyon, incidentally, has twenty-four of them — the remains of Roman temples or even a collection of shoes through the ages, will have to stick closely to the valley. Apart from an isolated tourist attraction, the hills only pander to those who enjoy wandering about during the summer and cross-country skiing in winter.

Ardèche

The Vallée du Rhône is divided into five *départements* — Ardèche and Loire to the west, with Drôme, Rhône and Ain occupying the remainder, most of it on the opposite side of the river. Although Ardèche is sandwiched between Lozère and Haute-Loire on one hand and the Rhône on the other, only a very small section can honestly claim to be part of the Massif Central. These uplands have more in common with their neighbours than with the low-lying sections which are full of orchards, market gardens, cereal crops and light industries. There

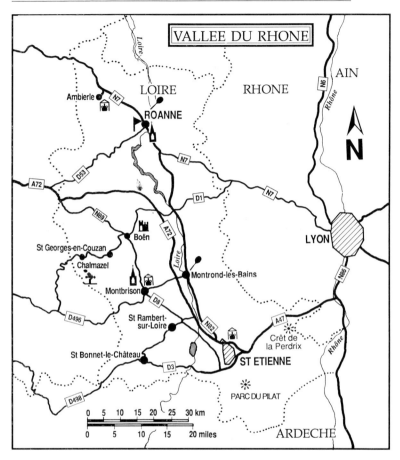

are extinct volcanoes, though they are by no means as numerous or as spectacular as those of Auvergne, a few natural and man-made lakes, wooded areas and rocky outcrops whose outlines are softened by clumps of gorse and heather.

The villages are mostly small and unassuming, with little or nothing of historic interest and very few hotels worth mentioning. However, determined attempts are being made to exploit the natural tourist possibilities of the area with the help of *gîtes*, farms willing to accept paying guests and sports facilities such as tennis courts,

View from one of the roads to Privas in Ardèche

riding stables, streams full of fish, bridle paths, cycle tracks and the occasional swimming pool.

It is said that some of the local boundaries have remained unchanged for the best part of 2,000 years but, at the same time, there has been a fairly steady shift in population, particularly since the end of the nineteenth century. Life is easier at the lower altitudes and many younger people gravitate towards the bright lights and job prospects offered by the main centres, most of which are crammed into a small proportion of the *département*. As a result, the highlands are sparsely populated, except by birds and butterflies, together with sheep and goats which do well on the open hillsides. Fields of wild flowers are undisturbed by amateur gardeners and the verges are blissfully free of litter. It is a no-man's-land for the 'five capitals in five days', luxury-loving fraternity but it has much to offer the traveller in search of peace and wide open spaces.

Driving in from the south-west on the line of the Cévennes, the first place to visit might well be **Les Vans**, especially as it has a very reasonable hotel standing quietly in its own park and providing both tennis and swimming on the premises. The town itself is an attractive little place with an old-world atmosphere and a fairly comprehensive museum that dabbles in archaeology, history and geology, yet still finds space for local arts and crafts. Another advantage is that it is only 3km (2 miles) from the point where the GR4 from the north joins

PLACES OF INTEREST IN ARDECHE

Les Vans
Municipal Museum
Items of local interest ranging
from archaeology to arts and
crafts.

Gerbier de Jonc
The source of the Loire.

Château de Rochebonne
Ruins. Near St Martin-de-
Valamas

St Agrève
Le Petit Train Touristique du
Velay-Vivaris

Annonay
Musée César Filhol.
Museum of local interest with
special reference to the Montgolfier brothers and Marc Séguin.

Safari de Peaugrès
Wild life park. Peaugrès.

forces with the GR44 soon after it crosses the border with Gard, so
hikers have three entirely different directions to choose from.

For the motorist, there is a direct link with Privas, the provincial
capital 66km (41 miles) away beyond Joyeuse and Aubenas, or a
scenic, if rather winding route that follows the Allier northwards to
Langogne. There are not many places to inspect en route and some
of the side turnings can be a bit unsure of their destination, if they
have one at all. Langogne is the most northerly crossing point from
Lozère with a main road that immediately heads into Auvergne on its
way to Le Puy-en-Velay but also offers a couple of routes back to
Ardèche, the second and larger of them being the main road to
Aubenas which it joins just beyond Pradelles.

In order to keep the Massif in view, it is necessary to head in the
general direction of **Coucouron**. However, as its local hotel is on the
modest side, it might be better to pause at the Auberge de Peyrebeille
where the management fortunately gave up the practice of murdering
travellers for their money a century or more ago. The old building is
no longer used for guests, though they are allowed to look at the
rooms. No doubt all the ghosts were laid when the innkeeper and his
wife were beheaded in the courtyard outside.

This part of Ardèche is very much ski country, with *logis* that cater
for individuals as well as groups, provide tuition where necessary and
charge realistic prices. When the weather warms up, some of them,
like those at Borne near La Croix de Bauzon, widen their horizons to
include organised walks, which may last for around 3 to 5 days, while

less energetic members of the party can attend classes in subjects ranging from geology to making myrtle jam. Coucouron goes one better, with tennis, swimming and a pedalo or two, in addition to country walks. For the benefit of anyone who decides not to drive down, there are cars for hire in Langogne or, alternatively, it is usually quite easy to find a taxi at the station.

Within easy reach of Coucouron is the Lac d'Issarlès, a smallish lake captured in an old volcanic crater with some pleasant views and opportunities for both boating and swimming. The village of the same name is somewhat isolated but it has two small hotels, a number of furnished premises and all the necessary shops for those who are self-catering. It also holds fêtes and festivals during the summer and is very popular with local people at the height of the season. Because of this, a certain amount of care is needed on the rather temperamental byway down to the Barrage de la Palisse. This is a winding, man-made lake with a self-effacing ruin nearby and a tunnel, originally planned for the railway, beyond St Cirgues-en-Montagne, which saves time on the way to Le Roux. From here a scenic road heads due north, nods at a small lake, edges its way round the Suc de Bauzon and soon afterwards offers the discerning driver a parallel shortcut along the young Loire to **Ste Eulalie**.

The most endearing thing about this sleepy little village is that, rather in the manner of Brigadoon, it only bursts into life for a single day each year. There is no specific date for the Foire-aux-Violettes, except that it always takes place in the spring, but the gypsies know exactly when it will be and invariably arrive in plenty of time. They are joined by people in search of unusual plants as well as homoeopathic doctors seeking alternatives to the various pills and potions churned out by modern scientific laboratories. They all browse knowledgeably among the wild flowers, medicinal plants and ancient remedies on display at what is said to be the largest event of its kind in Europe. At nightfall, when the crowds fade away, there is nothing left to distinguish the village from any other little hamlet in the district except for the fact that there may be no room that evening at either of the local inns.

From Ste Eulalie it is a very short drive to the **Gerbier de Jonc**, a large, rather nondescript hump standing all by itself and hardly worth a second glance were it not so widely publicised as the source of the Loire. There is a marked path up this old volcanic peak from a well maintained road at the bottom which is flanked with stalls full of predictable souvenirs. However, it is quite unnecessary to climb up the mountain unless you want to admire the view.

On the opposite side of the road, just inside the door of what looks like an antiquated cowshed, the Loire emerges from a wooden pipe, splashes over the edge of an oblong water trough and begins its 600-mile journey through France. There are a couple of glasses for anyone who is feeling thirsty but most people bring their own empty bottles as well as a few francs to buy a postcard from the display area inside. It is really best to go there out of season unless you are prepared to join a long queue. If one extinct volcano is insufficient for the day, there is always Mont Mézenc, at 1,754m (5,750ft), the highest peak in the locality, where anyone in search of more hills to climb can select whichever footpath is best suited to the amount of time and energy available.

Mézilhac, to the east, is another winter sports station with two ski lifts and every intention of becoming a popular holiday resort. To this end it provides both lessons and equipment for hire, with three pistes requiring varying degrees of competence. In summer the attractions include riding, fishing and walking, with maybe a trip up the Piton de la Croix to inspect the view. Alternatively, the Cascade du Ray-Pic is an ideal spot for an alfresco lunch, provided there is no objection to carrying all the provisions from the car park, about half an hour's walk away.

It is at this point that a note of doubt starts to creep in and controversy raises its ugly head. Are we, or are we not, running out of Massif Central? One map says yes, another says no, a member of staff at the main tourist office draws an arbitrary line, which fortunately just includes the Gerbier de Jonc, and leaves it at that. This leaves the visitor stranded in open country with the knowledge that there is a bit more to be found in Loire to the north, on the far side of a fistful of Auvergne. However, for the purposes of this chapter, we should try to stay on the right side of the boundary as far as possible. For this reason we are taking a liberty with the area in question and skirting along the edge, across the highlands with their herds of cattle and chestnut trees, towards the Parc du Pilat and Loire.

From Mézilhac a secondary road, with a number of side turnings to tempt the curious motorist, makes its way to **Le Cheylard** in the peaceful Valley of the Eyrieux. Once again there is nothing memorable in the way of hotels but anyone towing a caravan has a choice of camp sites near the river. The Circuit Equestre passes the door,

Gerbier de Jonc

travelling from the south-west to the north-east, with plenty of opportunities for a sudden change of direction. The local cycle club, on the other hand, is only too happy to advise, assist and point out the most attractive routes. It is possible to play tennis, go fishing, join in a game of *boules* or listen to an organ recital in the eleventh-century church. When the time comes to move on, another secondary road follows the course of the river to **St Martin-de-Valamas**. This is not a centre of any particular moment but it will be appreciated by seekers after old ruins because the remains of the Château de Rochebonne are quite close by.

St Agrève, a bit further up the road, has rather more to crow about. To start with there are half a dozen inns, all with restaurants, some with private parking and at least one with baths en suite. The most obvious attraction is Mont Chiniac which has a splendid view over the surrounding country including the Massif du Pilat. There are pine forests full of summer walks and winter trails as well as a man-made lake just short of Devesset which is a good place to sail, windsurf or swim.

It is an amiable little town with a fairly dominant church overlook-

214

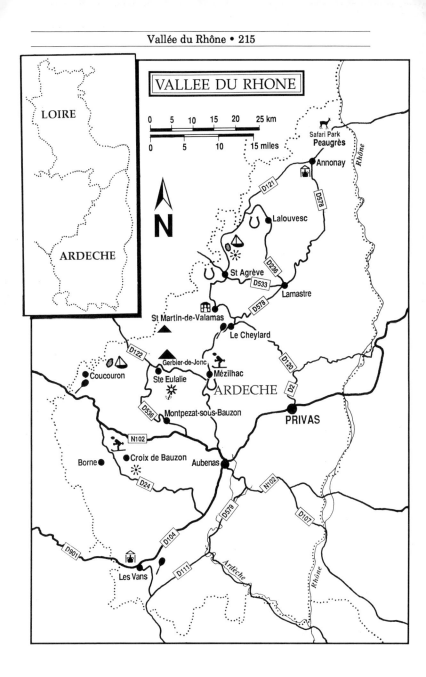

ing a collection of comparatively modern houses scattered across a gentle slope. It also has a hairdresser, various shops, banks, garages, a disco and a cinema. The GR7 wanders by, horses and bicycles are available, along with tennis courts, a gymnasium, furnished *gîtes* and *chambres d'hôtes*. Less well publicised is the little tourist train that runs between St Agrève and Dunières, 37km (23 miles) away in Haute-Loire, past the volcanoes of Velay and the Gorges du Lignon.

A choice of routes, all quite small and mostly scenic, press on to Lalouvesc, another tiny resort for all seasons with a similar range of facilities, and from there to **Annonay**, the ancient capital of Ardèche. It is by far the largest and busiest town in the *département*, with its industries concentrated in the suburbs. The old quarter is tucked away behind the Rue de la Valette, built over the River Déume which disappears quite suddenly at one end and reappears, apparently none the worse for its experience, a little further on.

The Musée César Filhol, on the far side of the church and its adjoining block, is concerned mainly with Annonay through the ages and particularly with the town's three most famous sons. Two of them, Joseph and Etienne Montgolfier, were the first people to take off in a hot air balloon. Their initial, rather crude experiments in 1783 were not only a landmark in aviation history but led directly to the invention of the hydrogen balloon. Marc Séguin, on the other hand, kept his feet firmly on the ground while designing the world's first iron suspension bridge. It was also a nineteenth-century achievement and can still be seen crossing the River Rhône.

There are fewer hotels to choose from in Annonay than one would expect but some of the restaurants do a nice line in traditional dishes that owe a certain amount to both Auvergne and Provence. Chestnuts add a local flavour and vegetables are plentiful, not to mention pheasant and guinea fowl which are both delicious and can be followed by goat's milk cheese and seasonal fruit.

Anyone who enjoys nature parks should visit the Safari de Peaugrès where there is a wide variety of animals, ranging from lions and tigers to wolves, monkeys and giraffe. There are also reptiles and birds including colonies of ducks and swans on a special lake which is a bread crumb's throw from the cafeteria. When the children get tired of the wild life there is a well equipped playground set aside for them where they can work off all their surplus energy. In addition, the park provides an area for picnics and somewhere to buy all the usual souvenirs. This is the end of the trip through Ardèche, beyond which the road heads for the Parc du Pilat, across the border in Loire.

Loire

Loire, certainly no bigger than Ardèche, is neatly bisected from south to north by its famous river, accompanied for much of the journey by an extremely busy highway that connects St Etienne with Roanne. From here it continues northwards into Saône-et-Loire or north-west across the border into Allier on its way to Paris. From the visitor's point of view, there is nothing particularly outstanding about the area although the hills are covered in a cobweb of attractive minor roads and byways as well as being peppered with small villages which may contribute a modest church, a wayside inn or a fairly limited view.

St Etienne is large, mainly industrial and does not reach first base in the list of popular holiday playgrounds. Nevertheless, there are some comfortable hotels, excellent restaurants and a very competent Museum of Art and Industry. **Roanne** is considerably smaller but almost as busy, with a couple of fairly run-of-the-mill churches, a river frontage of no great merit, a sports centre and a 9-hole golf course. However, it has an irresistible attraction for gourmets in the form of the Hôtel des Frères Troisgros, a first class establishment whose owners provide some of the most oustanding and delicious menus in France.

The Parc Régional du Pilat, in the far south of the *département*, is pleasant without being exceptional and takes its name from the hilly area in the middle whose Crêt de la Perdrix marks the end of the Cévénoles mountains. Its main attraction is an abyss known as the **Gouffre d'Enfer**, reached by either of two very minor roads which run in tandem for part of the way, one of them joining a slightly larger road in the shadow of a ruined château, the other carrying on towards the capital.

Try as you may, it is almost impossible to avoid the suburbs of St Etienne when travelling up from Ardèche and the effort is hardly worth it unless you are prepared to make a wide and not entirely satisfactory detour in and out of Auvergne to join the road to Montbrison near St Rambert-sur-Loire. On the other hand, this would give you an opportunity to see the Lac de Grangent, created by a barrage on the Loire and boasting at least three separate ruins, a small hermitage and some rewarding views.

After this, it is useful to know that **Andrézieux-Bouthéon**, less

PLACES OF INTEREST IN LOIRE

St Etienne
Museum of Art and Industry
Includes sections devoted to
armaments and modern
paintings.

Gouffre d'Enfer
In the Parc du Pilat. A deep
chasm off the scenic road to Le
Bessat.

Ambierle
Alice Taverne Forez Museum
A varied collection of items that
were commonplace in the region
during the nineteenth century.

Lac de Grangent
A man-made lake on the River
Loire.

Montbrison
Church of Notre-Dame
d'Espérance
A twelfth-century church, well
restored and with an interesting
interior.

Doll Museum
Boulevard de la Préfecture.
A collection of old dolls and
others in various peasant
costumes.

than 10km (6miles) due north of St Rambert-sur-Loire, has a large, comfortable but rather bland hotel with both a grill-room and a swimming pool. From here the river runs through a plethora of little lakes and ponds, linked by streams and boasting an occasional spa such as **Montrond-les-Bains**. The town provides a small but comfortable hotel with a good restaurant and a motel which, unfortunately, has nowhere to eat on the premises. In addition, there are facilities for tennis and opportunities for a flutter at the well-patronised casino.

Montbrison, to the west, is larger, older and rather more tourist-conscious but cannot compare when it comes to hotels, though there is some basic accommodation. Its most obvious attraction is the somewhat angular Church of Notre-Dame d'Espérance, built towards the end of the twelfth century and certainly worth looking round inside. It is the largest of its kind in the region and dwarfs the Church of St Pierre at the opposite end of the old town where there is also a solitary cross and the remains of some elderly ramparts.

The town is a pleasant place to wander with no special aim in view, inspecting the Vizézy as it drifts past under a series of small bridges and the narrow streets that never quite succeed in running parallel to each other. Very few are closed to traffic but, because of the lack of space, a one-way system has been devised which makes perfect sense to the local residents but is a trifle confusing for some visitors. Just outside the encircling boulevards, and almost behind the *hôtel de ville*, is the delightful Doll Museum which is backed by a small park. It has an enchanting display of antique dolls as well as more up-to-date models showing off traditional costumes. Folklore also plays a part in the Fourme Cheese Fair during which the townspeople are quite happy to include tourists in their celebrations but make little attempt to entertain them in any other way.

The main road continues without any further interruptions to Boën, where there is a château nearby and a small scenic road following the Lignon River down through St Georges-en-Couzan to **Chalmazel**. This is the only resort in the area which provides opportunities for both downhill and cross-country skiing. A cable car and half a dozen chair-lifts make life easier but on the debit side there is practically nothing in the way of accommodation, apart from a restaurant with some rooms attached. At the moment this is true of all the hill villages where a winter sports holiday is more of a family outing, with the innkeeper taking on the additional role of instructor and the farmers acting as guides.

During the summer, blazed footpaths, and in particular the GR3 and the GR3A, explore the wooded areas up to Renaison de la Tache where there is another man-made lake, an arboretum in the vicinity and a rather uninteresting road to **Ambierle**. The only reason for stopping in this village would be to visit the Alice Taverne Florez Museum which delves into every aspect of nineteenth-century life in the area. Thereafter, the road joins the main route to Lapalisse in Allier with, perhaps, a short pause at La Pacaudière to cast an eye over the Maison Papon at Le Crozet, 2km (1$^1/_4$ miles) away. From here there is a choice between returning to Auvergne or seeking fresh pastures along the Loire Valley as it swings round towards Nevers and out of the reach of the Massif Central.

USEFUL INFORMATION FOR VISITORS

ACCOMMODATION

Camp Sites

The French are keen on camping and there are a whole host of different sites available, ranging from one to four star and charging accordingly. They are often very well equipped with plenty of opportunities for all the usual sports, as well as a small shop, a restaurant and, in some cases, organised entertainments. However, they can quite easily be nothing more than a field set aside by a local farmer. The more popular sites are usually crowded to capacity during the holiday season when it is often essential to book in advance.

Gîtes

This term applies to most self-catering accommodation which can be a furnished apartment, a small house in a village, a country cottage, part of a private home or even self-contained rooms on a farm known as a *ferme de séjour*. Some *gîtes* stand in their own grounds while others have been built as small complexes. They are usually equipped with all the essentials but not a great many extras so it is as well to be prepared and check all such details in advance. This type of accommodation is easier to find in the country than in a large town or along the coast and there is usually an all-purpose shop within reach. *Gîtes* are normally let by the week and cost less than even quite modest hotels.

Hotels

Despite the scarcity of luxury and first class hotels, visitors will find plenty of *auberges* which are perfectly acceptable and provide amenities such as lifts, private bathrooms, restaurants, room service and parking space. The inns and taverns are rather more basic but they are usually clean, cheap and cheerful with traditional cooking and attentive service. The majority provide pillows as well as bolsters, in addition to extra blankets and probably central heating, but in the more out-of-the-way places anyone who needs a large bath towel or soap would be well advised to take their own.

The price of a room, which is always displayed on the back of the bedroom door, is invariably given for two people and, with few single rooms on offer, one should remember that a person alone will pay more than half the amount whereas an extra bed, sometimes folded up in the cupboard, will only add about 30 per cent to the bill. Meals are priced per head, based on the cheapest menu, and breakfast is always extra unless there is a notice saying that it is included. If in doubt, always ask to see the room because nobody minds if you turn it down.

The majority of small hotels close one day a week. Guests already in residence are not affected, though breakfast will almost certainly be the only meal available. A great many establishments, apart from some of the larger commercial ones, close for their annual holiday and in the winter sports areas this could well be during the summer months. Finally, nearly all the hotels and inns are ready and equipped to welcome children but some are less enthusiastic about animals.

Logis and Auberges

These are the traditional hostelries of France and can be easily identified by their distinctive signs — a yellow stone fireplace with logs burning in the grate, on a bright green shield edged with black. Generally speaking, they are delightful, often atmospheric, and frequently take great pride in their traditional cooking. It is usually possible to find a room with a bath but only occasionally a lift; some have a great many stairs and there is seldom anybody about to help with the luggage, so it is a good idea to travel light.

Other Accommodation

The equivalent of bed and breakfast accommodation, either chambres d'hôtes or tables d'hôtes, can be found and some families are happy if their guests opt for an evening meal as well. There are also centres for children on holiday alone, as well as youth hostels. Overnight stopping places are provided for riders, cyclists canoeists and long distance ramblers, conveniently sited along the various rivers and randonnées. Some organisations which offer trips lasting for a number of days also arrange for food and a change of clothing to be waiting for the members of the party when they arrive. This is particularly true when a refuge or a camp site is involved rather than a small auberge. Fishermen also have a choice of special accommodation — anything from a tiny waterside chalet to a hôtel de pêche where meals are flexible, the catch is put on ice or prepared for dinner and, in some cases, alternative activities are provided for the rest of the family.

FAIRS, FESTIVALS AND FETES

The Massif Central celebrates as often and as enthusiastically as anywhere else in France without adding many of the more obvious trappings of tourism. That side of things is left to events such as an international festival of music or art, the biennial exhibition of enamels in Limoges or the Jean Giraudoux Festival at Bellac during the height of the summer. In addition to these there are a great many celebrations with a religious flavour, from colourful processions in most large towns to less ambitious pilgrimages in honour of the Virgin or the local patron saint.

There are son et lumière performances, village fêtes and folklore festivals complete with people in traditional dress reviving old customs and keeping the ancient songs and dances alive. Some of the fairs and markets are designed to give farmers an opportunity to buy and sell horses, sheep and cattle. Others, especially round the various spas, are more in the nature of entertainments laid on for visitors, which the local people appear to enjoy every bit as much as their guests.

Complete lists of all the current events can be obtained from the various tourist offices in addition to the main annual celebrations, some of which are listed here.

Auvergne

Besse-en-Chandesse — The 'Ascent' and 'Descent' of the Black Madonna; in early July and late September respectively.

La Chaise-Dieu — Music Festival in late August and early September.

Clermont-Ferrand — Pilgrimage to Notre-Dame du Port. First Sunday after 15 May.

Le Puy-en-Velay — Processions to mark the Assumption. 15 August Fête du Roi de l'Oiseau, September.

Riom — St Amable's Day Festival with a procession of farmers in traditional costumes. Mid-June.

St Nectaire — Torchlit procession to Notre-Dame du Mont. 15 August.

Vichy Procession in honour of Notre-Dame-des-Malades. 15 August.

Classical concerts, drama and opera during the summer.

Limousin

Argentat — International Canoe Rally. First Sunday in July.

Brive — Twelfth Night Fair. 7 January.

Chénérailles — Medieval Pageant. First Sunday in July.

Limoges — Exhibition of Porcelain. Mid-June to mid-September.

Folk dance and song events. Tuesdays and Fridays July-August. Parish Feast of the Butchers Brotherhood, third Friday in October.

St Just-le-Martel — International Comic Cartoons Exhibition. First half of October.

St Léonard-de-Noblat — Concerts of classical music, June-August. Tilting at the Quintain. Second Sunday after 6 November.

Tours de Merle — Medieval displays and son et lumière, July-August.

Tulle — International Accordion Festival. First half of July.

Elsewhere in the Massif Central

Albi — Festival of Music. Mid-July to mid-August.

Brantôme — Festival of the Sabot de Bois. Early May. Dance Festival. Early July. Concours Hippique National. 15 August.

Cordes — Festival of Music. August.

Estaing — Procession of St Fleuret. First Sunday in July.

Marvejols — Fête de Marvejols. 15 August.

Mazamet — Bach Festival. Early September.

Mende — Fête de Mende et du Gévaudan. Mid-July.

Rocamadour — son et lumière. Le Livre d'Or de Rocamadour. Summer

Sarlat — Theatre Festival. Late July to early August.

Public Holidays

There are eleven public holidays in the French calendar when banks and most public places are closed but shops and restaurants may be open. They are:- New Year's Day, Easter Monday, Labour Day (1May), Ascension Day (6 weeks after Easter), VE Day (8 May), Whit Monday (10 days after Ascension Day), Bastille Day (14July), Assumption Day (15August), All Saints Day (1November), Remembrance Day (11 November) and Christmas Day.

MISCELLANEOUS

Credit Cards

Most of the hotels and restaurants, except the very small ones, accept credit cards. Visa, incidentally, is better known as *Carte Bleue*. A lot of garages also take credit cards but it is as well to make quite sure before filling up the tank. Usually a Eurocheque is perfectly acceptable but the wise motorist will also have some ready cash for such eventualities, particularly in small villages and outlying areas.

Currency Regulations

There is no restriction on the amount of cash which may be taken into France but visitors must declare 12,000 francs or more if they intend to take it out of the country.

Electricity

France operates on 220 volts but adapters will be needed by the majority of people who use anything other than continental two-pin plugs at home.

Health Care

British tourists should check with the DHSS to see if they are eligible for an E111 form that provides cover for emergencies. Otherwise, it is a good idea to take out an insurance policy for the visit, including the period spent in travelling. Americans should check that they are covered by their health insurance. There are plenty of doctors, dentists and hospitals but the pharmacies, clearly marked with a green cross, can usually deal with minor ailments, provide first aid and advise people where to go if any additional help is needed.

Opening Hours

Banks are open on weekdays from 9am-12noon and from 2-4pm but are closed on either Saturdays or Mondays, in addition to which they close early on the day before a Bank Holiday. Post Offices are open from 8am-7pm during the week and from 8am-12noon on Saturdays. Most shops open from 9am to about 6.30 or 7.30pm but close on Mondays for all or part of the day, while those in smaller towns take a lunch break from 12noon-2pm. The main exceptions are food shops which may vary their hours considerably and bakers who are frequently open on Sunday mornings. Churches, châteaux and museums also close for lunch as a rule but tend to vary their hours according to the season. Some of them, along with grottoes and other places of interest, are quite capable of staying open all day without a break during July and August.

Souvenirs

The Massif Central has a fair amount to offer in the way of souvenirs. Apart from all the cheap and cheerful keepsakes, there are articles of every shape and size in an equally wide range of prices. Top of the list are tapestries and expensive china from Limousin, though you do not have to pay the earth for some really delightful porcelain. Copper, brass and pewter are also good buys and so are local semi-precious stones like amethysts and topazes as well as carved lava. Walnut, cherry and pear woods are all used for furniture and some of the pottery is both attractive and useful. Cheeses, tripe cooked with sheep's trotters, crystallized fruits and bottles of liqueur are all worth buying.

Tipping

Almost every bill has service and VAT included but nobody will be offended if customers add a small amount to show their appreciation of high quality, good service or a pleasing atmosphere. The same thing applies to anyone who goes out of their way to be helpful, such as hotel staff, the caretaker of a church or château and others whose jobs bring them into contact with visitors.

MUSEUMS AND PLACES OF INTEREST

Nearly all museums and other places of interest vary their opening and closing times, not only according to the season but also from one year to the next and sometimes for no apparent reason at all. It is therefore worth checking if time is short or extra travelling is involved. Most of them also charge an entrance fee which can be very minimal, perfectly reasonable or, in a few cases, rather expensive. Some churches regard their treasures as mini-museums, with opening and closing hours and entrance fees, while others favour the coin-in-the-slot method which illuminates dark corners, a valuable painting or even the whole church itself. Some close for

lunch and others will not allow visitors inside during services unless they are part of the congregation.

Auvergne

PUY-DE-DOME

Arlanc
Lace Museum
No specific times available.
Enquire at the tourist office.

Aulteribe. Château d'
☎ 73 53 14 55
Open: 9am-12noon and 2-6pm May to September. 10am-12noon and 2-5pm October to April. Closed Tuesdays.

Busséol. Château de
☎ 73 69 00 84
Open: 10am-12noon and 2-7pm mid-June to mid-September. 2.30-5.30pm Sundays and holidays mid-September to mid-June.

Chapelle de Vassivière
Open: 8am-8pm July to mid-September.

Chazeron. Château de
☎ 73 86 65 42
Open: 3-6pm May to September.

Clermont-Ferrand
Bargoin Museum
☎ 73 91 37 31
Open: 10am-12noon and 2-6pm May to September. Otherwise 10am-12noon and 2-5pm. Closed Sunday mornings, Mondays and holidays.

Cathedral
Tower can be climbed on request.

Fontaines Pétrifiantes
☎ 73 37 15 58
Open: 8am-7.30pm July and August. Otherwise 9am-12noon and 2-6pm.

Lecoq Museum
☎ 73 91 93 78
Open: 10am-12noon and 2-6pm
May to September. Otherwise
10am-12noon and 2-5pm. Closed
Sunday mornings, Mondays and
holidays.

Ranquet Museum
☎ 73 37 38 63
Open: 10am-12noon and 2-6pm
May to September. Otherwise
10am-12noon and 2-5pm. Closed
Sunday mornings, Mondays and
holidays.

Cordès. Château de
☎ 73 65 81 34
Open: 10am-12noon and 2-6pm
throughout the year.

Davayat. Château de
☎ 73 63 30 04
Open: 2.15-6.45pm during the
summer.

Denone. Château de
☎ 73 63 64 02
Open: 2-7pm July and August.

Effiat. Château d'
☎ 73 63 64 01
Open: 9am-12noon and 2-7pm
June to September. 9am-12noon
and 2-7pm weekends and holidays
March to June and during October
and November.

Egliseneuve-d'Entraigues
Cheese House
☎ 73 71 93 69
Conducted tours at 10am, 11am,
2pm, 3pm, 4pm, 5pm and 6pm
mid-June to September.

Grottes de Jonas
Open: 10am-7pm July and August.
10am-12noon and 2-7pm June
and September. 2-6pm at Easter.
Thereafter 10am-12noon and 2-
6pm on Sundays until end May,
during October and until mid-
November.

Marsac-en-Livradois
Museum of the White Penitents
Open: 9-11.30am and 2-5.30pm
June to September. Otherwise
2-5.30pm Sundays and holidays.

Martinanches. Château des
☎ 73 70 80 02
Open: 2-7pm mid-June to mid-
September. Mornings on request.
2-7pm Sundays and holidays mid-
September to mid-June.

Montfleury. Château de
☎ 73 69 02 55
Open: 10am-12noon and 2-7pm
Easter to mid-October.

Montmorin. Château de
☎ 73 68 30 94
Open: 3-7pm July and August.
Otherwise 3-7pm Saturdays and
Sundays Easter to October.

Moulin Richard-le-Bas
☎ 73 82 03 11
Open with guided tours 9am-7pm
July and August. Otherwise
9-11am and 2-5pm. Closed
1January and 25 December.

Murol
Castle ruins
☎ 73 88 67 11
Open: 10am-7pm April to mid-
October. Otherwise on request.

Parc Zoologique du Bouy
☎ 73 82 13 29
Open: daily June to September.
Otherwise Saturdays, Sundays
and holidays only.

Pontgibaud
Château-Dauphin
☎ 73 88 73 39
Open: 2-7pm mid-July to end
August. Closed Mondays.

Puy-de-Dôme
Exhibition and information office at
the summit.

Open: 10am-12.30pm and 2.30-7pm mid-June to September.

Puy-de-Sancy
Cable car operates from 9am-12noon and 1.30-5.30pm.

Ravel. Château de
☎ 73 68 44 63
Open: 10am-12noon and 2-7pm July to September. Otherwise 2-6pm Easter to October.

Riom
Hôtel Guimoneau
Open: 9am-12noon and 2-6pm. Closed Sundays, holidays and second half of August.

Mandet Museum
Open: 10am-12noon and 2-5.30pm April to September. Closed Tuesdays. Otherwise 10am-12noon and 2-4.30pm. Closed Mondays and Tuesdays out of season and some holidays.

Musée Régional d'Auvergne
Open: 10am-12noon and 2-5.30pm April to September. 10am-12noon and 2-4.30pm October to March. Closed Mondays and Tuesdays out of season and some holidays.

Palais de Justice
Open: 9am-12noon and 2-6pm. Closed Saturdays, Sundays and holidays. Enquire from the caretaker from mid-July to end of August.

St Amable Church
Closed Sunday afternoons October to May. Enquire at the tourist office to visit the sacristy.

Roche. Château de la
☎ 73 63 65 81
Open: 9am-12noon and 2-6pm June to October. Otherwise 9.30am-12noon and 2-6.30pm except Tuesdays.

Royat
Taillerie des Pierres Fines
Conducted tours 9.30-11.30am and 2-5.30pm mid-June to mid-September. Closed Tuesdays, 1 January, Easter, 1 November, 25 December except for exhibitions.

St Nectaire
Church
Open: 10am-12noon and 2.30-6pm June to mid-September. Otherwise closed Mondays and also Tuesdays from November to April.

Fontaines Pétrifiantes
☎ 73 88 50 80
Open: 8.30am-12noon and 2-7pm during the season. Otherwise 9.30am-12noon and 2-5.30pm. Closed mid-November to mid-December.

Thiers
Maison des Couteliers
Open: 10am-12noon and 2-6.30pm June to September. Otherwise 2-6pm. Closed Mondays out of season, 1 January, 1 May, 14 September, 1 November, 11 November and 25 December.

Tournoël. Château de
☎ 73 33 53 06
Open: 9am-12noon and 2-7pm Easter to September. 9am-12noon and 2-6pm October. Closed Tuesdays.

Vollore. Château de
☎ 73 53 71 06
Open: 2-7pm July and August.

Volvic
Maison de la Pierre
Conducted tours 10-11.30am and 2.15-6pm mid-March to mid-November. Closed Tuesdays.

CANTAL

Albepierre-Bredons
Church can be seen from mid-July to mid-August by enquiring at the tourist office in Murat.

Anjony. Château d'
☎ 71 47 61 67
Open: 2-6.30pm Palm Sunday to end October.

Aurillac
Maison des Volcans
Open: 10am-12noon and 2-7pm July and August, except Sunday mornings and holidays. Otherwise 8.30am-12noon and 2-5.30pm. Closed Monday mornings, Saturday afternoons, Sundays and holidays.

Musée de Cire
Open: 10am-12noon and 2-7pm mid-June to mid-September except on Sunday mornings. 2-7pm mid-September to mid-November and mid-December to mid-June.

Musée Hippolyte-de-Parieu
Open: 10am-12noon and 2-6pm. Closed Sunday mornings, Tuesdays and holidays.

Musée de Vieil Aurillac
Open: 10am-12noon and 2-6pm. Closed Sundays, Tuesdays and holidays.

Musée Jean-Baptiste Rames
Open: 10am-12noon and 2-6pm. Closed Sunday mornings, Tuesdays and holidays.

Palais de Justice
Open: 9am-12noon and 2-6pm. Closed Saturday afternoons and Sundays.

Auzers. Château d'
☎ 71 78 62 59
Open: 2-6.30pm July, to mid-September.

Brezons
La Bohal
☎ 71 73 40 82 or 71 73 40 24
Open: August and September by appointment only.

Chapelle de Notre-Dame-de-Consolation
To see inside enquire at the church in Thiézac or at the school.

Conros. Château de
☎ 71 63 50 27
Open: 2-6pm mid-July to end August.

Etablissement de Pisciculture, near Thiézac
Open: 2-4pm.

Laveissière
The Buronnier's House
Open: 10am-12.30pm and 2.30-7pm mid-June to mid-September. Closed Tuesdays.

Maison de la Gentiane et de la Flore
Near Riom-ès-Montagnes
☎ 71 78 10 45
Open: 10am-12.30pm and 2.30-7pm mid-June to mid-September.

Mauriac
Notre-Dame-des-Miracles
Ask if you would like the lights turned on.

Pesteils. Château de
☎ 71 47 44 36
Open: 10am-12noon and 2.30-6pm July and August. 2.30-5.30pm May, June and September.

Plomb du Cantal
Cable car operates 9.30am--6.30pm in summer and 9am-5.30pm in winter. About every 15 minutes.

Rochebrune. Château de
☎ 71 23 82 72

Open: 2.30-6pm mid-July to end
August. Closed Tuesdays.
Otherwise on request.

St Flour
Alfred Douet Museum
Open: 9-11.15am and 2-6.15pm
July and August.

Musée de la Haute-Auvergne
Open: 9am-12noon and 2-7pm
June to September. 9am-12noon
and 2-6pm October to May. Closed
Saturdays and Sundays in winter,
Easter, Whitsun and 25 December.

Salers
Ancien Bailliage
Open 10am-12noon and 2-6pm.
Closed January and February.

Maison de Bargues
Open: 10am-12noon and 2-7pm
Easter to All Saints Day.

Maison des Templiers
Open: 10am-12noon and 2-6pm
mid-July to the first week in
September.

Trémolière. Château de la
☎ 71 40 00 02
Open: 2.30-7pm July and August.

Vigne. Château de la
☎ 71 69 00 20
Open: 2.30-7pm. July and August.

HAUTE-LOIRE

Arlempdes
Ruins and Chapel
Open: all year. Enquire at the
Hôtel du Manoir

Auvers
Museum of the Resistance
Movement
Open: 8am-12noon and 1.30-7pm
May to mid-October.

Auzon
To see inside the church enquire
on the premises.

Blassac
To see inside enquire from the
guardian next door.

Blesle
To see the treasure at the church
enquire at the Mairie.

Chaise-Dieu
Abbaye St Robert
Tombs, stalls, murals and
tapestries. Conducted tours 9am-
12noon and 2-7pm June to
September. Otherwise open 10am-
12noon and 2-5pm. Closed
Tuesdays out of season.

Historial de la Chaise-Dieu
Open 9am-12noon and 2-7pm.
Closed October to March.

Chambon-sur-Lignon
Museum
Open: 3-6.30pm July and August.
Closed Tuesdays.

Chavaniac-Lafayette
☎ 71 77 50 32 or 71 77 52 85
Open: 10am-12noon and 2-7pm
throughout the year.

Lavaudieu
Cloister and museum
☎ 71 76 43 15
Open: 10am-12noon and 2-6pm.
Closes at 5pm out of season, also
Tuesdays, 1 January, 1 November
and 25 December. Otherwise
enquire at the house with a
wooden balcony near the church.

Maison de l'Artisanat de
Bilhac-Polignac
☎ 71 09 50 94

Monastier-sur-Gazeille (Le)
Exhibitions in the château during
July and August.

Church treasure and museum
Open: 9am-12.30pm and 2.30-
6.30pm July to September. Closed
Tuesday mornings and Thursday
afternoons.

Moudeyres
Ferme des Frères Perrel
Open 10am-12noon and 3-7pm
July to mid-September. Closed
Wednesdays.

Polignac
Château
☎ 71 09 32 24
Open: 9.30am-12noon and 2-7pm
July and August.
Otherwise 10am-12noon and
2-5.30pm. Closed October to April.

Pradelles
L'Oustalou
☎ 71 00 83 65
Open: 10am-12noon and 2-6pm
July to September.

Puy-en-Velay (Le)
For a detailed visit to the cathedral
enquire from the sacristy.

Chapel des Reliques
Open: 9am-12.30pm and
2-6.30pm July and August. 9am-
12noon and 2-6pm April, May,
June and September. Otherwise
10am-12noon and 2-4pm. Closed
Tuesdays and holidays.

Cloister
The same times as the Chapel des
Reliques.

Maison du Prieur
Open: 9am-12noon and 2-6pm.
July and August.

Treasure
Open: 8am-7pm Easter to All
Saints Day. Otherwise 8am-5pm.

Rocher Corneille
Open: 9am-8pm July and August,
9am-7pm May, June and September. 9am-6pm mid-March to the
end of April. 10am-5pm October to
mid-March. Closed December and
January and Tuesdays from
November to March.

Son et lumière
Tuesdays and Fridays during July
and August.

Chapelle St Michel d'Aiguilhe
Open: 9am-12noon and 2-7pm
mid-June to mid-September.
10am-12noon and 2-6pm mid-
September to end of October and
mid-March to mid-June. 2-4pm
during school holidays and in
February except on 25 December
and 1 January.

Musée Crozatier
Open: 10am-12noon and 2-6pm.
Closes at 4pm from October to
April. Also Tuesdays and Sunday
mornings, throughout February
and 1 January, 1 November,
25 December.

Rocher St Joseph
Open: 8am-7pm.

Rochelambert. Château de la
Open: 10.30-11.30am and
2-5.30pm. Closed October and
Tuesdays and Fridays out of
season. Otherwise enquire from
the caretaker in the house to the
right of the gates.

St Vidal. Château de
Open: 2-6.30pm July and August.

Sauges
Musée de la Forêt
Open: 10am-12noon and
2-6.30pm July and August.
Otherwise ☎ 71 77 81 22.

Tour des Anglais
Open: 10am-12noon and
2-6.30pm July and August.

Yssingeaux
Musée des Arts et Traditions
Populaires de Versilhac
Open: 2-6.30pm July and August.
Closed Tuesdays.

ALLIER

Balaine
Château and botanical garden
☎ 70 43 30 07
Open: 10am-12noon and 2-7pm
May to October. Closed Tuesday
mornings, Friday mornings and
Saturday mornings. Otherwise by
appointment only.

Beauvoir. Château de
Grounds only. Open: 9am-7pm but
closes at 5pm out of season.

Billy
Fortress
☎ 70 43 50 14
Open 10am-12noon and 2-6pm
July to mid-September. Weekends
only at the same times May and
June.

Bourbon-l'Archambault
Augustin-Bernard Museum
Open: 3-6pm Wednesdays,
Saturdays, Sundays and holidays
April to October.

Château
Open: Sundays 10am-12noon and
2-6pm. Otherwise 2-6pm only mid-
April to mid-October.

Gannat
Musée des Trésors des Portes
Occitanes
Open: 3-6pm April to September.
Closed Tuesdays, 14 July and
15 August.

Gouttes. Parc des
☎ 70 34 73 01
Open: 9am-7pm April to October.

Lapalisse
Château
☎ 70 99 08 51
Open 9am-12noon and 2-6pm late
March to October. Closed
Tuesdays in April, May, September
and October.

Montluçon
Musée Folklorique
Open: 10am-12noon and 2-6pm
mid-March to mid-October. Closed
Tuesdays. Otherwise 2-6pm
except Mondays and Tuesdays.
Closed on certain holidays.

Musée International de la Vielle
Open: the same times as the
Musée Folklorique

Moulins
Cathedral
Treasures on view 9am-12noon
and 2-6pm. Closed Tuesdays
November to April.

Mausolée du Duc de Montmorency
Enquire at the tourist office.

Museum of Art and Archaeology
Open: 10am-12noon and 2-6pm
April to September. 10am-12noon
and 2-5pm October to March.

Musée du Folklore et du Vieux
Moulins
Open: 10am-12noon and 3-
6.30pm Palm Sunday to Septem-
ber. Otherwise 2-5pm. Closed
Thursdays and Sunday mornings
out of season, 1 May and over
Christmas.

Musée Historique du Bourbonnais
Yzeure
Open: 8am-12noon and 2-6pm.
Closed Saturdays, Sundays and
holidays.

Néris-les-Bains
Musée Rieckotter
Open: 5.30-7pm May to Septem-
ber. Closed Sundays and holidays.

Pal. Zoo du
☎ 70 42 00 38 or 70 42 03 60
Open: 10am-7pm.

Riau. Le
Villeneuve-sur-Allier
☎ 70 43 30 74

Open: 3-7pm except Tuesdays in summer. 2-5pm except Tuesdays and Sundays in winter.

St Augustin. Château de
Wild life park
☎ 70 66 42 01
Open: 2-6pm June to mid-September. Otherwise 2-6pm Wednesdays, Saturdays, Sundays and holidays only.

St Pourçain-sur-Sioule
Abbey church
Open for guided tours from mid-June to early September. Arrange through the tourist office.

Souvigny
Church of St Pierre
Open: daily but with conducted tours during July and August.

Eglise-Musée St Marc
Open: 10am-12noon and 3-6pm July and August. Closed Tuesday.

Toury. Château de
☎ 70 42 00 41
Open: 10am-12noon and 2-6pm April to November.

Vichy
Centre des Recherches Archéologiques de Vichy
Open: 2-6pm Wednesdays and Saturdays, June to mid-September.

Maison du Bailliage
Open with guided tours at 3pm, 4.15pm and 6.30pm Fridays and Saturdays July to September.

Maison du Missionnaire
Open: 3-6pm mid-May to mid-September. Closed Mondays.

Limousin

HAUTE-VIENNE

Bellac
Jean Giraudoux House.
Open daily 3-7pm July and August. Otherwise enquire at the tourist office, except on Saturdays and Sundays.

Billanges (Les)
Fortified church. If closed enquire at the tobacconist opposite.

Brie
Château
Open with guided tours afternoons only on Sundays and public holidays from April to September.

Châlus
Château de Châlus-Chabrol
☎ 55 78 56 61
Open with guided tours mornings and afternoons July to mid-September. Sundays and public holidays afternoons only mid-April to end of June.

Musée des Feuillardiers
Open: 10am-12noon and 2-6pm daily in the summer. 2-7pm Sundays and holidays only April to June.

Chassenon
Ruins
Open for guided tours 10am-12noon and 2-6pm on weekdays and 9am-12noon and 2-7pm on Sundays and public holidays from July to mid-September.

Châteauponsac
René Bauderot Museum
Open daily 2-6pm July to mid-September. Otherwise Sundays and public holidays only 2-6pm.

Coussac-Bonneval
Château
Open for guided tours, afternoons only on Wednesdays, Saturdays and Sundays mid-March to end November. Also Thursdays during July and August.

Dorat (Le)
Church of St Peter
Crypt open for guided visits all day June to September. Otherwise mornings and afternoons only.

Lastours
Château
☎ 55 58 38 47
Open for guided tours daily mid-July to mid-August. Otherwise visiting hours are posted up on the main entrance.

Limoges
Adrien Dubouché National Museum
Place Winston-Churchill
☎ 55 77 45 58
Open: daily 10am-12noon and 1.30-5pm. Closed Tuesdays and public holidays.

Crypt of St Martial
Below the Place de la République
☎ 55 34 46 87
Open for guided tours mornings and afternoons July to September.

Municipal Museum
In Bishops' Palace near cathedral.
☎ 55 33 70 10
Open: daily 10-11.45am and 2-6pm. Closed Tuesdays except during July, August and September.

St Pierre-du-Queyroix Church
Rue Rafilhoux
Open: daily except on Sunday afternoons.

Workshops. Enamel
Atelier Veisbrot
19 Rue des Tanneries

Open: during working hours. For details of other workshops enquire at the tourist office.

Workshops. Porcelain
Maison de la Porcelaine
14 Avenue du Président-Wilson
Open: during working hours.

Centre de Démonstration des Porcelaines Limoges-Castel
Z.I. Magré
☎ 55 30 21 86
Open: daily 8.30am-7.30pm. Closed Sundays out of season. For details of other workshops apply to the tourist office.

Montbrun
Château
Open: daily for guided tours 9am-12noon and 2-7pm.

Mortemart
Church
Open: Saturday and Sunday afternoons during the summer. Otherwise enquire at the café opposite the château.

Oradour-sur-Glane
Church and Memorial Museum
Open: 9am-12noon and 2-6.30pm daily throughout the year.

Rochebrune
Château
☎ 45 89 20 65
Open for guided tours each afternoon from Palm Sunday to mid-November. Also mornings during July and August. Closed Tuesdays except in July and August.

Rochechouart
Château and Museum
Open for guided tours 10am-12noon and 3-6.30pm from Palm Sunday to All Saints Day. Otherwise Saturdays, Sundays and public holidays only. Closed Tuesdays.

St Léonard-de-Noblat
Gay-Lussac Museum
Open: mornings and afternoons
during July and August. Otherwise
afternoons only mid-June to mid-
September. Closed Sunday
mornings and public holidays.

St Junien
Chapel of Notre-Dame-du-Pont
Enquire at 16 Bis Avenue Maryse-
Bastié

St Yrieix-la-Perche
Porcelain Museum
At Les Palloux near the lake
Open: daily mornings and
afternoons. Closed Sundays,
Mondays and public holidays
Enquire at the *hôtel de ville* in
order to see the old Bible.

CREUSE

Ahun
Church
To visit the crypt enquire at the
Lamiraud pharmacy.

Aubusson
Maison du Vieux Tapissier
Rue Vieille
☎ 55 66 32 12
Open: 9am-12noon and 2-6pm
mid-June to end of September.

Tapestry Museum
Jean-Lurçat Cultural Centre
Avenue des Lissiers
☎ 55 66 33 06
Open: 9am-12noon and 2-7pm
mid-June to end September.
Otherwise 9.30am-12noon and
2-6pm. Closed Tuesdays and first
week in October.

Town Hall
Open: daily from mid-June to end
September.

Workshops. Tapestry
Andraud Père et Fils
2 Place Maurice-Dayras

Open: during working hours.

Braquenie et Cie
8 Avenue de la République
Open: during working hours. For
other workshops enquire at the
tourist office.

Bourganeuf
Tour Zizim
☎ 55 64 02 37
Open: for guided tours afternoons
during July and August.

Town Hall
☎ 55 64 07 61
Open to visitors mornings and
afternoons Mondays and Fridays.
Closed 1 January, Easter Monday,
14 July, 15 August, Whit Monday,
1 and 11 November and
25 December.

Boussac
Château
Open: daily 9am-12noon and
2-6pm.

Chambon-sur-Voueize
Church of Ste Valérie
Open: mornings and afternoons
July and August. Treasure can be
seen on request.

Chénérailles
Church
Open: daily but closed Sunday
afternoons.

Crozant
Ruins
Open: all day from Easter to end
September.

Excursions to the Barrage
d'Eguzon, leaving 2.45pm and
4pm from mid-July to end August.
5.30pm for parties of not less than
twenty. The minimum number also
applies on Sundays from May to
mid-July and in September.
☎ 55 89 81 96

Glénic
Church
☎ 55 52 22 09
Enquire at the *mairie*.

Guéret
Creuse Museum
In the market place
Open: daily. Closed Tuesdays.

Municipal Museum
Avenue Sénatorerie
☎ 55 52 07 20
Open: 10am-12noon and 2-6pm.
Closes 5pm in winter and every
Tuesday.

Lavaufranche
Boussac
La Commanderie
Open: 2-6pm July and August.

Moutier-d'Ahun
Church
Open: daily May to October.
Otherwise visiting hours are
posted at the main doorway.

St Germain-Beaupré
Open: 9am-12noon and 2-6pm
Mondays, Tuesdays and Satur-
days.

Souterraine (La)
Church of the Assumption
Crypt open during July and
August.

Théret
Château
Open for guided tours after midday
from July to September.

Vassivière (Lac de)
☎ 55 69 20 45
Trips by motor launch from May to
September.

Villemonteix
Château
☎ 55 62 33 92
Open for guided tours 10am-

12noon and 2-7pm June to All
Saints Day.

CORRÈZE

Arnac-Pompadour
Castle terraces
Open: 9am-12noon and 2-6pm.
Special opening hours on race
days.

Haras
Open: 2.30-5pm weekdays. 10-
11.30am and 2.30-5pm Sundays.
10am-12noon and 6-7pm race
days.

La Jumenterie de la Rivière
Open: 2-4pm weekdays July to
October. 2-6pm Sundays and
holidays. 10am-12noon and 6-7pm
race days.

Aubazine
Monastery
Open: 2-5.30pm June to mid-
September. Closed Mondays.
Otherwise Saturday and Sunday
afternoons only.

Bort-les-Orgues
Near Lac de Bort
Hydro-electric powerhouse open
9am-6pm.

Brive-la-Gaillarde
Edmond Michelet Museum
Open: 10am-12noon and 2-6pm.
Closed Sundays and public
holidays.

Chapelle aux Saints (La)
Open 9am-12noon Sundays and
Mondays.

Gimel-les-Cascades
☎ 55 21 26 49
Waterfalls open daily from March
to October.

Gouffre de la Fage (Le)
Museum
Open: 9am-7pm July and August.

2-7pm April, May, June and
September.

Lubersac
Church
Closed Saturday and Sunday
afternoons.

Meymac
Marius-Vazeilles Museum
Place du Bûcher
Open: 10am-12noon and 3.30-
6.30pm July and August. Other-
wise 3-5pm Saturdays, Sundays
and public holidays May to mid-
October. Closed Tuesdays.

Museum of Contemporary Art
At the same address
Open: 10am-12.30pm and 3-7pm
June to October. Closed
Tuesdays.

Neuvic
Henri Queville Museum
☎ 55 95 96 87
Open: 10am-12noon and 3-6pm
mid-June to mid-September.

Reygade
Chapel with son et lumière
Open: 9am-10pm throughout the
year.

Sédières
Château
☎ 55 27 82 40
Open for guided tours morning and
afternoon during July and August.

Tours de Merle
Ruins
Medieval show and son et lumière
mid-July to mid-August. Nightly
son et lumière during remainder of
July and August. Saturday
evenings only in June and
September.

Treignac
Maison Marc Sangnier
Open: 10.30am-12noon and

5-7pm July and August. Closed
Sundays.

Tulle
Andre Mazeyrie Cloister Museum
☎ 55 26 22 05
Open: 9.30am-12noon and 2-6pm
mid-June to mid-September.

Cathedral
Closed on public holidays.

Musée Départemental de la
Résistance et de la Déportation
2 Quai Edmond-Perrier
Open: 9am-12noon Tuesdays,
2-5pm Wednesdays and 9am-5pm
Fridays throughout the year.

Turenne
Castle ruins
Open: 9am-12noon and 2-7pm
Easter to October. Sundays from
10am.

Ussel
Hôtel du Juge Choriol
Open: 10am-12noon and 3-7pm
July and August.

Vâl. Château de
On the Lac de Bort
Open: 9am-12noon and 2-6.30pm
mid-June to mid-September.

Midi-Pyrénées

LOT

Aynac. Château d'
☎ 65 38 93 16
No specific opening times.

Bonaguil. Château de
Open for conducted tours 10am,
11am, 3pm, 4pm and 5pm June to
August. 10.30am, 2.30pm, 3.30pm
and 4.30pm March to May and
during September 3pm and
4.30pm February, October and
November.

Cahors
Cathedral Cloister
Open: 9am-12noon and 2-6pm
July and August. Closed Sundays
and holidays.

Maison de Roaldes
Open: 10.30am-12noon and 2.30-
6pm July to September. Closed
Sundays and holidays.

Municipal Museum
Open: 10am-12noon and 2-7pm
June to September 2-6pm April
and May. Closed Sundays,
Mondays and holidays.

Pont Valentré. Centre tower open
9am-12noon and 2-7pm July and
August.

Castlenau-Bretenoux.
Château de
☎ 65 38 52 04
Open: 9am-12noon and 2-6pm
April to September. 10am-12noon
and 2-5pm October to March.
Closed Tuesdays.

Cénevières. Château de
Open: 10am-12noon and 2-7pm
mid-June to mid-September and at
Easter.

Coste. Château de la
☎ 65 21 34 18
Open for guided tours 5pm on
Sundays June to September.
Otherwise enquire.

Cougnac. Grottes de
Open: 9.30-11am and 2-5pm Palm
Sunday to end of June and
21 September to All Saints Day.
9am-6pm July to 20 September.

Eyzies. Les
Combarelles. Grotte de
☎ 53 08 00 94
Open: 9am-12noon and 2-6pm
April to September. 10am-12noon
and 2-4pm October to March.

Closed Tuesdays and some
holidays. Tickets are sold before
opening times and visitors are
restricted so it is wise to arrive
early.

National Museum of Prehistory
☎ 53 06 97 03
Open 9.30am-12noon and 2-6pm
March to November. 9.30am-
12noon and 2-5pm December to
February. Closed Tuesdays.

Figeac
Hôtel de la Monnaie
Open: 10am-12noon and 2-7pm
mid-June to mid-September.
Otherwise 10am-12noon and
2-4pm Tuesdays and Fridays.

Musée Champollion
☎ 65 34 40 40
Open: 10am-12noon and 2.30-
6.30pm as well as school holidays
at Christmas and Easter. Closed
Mondays, January to April and
Christmas Day.

Gramat
Centre de Formation des Maîtres
de Chien de la Gendarmerie
Visitors can watch the dogs in
training at 3.30 and 5.30pm
Thursdays during July and August.

Lacave. Grottes de
Open: 9am-12noon and 2-6.30pm
June and July. 9am-7pm August.
9am-12noon and 2-6pm late
March to May, also September and
October.

Larroque-Toirac. Château de
Open 10am-12noon and 2-6pm
mid-July to mid-September and
also at Easter and Whitsun.

Lascaux II
☎ 55 53 44 35
Open: 10am-12noon and 2-5pm
February to June and mid-
September to mid-December.

9.30am-7.30pm July to mid-September. 10am to 12noon and 2-6pm Sundays and holidays. Closed Mondays. Visitors estricted to forty people at a time and a maximum of 2,000 a day so it is as well to get there early.

Luzech
Armand Viré Museum
☎ 65 20 17 27
Open: 9.30am-12noon and 2.30-7pm July to mid-September.

Martel
Cloître de Mirepoises
Open: 8.30-11.30am and 2.30-5.30pm June to September. Closed Sundays and holidays. Also enquire at the tourist office.
Hôtel de la Raymondie
No specific times given. Enquire at the tourist office.

Montal. Château de
☎ 65 38 13 72
Open: 9.30am-12noon and 2.30-6pm July. 3-7pm August. 9.30am-12noon and 2.30-6pm Palm Sunday to June and September to All Saints Day.

Moustier. Le
Prehistoric site in the village
☎ 53 50 72 89
Open: 9am-12noon and 2-6pm during the season. Closed Tuesdays. View out of season by appointment.

Site of Le Ruth
☎ 53 50 74 02
Open: all day every day.

Troglodyte cliff settlement
☎ 53 50 70 45 or 53 06 23 22
Open: 9.30am-12noon and 2-6.30pm July to mid-September. 9am-12noon and 2-6pm mid-April to October.

Padirac. Gouffre de
Open: 8am-12noon and 2-7pm June to mid-September. 8am-7pm without interruption during August. 9am-12noon and 2-6pm Easter to May and mid-September to early October.

Pech-Merle. Grotte du
Open for conducted tours 9am-12noon and 2.30-6pm Palm Sunday to September. 10.30am, 11.30am, 3pm and 5pm weekdays during October.

Rocamadour
Basilique St Sauveur
Chapels open 9am-6pm June to mid-September. Enquire at the sacristy or the shop selling religious souvenirs. Treasure open 8am-7pm July and August. 9am-12noon and 2-6pm April to June and September and October.

Château
Open: 8am-7pm Easter to All Saints Day.

Hôtel de Ville
Open: 9am-12noon and 2-7pm Easter to September.

Musées des Cire Roland-le-Preux et l'Historial
Open: 8am-12noon and 1.30-10pm Easter to All Saints Day.

St Céré
Tapestry Exhibition
Closed Tuesdays out of season.

Vintage Car Museum
Open: daily from Easter to September but closed Tuesdays from Easter to the end of May.

St Cirq-Lapopie
Musée la Gardette
Open: 10am-12noon and 2.30-6pm April to November.

Sarlat
Aquarium Museum
☎ 53 59 44 58
Open 10am-7pm June to September. 2.30-6pm April, May, October and school holidays. Otherwise 2.30-6pm Saturdays and Sundays.

Chapel of the White Penitents Museum
Open: 10am-12noon and 3-6pm Easter to mid-October.

AVEYRON

Bosc. Château de
Open: 9am-12noon and 2-7pm Easter to mid-November.

Conques
Cathedral Treasure
Open: 9am-12noon and 2-6pm. Closed Tuesdays in winter and throughout February.

Espalion
Eglise St Jean
Open: 10am-12noon and 3-7pm May to November. Closed Sunday mornings.

Estaing. Château
Open: 9am-12noon and 2.30-6pm on request. Closed 16 to 24 May.

Las Planques
Eglise de
Collect the key from the town hall in Tanus.

Millau
Beffroi
Open: 10am-12noon and 3-7pm July and August. Otherwise 3-6pm Wednesdays and Saturdays. Closed Sundays and holidays.

Museum
Open: 10am-12noon and 3-7pm July and August. Otherwise 3-6pm Wednesdays and Saturdays. Closed Sundays and holidays.

Najac
Château
Open: 10am-12noon and 2-7pm Easter to September. 10am-12noon and 2-5pm October, Sundays and holidays only.
Church
Open: from Palm Sunday to All Saints Day.

Perse. Eglise de
Open: 10am-12noon and 2.30-6.30pm July to September.

Rodez
Musée des Beaux Arts
Open: 9-11am and 2-5pm. Closed Sundays and holidays.

Musée Fenaille
Open: 10am-12noon and 2.30-6pm July and August. Closed Sundays, Mondays and holidays.

Roquefort-sur-Soulzon
Cheese caves
☎ 65 60 23 05
Open: 9-11am and 2-5pm. Hours may be extended during the tourist season.
No animals allowed inside.

Museum
Open: 9am-12noon and 2-6pm. Closes at 5pm in winter.

Villefranche-de-Rouergue
Ancienne Chartreuse St Sauveur
Open: 9.30am-12noon and 2.30-6.30pm July and August for conducted tours. Otherwise at the same times but without guides.

Chapelle des Pénitents Noirs
Open: 9.30am-12noon and 2.30-6.30pm July and August.

TARN

Albi
Cathedral of Ste Cécile
Open: 12noon-2pm in summer and in the evening.

Toulouse-Lautrec Birthplace
Open: 9-11.45am and 3-6.45pm
mid-June to mid-September.
Closed Sunday mornings and
holidays.

Toulouse-Lautrec Museum
Open: 9am-12noon and 2-6pm
mid-June to September. Otherwise
10am-12noon and 2-5pm. Closed
Tuesdays October to March. Also
1 January, 1 May, 1 November
and 25 December.

St Salvy Church
The sacristy closes from 10am-
5pm except Saturdays and is open
on Sunday mornings.

Castres
Musée Goya
Open: 9am-12noon and 2-6pm but
opens at 10am on Sundays and
closes at 5pm in winter. Closed
Mondays, 1 January, 1 May,
Easter Monday, Whit Monday,
1 November and 25 December.

Musée Jean Jaurès
Open: same times as the Musée
Goya.

Cayla. Château du
Open: 10am-12noon and 2-6pm
April to October. Closes at 5pm
November to March and on
Fridays.

Cordes
Charles Portal Museum
Open: 10am-12noon and 2-6pm
April to mid-November.

St Michel Church
If closed enquire at the tobacconist
opposite.

Yves Brayer Museum
Open: 10am-12noon and 2.30-
6.30pm (2-6pm Sundays and
holidays) mid-June to September.
9am-12noon and 2-6pm Mondays
and Fridays only October to mid-
June.

Ferrières
Musée du Protestantisme en Haut-
Languedoc et Maison du Luthier
Open: 10am-12noon and 3-7pm
mid-April to mid-October. Closed
Sundays and holidays. Otherwise
enquire at the Centre d'Art de
Ferrières.

Limousis. Grottes de
Open: 9am-12noon and 2-7pm
June to September. 2-6pm
Sundays and holidays October to
mid-May. 2-6pm daily during
Easter and the second half of May.

Monestiés
St Jacques Chapel
Open: 10am-12noon and 2-6pm.
Enquire from the caretaker.

St Michel de Lescure
Musée de la Carte Postale
Open: 1.30-7pm August to late
September.

Languedoc-Roussillon

LOZERE AND GARD

Aven Armand
Grotto
☎ 66 45 61 31
Open: 9am-7pm June to August.
9am-12noon and 1.30-6pm April
and May. 9am-12noon and 1.30-
5.30pm September and October.
Otherwise 2-4pm.

Castanet. Château de
☎ 66 46 81 11
Open: 10am-7pm July and August.

Dargilan. Grotte de
☎ 66 45 60 20
Open: 9am-12.30pm and 1.30-
6.30pm July to September. 9am-
12noon and 2-6pm Palm Sunday
to June and to mid-October.

Malène. La
☎ 66 48 51 10

Point of departure for river trips along the Gorges du Tarn.

Mende
Musée Ignon Fabre
Open: 10am-12noon and 3-7pm July to mid-September. Closes at 6pm during the rest of the year. Closed Tuesdays, Sundays and holidays.

Musée du Désert
near Mialet
Open: 9.30am-6.30pm July and August. 9.30am-12noon and 2.30-6pm March to June, September and October.

Parc de Prafrance
Open: 9am-7pm July and August. 9am-12noon and 2-7pm March to June, September and October.

Pont-de-Montvert
Ecology Museum
Open: daily June to September. Otherwise Thursdays, Saturdays and Sundays only.

St Jean du-Gard
Musée des Vallées Cévenoles
☎ 66 85 10 48
Open: daily June to September. Closed Sunday mornings and Mondays.

Tourist train
☎ 66 85 13 17
Runs Thursdays, Fridays and Sundays May to September. Also public holidays.

Ste Enimie
Le Vieux Logis Museum
Open: 10am-12.30pm and 2.30-10pm July and August. 10am-12noon and 2.30-6pm April to June and September.

Twelfth-century church can be seen on request.

Ste Lucie
Wolf Park and Museum
☎ 66 32 09 22
Open: 10am-6pm. Early June to early September.

Trabuc. Grottes de
☎ 66 85 33 28
Open: 9.30am-6.30pm mid-June to early September. 12noon to 2pm mid-March to mid-June and mid-September to mid-October. Otherwise enquire.

Vigan. Le
Musée Cévenol
Open: 10am-12.30pm and 2-6.30pm April to October. Otherwise Wednesdays only. Closed Tuesdays.

Vallée du Rhône

ARDECHE

Annonay
Musée César Filhol
Open: 2-6pm Wednesdays, Saturdays and Sundays throughout the year and daily during August.

Petit Train Touristique du Velay-Vivaris
St Agrève
Operates from May to October. For seasonal details ☎ 77 90 26 90 or 77 25 45 01.

Safari de Peaugrès
☎ 77 33 00 32
Open: 9.30am-6pm or 7pm daily during the summer. 11am-5pm daily during the winter.

Les Vans
Municipal Museum
Open: 10am-12noon and 1.30-5pm Tuesdays to Fridays and 2-5pm Saturdays July and August. Otherwise Thursdays 2-5pm.

LOIRE

Ambierle
Alice Taverne Forez Museum
☎ 77 65 60 99
No specified opening times.

Montbrison
Doll Museum
Opening times vary, enquire at the tourist office or ring ☎ 77 58 33 07

FOOD AND DRINK

There is a rich variety of food and drink in the Massif Central and plenty of people who take great pride in serving up well tried recipes in the appropriate manner. Most of them rely on local produce so the basic ingredients remain the same even if the quality of meat such as beef varies quite considerably. The different results depend mainly, though, upon preparation and presentation. For example, leg of lamb cooked with wild mushrooms is particularly mouthwatering, as is *foie gras* and other local pâtés that can be made from meat, duck or even potatoes. *Coq-au-vin* is a speciality in Auvergne and it is well worth ordering *ris de veau*, which can be lightly cooked under a pastry crust 3-4in high and as light as a feather. Wild boar is another speciality and stews are a good choice in rural areas for anyone with a healthy appetite. They frequently consist of pork and cabbage, with perhaps a few carrots, but the selection of herbs that make them distinctive is nearly always a closely guarded secret.

Limousin has dozens of different and delectable ways of preparing fish. Fruit tarts are served practically everywhere but the sweets can prove to be something of a disappointment. The Massif Central area is famous for its cheese and produces varieties such as Roquefort, St Nectaire, Fourme d'Ambert, Chèvreton and Gaperon among many others. Some are quite delicate but those made from ewe's or goat's milk are very much stronger. Fresh fruit is always a good bet, especially strawberries, peaches and cherries.

Local wines vary considerably, some are superb and world famous like those of Burgundy on the north-eastern fringe of the Massif Central. Others are very drinkable while a few take a bit of getting used to. *Eaux-de-vie* (spirits) come in a variety of flavours ranging from raspberry to verbena and gentian to walnut.

Restaurants
Restaurants follow much the same pattern as hotels. There are one or two outstandingly good ones, situated for the most part in large towns and tourist centres. A few even provide limited accommodation, in which case the quickest way to the owner's heart is to enquire if he has a table free and only mention the room as an afterthought. The best of the rest are sometimes very good and sometimes a little ordinary but it is rare to find one that serves dull or badly cooked food. The *logis* and *auberges* which concentrate on traditional dishes are almost invariably a good bet, with interesting menus, farm produce attractively served, unfailing attention and a cheerful atmosphere, all at a reasonable price.

Three or four set menus are always posted up outside. The cheapest usually has about three courses with a choice in each one, while the most expensive offers at least double that number and expects the customer to have a healthy appetite. *A la carte* always tends to be a bit more expensive and so do the majority of snacks. Lunch is usually served at about noon and dinner starts at around 7pm and can be over by 8.30pm.

Shopping

Anyone choosing a self-catering holiday will find shopping very simple. The markets are functional rather than quaint with plenty of seasonal produce displayed to good advantage. There are also small shops specialising in one particular item such as bread or meat while others carry a range of goods. Supermarkets are catching on fast, along with convenience foods, a whole range of things in the deep freeze and a certain amount of pre-packaging with everything already weighed and priced.

SPORTS

The Massif Central is very much a sporting area and provides a wide range of facilities, including the following.

Climbing and Potholing

These are popular pastimes in the mountains to the north and in the vicinity of canyons and gorges further south. There are clubs and societies which provide assistance and advice as well as organising special parties for specific trips.

Cycling

Cycling is equally popular and detailed maps of various routes are available from cycle clubs and local tourist offices.

Fishing

Fishermen have a wide choice of lakes, rivers and streams, but only after obtaining a licence. These are available from the appropriate shops which will also advise on the best areas and draw the attention of their customers to the rules governing such things as the different open seasons and the size of the permitted catch.

Golf

Golf is not a widely played game in the Massif Central but there are courses with clubs open to visitors, mainly in Auvergne.

Riding

Riding stables and equestrian centres provide tuition where needed, horses for short outings or longer excursions and organise guided tours. Some of them also have horse-drawn caravans for hire. They can be found all over the region and brochures are available from the tourist offices setting out all the relevant details.

Tennis

Tennis is becoming increasingly popular and most sports centres as well as several hotels have their own courts which are open to visitors.

Walking

Walking, rambling and hiking in the Massif Central attract hordes of outdoor enthusiasts every year. The blazed footpaths range from *Les sentiers de grande randonnée*, which stretch from one end of the country to the other, to *les sentiers de promenade*, covering much shorter distances. The footpaths designed for casual strolls are undemanding whereas others down into gorges and up craggy mountainsides sometimes call for the determination and agility of a mountain goat.

Water Sports

Water sports include everything from windsurfing, waterskiing and sailing on the lakes to rafting and canoeing along the rivers and through the gorges. Tuition is available if required and there are stretches of water which are suitable for beginners as well as others for the more experienced.

Winter Sports

Winter sports, particularly cross-country skiing, are becoming increasingly popular. There are winter sports centres in Auvergne, Lozère and mountainous areas of the Vallée du Rhône, some of which have ski-lifts or even cable cars, but for the moment they cannot compare with the majority of alpine resorts.

Other Sports

Less popular sports are also on offer in specific areas and include such things as archery, hang gliding, hot air ballooning, skin diving and parachuting.

SERVICES FOR VISITORS

When arriving in a strange town it is a good idea to call at the local *Office de Tourisme* or *Syndicat d'Initiative*. The staff are extremely helpful and have a great deal of information about their own individual areas. They will give advice on almost every subject, from the location of hotels and places of interest to the departure times for conducted tours and the availability of cars and bicycles.

The Accueil de France Tourist Offices, which are open throughout the year, will make hotel bookings for the same day or up to a week in advance, provided you call in personally and pay a small fee to cover the cost of a telephone call.

The Loisirs-Accueil Offices, which have been set up by a number of *départements*, will reserve hotel rooms, *gîtes* or

space on a camp site as well as arranging holidays of special interest such as a tour of ancient châteaux or one involving a particular sport. There is always someone who speaks English on the staff and a complete list is available from your French Government Tourist Office. However, if you write instead of calling in, do remember to send a stamped addressed envelope.

For British visitors the address of the office in London is:-
The French Government Tourist Office
178 Piccadilly
London WIV 0AL

For American visitors there are several offices including
The French Government Tourist Office
610 Fifth Avenue
New York
NY 10020-2452

TOURIST OFFICES

Auvergne

PUY-DE-DOME

Ambert
Syndicat d'Initiative
4 Place Hôtel de Ville
☎ 73 82 01 55
Open: mid-June to mid-September.

Besse-en-Chandesse
Office de Tourisme
Place Grand-Mèze
☎ 73 79 52 84

Billom
Syndicat d'Initiative
13 Rue Carnot
☎ 73 68 39 85
Open: June to August.

Bourboule (La)
Office de Tourisme
Place Hôtel de Ville
☎ 73 81 07 99

Châteauneuf-les-Bains
Office de Tourisme
☎ 73 86 67 86
Open: afternoons only May to
September.

Châtelguyon
Office de Tourisme
Parc Etienne Clémentel
☎ 73 86 01 17
Open: April to early October.

Clermont-Ferrand
Office de Tourisme
69 Boulevard Gergovia
☎ 73 93 30 20

Also at the station
☎ 73 91 87 89

A.C. Place Galliéni
☎ 73 93 47 67

Issoire
Syndicat d'Initiative
At the Mairie
☎ 73 89 03 54
Also on the Place Général De
Gaulle, mid-June to the beginning
of September.
☎ 73 89 15 90

Mont-Dore (Le)
Office de Tourisme
Avenue Général-Leclerc
☎ 73 65 20 21

Murol
Syndicat d'Initiative
At the Mairie
☎ 73 88 62 62

Riom
Office de Tourisme
16 Rue Commerce
☎ 73 38 59 45
Open: afternoons only November
to March.

Royat
Syndicat d'Initiative
Place Allard.
☎ 73 35 81 87
Closed November.

St Nectaire
Office de Tourisme
Anciens Thermes
☎ 73 88 50 86

CANTAL

Aurillac
Office de Tourisme
Place Square
☎ 71 48 46 58

Chaudes-Aigues
Office de Tourisme
1 Avenue Georges Pompidou
☎ 71 23 52 75
Open: May to mid-October.

Massiac
Office de Tourisme
Rue Paix
☎ 71 23 07 76

Mauriac
Office de Tourisme
Place Georges Pompidou
☎ 71 67 30 26

Montsalvy
Office de Tourisme
☎ 71 49 21 43

Murat
At the Mairie
☎ 71 20 03 80
Also Avenue Dr Mallet
☎ 71 20 09 47
Open: June to mid-September.

Riom-ès-Montagnes
Office de Tourisme
Place Général de Gaulle
☎ 71 78 07 37
Open: afternoons only except in
July and August.

St Flour
Office de Tourisme
2 Place Armes
☎ 71 60 22 50

Thiézac
Syndicat d'Initiative
☎ 71 47 01 21
Mid-June to end of August.

Vic-sur-Cère
Office de Tourisme
Avenue Mercier
☎ 71 47 50 68

HAUTE-LOIRE

Brioude
Office de Tourisme
Boulevard Champanne
☎ 71 50 05 35
Open: mornings out of season.

Chaise-Dieu (La)
Syndicat d'Initiative
Place Mairie
☎ 71 00 01 16
Open: Easter to October.

Chambon-sur-Lignon (Le)
Office de Tourisme
Place Marché
☎ 71 59 71 56

Puy-en-Velay (Le)
Office de Tourisme
Place du Breuil
☎ 71 09 38 41
Also 23 Rue Tables during July
and August.
☎ 71 09 27 42

ALLIER

Bourbon-l'Archambault
Syndicat d'Initiative
1 Place Thermes
☎ 70 67 09 79
Open: April to mid-October.

Cusset
Syndicat d'Initiative

Rue St Arloing
☎ 70 31 39 41
Open: mornings only July and
August.

Ebreuil
Syndicat d'Initiative
Hôtel de Ville
☎ 70 90 71 33
Open: July and August.

Lapalisse
Syndicat d'Initiative
Place Charles-Bécaud
☎ 70 99 08 39
Open: mid June to mid-September.

Montluçon
Office de Tourisme
1 Avenue Marx-Dormoy
☎ 70 05 05 92
Also Place Piquand
Open: afternoons July to
September. ☎ 70 05 50 70
A.C. 128 Boulevard Courtais
☎ 70 05 15 52

Moulins
Office de Tourisme
Place Hôtel de Ville
☎ 70 44 14 14
A.C. 62 Rue Pont-Guinguet.
☎ 70 44 00 96

Néris-les-Bains
Office de Tourisme
Carrefour des Arènes
☎ 70 03 11 03
Open: early May to late October.

St Pourçain-sur-Sioule
Syndicat d'Initiative
Boulevard Ledru-Rollin
☎ 70 45 32 73
Open: mid-June to mid-September.

Vichy
Office de Tourisme
19 Rue Parc
☎ 70 98 71 94

Accueil de France will help with hotel reservations up to five days in advance. Same telephone number and address.

Limousin

HAUTE-VIENNE

Bellac
Office de Tourisme
Ibis Rue L-Jouvet
☎ 55 68 12 79

Dorat (Le)
Office de Tourisme
Place Collégiale
☎ 55 60 76 81
Open: June to September.

Limoges
Office de Tourisme and Accueil de France
Boulevard Fleurus
☎ 55 34 46 87

St Junien
Office de Tourisme
Place Champ-de-Foire
☎ 55 02 17 93
Open: June to mid-September.

St Léonard-de-Noblat
Office de Tourisme
Rue Roger-Salengro
☎ 55 56 25 06

St Yrieix-la-Perche
Office de Tourisme
6 Rue Plaisances
☎ 55 08 14 95
Open: July and August.

CREUSE

Aubusson
Syndicat d'Initiative
Rue Vieille
☎ 55 66 52 12

Boussac
Office de Tourisme

Hôtel de Ville
☎ 55 65 07 62

Chambon-sur-Voueize
Syndicat d'Initiative
Hôtel de Ville and Avenue Georges Clemenceau
☎ 55 82 11 36
Open (the latter): afternoons only, July and August.

Guéret
Office de Tourisme
1 Avenue Charles de Gaulle
☎ 55 52 14 29

Souterraine (La)
Office de Tourisme
Place Gare
☎ 55 63 10 06
Open: mornings only out of season.

CORREZE

Argentat
Office de Tourisme
Avenue Pasteur
☎ 55 28 16 05
Open: mid-June to mid-September.

Arnac-Pompadour
Syndicat d'Initiative
At the château.
Closed in November.

Beaulieu-sur-Dordogne
Syndicat d'Initiative
Place Marbot
☎ 55 91 09 94
Open: July to September.

Bort-les-Orgues
Office de Tourisme
Place Marmontel
☎ 55 96 02 49

Brive-la-Gaillarde
Office de Tourisme
Place 14 Juillet
☎ 55 24 08 80

Meymac
Syndicat d'Initiative
Place Hôtel de Ville
☎ 55 95 18 43

Neuvic
Syndicat d'Initiative
Rue Poste
☎ 55 95 88 78
Open: mornings only.

Tulle
Office de Tourisme
Quai Baluze
☎ 55 26 59 61

Ussel
Office de Tourisme
Place Voltaire
☎ 55 72 11 50

Uzerche
Office de Tourisme
Place Lunade
☎ 55 73 15 71
Open: April to September.

Midi Pyrénées

LOT

Cahors
Office de Tourisme
Place Briand
☎ 65 35 09 36

Figeac
Office de Tourisme
Place Vival
☎ 65 34 06 25

Gramat
Office de Tourisme
Place République
☎ 65 38 73 60
Open: June to mid-September.

Martel
Syndicat d'Initiative
At the Mairie
☎ 65 37 30 03

Rocamadour
Office de Tourisme
Hôtel de Ville
☎ 65 33 62 59
Open: Palm Sunday, Easter, and
April to mid-September.

St Céré
Office de Tourisme
Place République
☎ 65 38 11 85
Closed Monday out of season.

Sarlat-la-Canéda. (Dordogne)
Office de Tourisme
Place Liberté
☎ 53 59 27 67

AVEYRON

Espalion
Office de Tourisme
At the Mairie
☎ 65 44 05 46

Estaing
Syndicat d'Initiative
At the Mairie
☎ 65 44 70 32
Open: June to September.

Millau
Office de Tourisme
Avenue Alfred-Merle
☎ 65 60 02 42

Najac
Syndicat d'Initiative
Place Faubourg
☎ 65 29 72 05

Rodez
Office de Tourisme
Place Foch
☎ 65 68 02 27

Villefranche-de-Rouergue
Office de Tourisme
Promenade Guiraudet
☎ 65 45 13 18

TARN

Albi
Office de Tourisme et A.C. Palais
Berbie
☎ 63 54 22 30

Castres
Office de Tourisme
Place République
☎ 63 59 92 44

Cordes
Syndicat d'Initiative
Maison du Grand Fauconnier
☎ 63 56 00 52

Languedoc-Roussillon

LOZERE

Canourgue. La
Office de Tourisme
At the Mairie
☎ 66 32 81 47

Florac
Office de Tourisme
Avenue Jean-Monestier
☎ 66 45 01 14

Langogne
Office de Tourisme
15 Boulevard Capucins
☎ 66 69 01 38
Open: during school holidays.

Malène. La
Syndicat d'Initiative
At the Mairie
☎ 66 48 51 16

Marvejols
Syndicat d'Initiative
Avenue de Brazza
☎ 66 32 02 14

Mende
Syndicat d'Initiative
16 Boulevard Soubeyran
☎ 66 65 02 69

A.C. 3 Rue Chapitre
☎ 66 65 17 17

Meyrueis
Office de Tourisme
Tour de l'Horloge
Open: June to September.
Otherwise at the Mairie
☎ 66 45 60 33

Rozier. Le
Syndicat d'Initiative
☎ 65 62 60 89
Open: Mid-June to mid-
September.

St Alban-sur-Limagnole
Syndicat d'Initiative
At the Mairie
☎ 66 31 50 29

Ste Enimie
Office de Tourisme
At the Mairie
☎ 66 48 53 44

Villefort
Office de Tourisme
Rue Eglise
☎ 66 46 87 30

GARD

Anduze
Syndicat d'Initiative
Plan de Brie
☎ 66 61 98 17

Génolhac
Syndicat d''Initiative
At the Mairie
☎ 66 61 10 55

St Jean-du-Gard
Office de Tourisme
Place Rabot
☎ 66 85 32 11

Vigan. Le
Syndicat d'Initiative
Place Triaire

☎ 67 81 01 72
or Place du Marché
☎ 67 81 01 72

Vallée du Rhône

ARDECHE

Annonay
Office de Tourisme
Place des Cordeliers
☎ 75 33 24 51

St Agrève
Syndicat d'Initiative
At the Mairie
☎ 75 3015 06
Open: mid-June to mid-
September.

St Martin-de-Valamas
Syndicat d'Initiative
At the Marie
☎ 75 30 41 76

Les Vans
Office de Tourisme
Place Ollier
☎ 75 37 24 48
Open: mornings only.

LOIRE

Montbrison
Office de Tourisme et A.C. Cloître
des Cordeliers
☎ 77 96 08 69

Roanne
Office de Tourisme et A.C. Cours
République
☎ 77 71 51 77

St Etienne
Office de Tourisme
12 Rue Gérentet
☎ 77 25 12 14
A.C 9 Rue Général-Foy
☎ 77 32 55 99

TRAVEL

By Air
Apart from the region's main
airports, serving provincial capitals
like Clermont-Ferrand, Limoges,
St Etienne and Vichy, there are
several local airfields which handle
charter flights and are used
extensively by light aircraft.
Information about Air Inter, the
national domestic airline, can be
obtained from Air France but
details of local flights are only
available in the different areas
concerned.

By Rail
Although the French railways
operate an extensive network
throughout the country, there are
many places in the Massif Central
which are not easy to get to by
train. Fast lines to the south run
from Paris to Clermont-Ferrand
and on through the area, stopping
at main towns such as Limoges
and Brive on the way, with
additional services to centres like
Aurillac and Cahors. Less direct
lines go to places like Guéret and
St Etienne but in order to change
direction it may be necessary to
change trains. In addition, you can
send your car by rail to either
Clermont-Ferrand or Brive and
special cut-price tickets are
available for young travellers and
holiday tours. Precise details can
be obtained from the overseas
offices of the French Railways and
from railway stations in the larger
towns.

By Bus or Coach
Long distance buses are almost
impossible to find in France and
the local services in the Massif
Central are somewhat restricted.
Most of these are either in the
bigger towns or the popular tourist

areas and are not designed for passengers who want to inspect the more remote parts of the countryside. Coach excursions are arranged in the normal way during the season, stopping at all the main tourist attractions, both scenic and historic, but seldom deviate far from the beaten track. Details of fares and schedules are available from the local tourist offices and from the various bus and coach stations.

By Road

Cars can be hired in most of the large towns, subject to all the usual conditions. Taxis can only be ordered by telephone or found on a rank and it is very unusual for a driver to stop anywhere in answer to a casual request. Motorists travelling in their own cars should have no trouble provided they observe the rules, which are much the same as those operating everywhere else. One thing to remember is that the police carry out random breath tests any time, anywhere. The restrictions on drinking and driving are rigidly enforced, with heavy fines payable on the spot, in cash, and the driver is not allowed to continue on his or her way.

No child under 10 years old is allowed on the front seat, the driver must be over 18 and have a valid driving licence, not a provisional one, and safety belts are obligatory. Stop signs mean exactly what they say and it is an offence to creep up to the line and then move out, even if there is nothing coming in either direction.

There is only one motorway in the Massif Central at the moment. This passes through Clermont-Ferrand, connecting the capital with St Etienne. A dual carriageway of almost equal importance

heads due south, only to end abruptly as it crosses the border between the *départements* of Puy-de-Dôme and Haute-Loire.

Well maintained major routes link all the larger towns, with a cobweb of secondary roads covering the areas on either side. There are also hundreds of short cuts, some fairly wide and well maintained, others serving small and sometimes isolated communities. It is fortunate for anyone exploring the area that most of the byways have a definite purpose in view and it is only on very rare occasions that one of them fails to make contact with another road a few kilometres ahead.

By Other Means

Bicycles can be hired or obtained from many of the large railway stations and there are extensive cycle tracks throughout the area. Advice is available on the best places to go, the most attractive ways of getting there and the location of conveniently placed *auberges* or refuge huts where cyclists can stop for the night.

Riding stables are widely scattered throughout the region and supply horses for both short outings and longer excursions as well as gipsy-type caravans and sometimes donkeys. There are well marked bridle paths, many of them with overnight stopping places, en route. There are also hundreds of miles of footpaths and trails, known as *grandes randonnées*, which are clearly marked for long distance hikers.

Canoes and kayaks are available on most of the main rivers where the conditions are suitable, along with advice on the kind of water to be encountered and the location of various accommodation along the banks.

Special Routes

For visitors with a definite purpose in view there are a number of specific routes to choose from, some of which have historical connections. One can follow in the steps of Richard Coeur-de-Lion, or even those of the Black Prince, discover the old mule tracks along the Salt Road between Aveyron and Aigues-Mortes on the far side of the Camargue or join the famous Pilgrims' Way from Le Puy, into Aquitaine and on across the Spanish frontier to Santiago de Compostela. One route takes in the main châteaux of Auvergne while another is devoted to tapestries in Limousin. American tourists in particular might opt for a trip round the mansions and museums associated with Lafayette, the eminent soldier-statesman who was one of their staunchest supporters during the War of Independence. Scenic routes cover everything from volcanoes to gorges, to say nothing of the trail blazed by Robert Louis Stevenson which can be followed either with or without a donkey.

INDEX